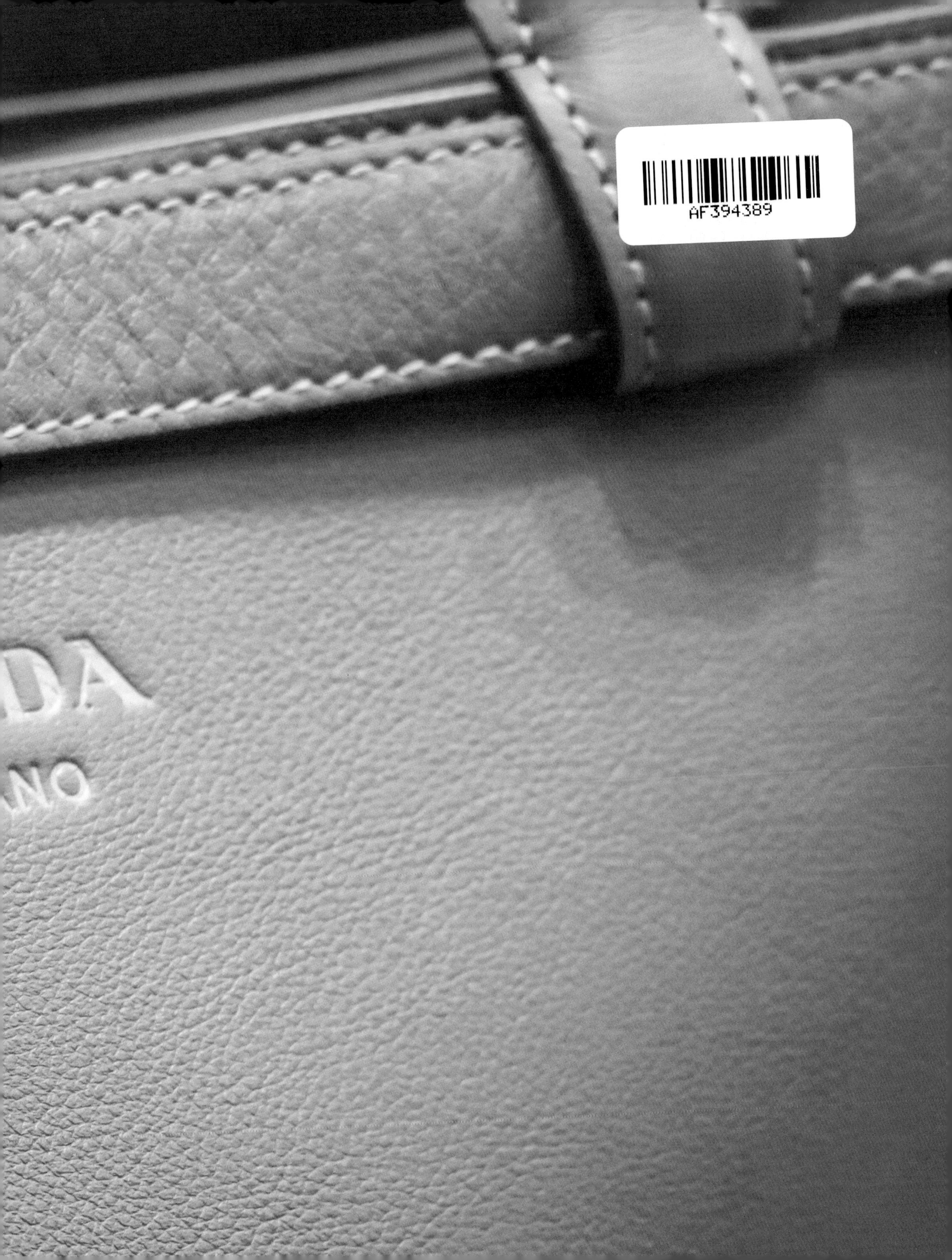
AF394389
PRADA
MILANO

THE FASHION ICONS

PRADA

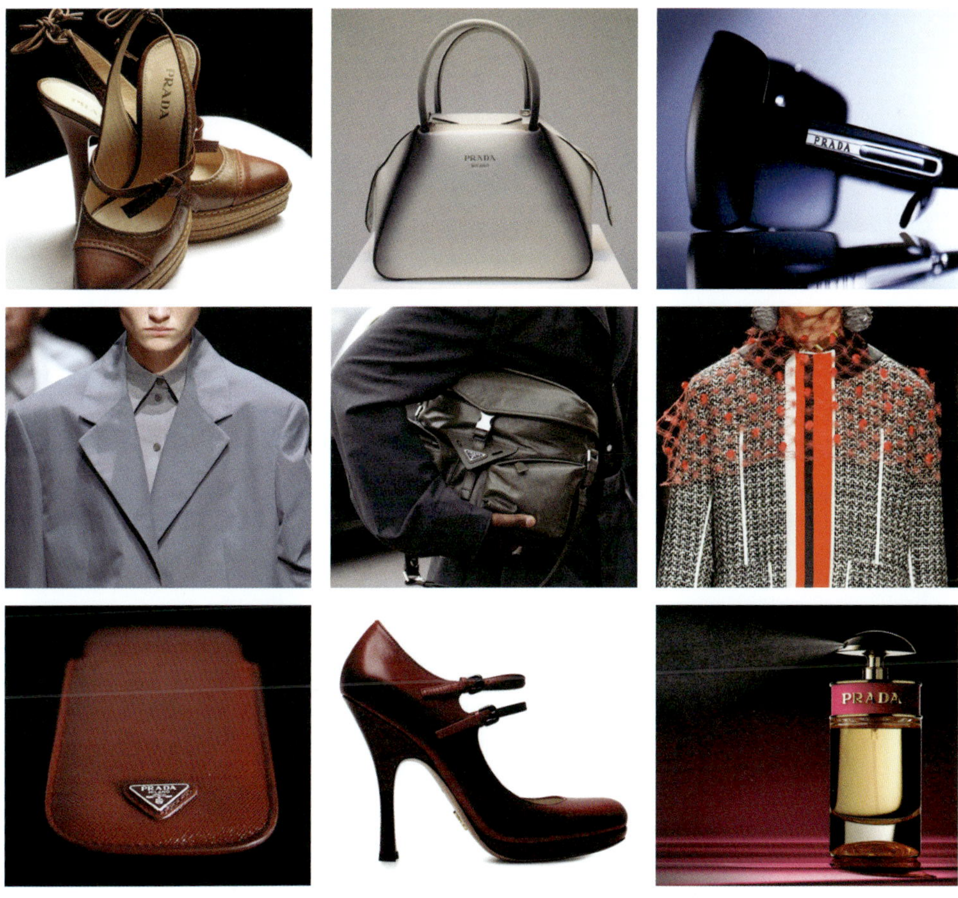

Alison James

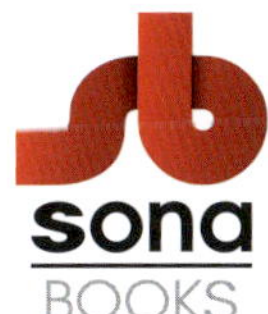

sona
BOOKS

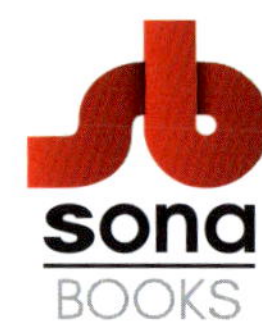

sona BOOKS

© Danann Media Publishing Limited 2026

First published in the UK 2026 by Sona Books an imprint of Danann Media Publishing Ltd.

CAT NO: SON0632

Photography courtesy of

Getty images:

Daniele Venturelli	Chris Jackson	Anadolu	Fairchild Archive	Rebecca Sapp
Victor Virgile	Dominique Charriau	Jacopo M. Raule	Ian Gavan	Jeff Kravitz
WWD	Penske Media	Stringer	Bennett Raglin	Giuseppe Cacace
Piero Cruciatti	Christian Vierig	Jeremy Chan	Pietro S. D'Aprano	Streetstyleshooters
Lexie Moreland	Jeremy Moeller	Frazer Harrison	Dimitrios Kambouris	
Pascal Le Segretain	Melodie Jeng	Variety	Axelle/Bauer-Griffin	
Edward Berthelot	Christophe Simon	Vanni Bassetti	Steve Granitz	

Alamy images:

Neil Setchfield	Patti McConville	Associated Press	Image Press Agency	Everett Collection Inc
Photolime	Zuma Press, Inc	Magicinfoto	Patti McConville	Abaca Press
David Hancock	Imaginechina Limited	Heorshe	DPA Picture Alliance	AFF
Zerilli Media	Retro AdArchives	Glenn Harper	Sipa US	
Andrei Antipov	AdsR	PictureLux	Imago	

Other images Wiki Commons

Book cover design Darren Grice at Ctrl-d
Layout design Alex Young at Cre8lve
Proof reader Juliette O'Neill
Editor Sofia Della Valle

Made in EU.
ISBN: 978-1-917259-10-1

CONTENTS

INTRODUCTION

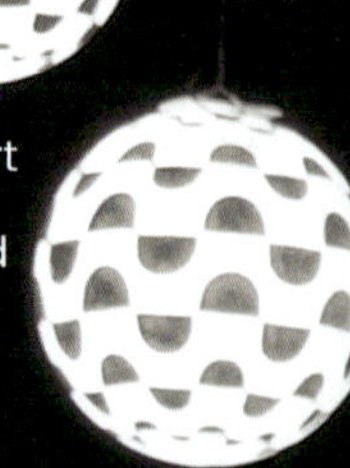

In the ever-changing landscape of fashion, few brands have captivated and transformed the industry quite like Prada. What began as a small leather goods shop in Milan's Galleria Vittorio Emanuele II in the early 20th century has evolved into a global symbol of sophistication, daring creativity, and subtle rebellion. Prada has always been more than just fashion - it represents an idea, a spirit that embraces inspiration, reinvention, sophistication.

This book explores Prada's journey - a path paved with bold choices, defiant design and an unapologetic embrace of both elegance and eccentricity. From Miuccia Prada's radical reimagining of the brand in the late 1970s, through its iconic 'ugly chic' aesthetic and experimental use of materials, to her ground-breaking collaborations with Belgian designer Raf Simons - whom she appointed as her fellow Creative Director in 2020 - La Casa di Prada has continuously blurred the lines of fashion. It inhabits the space between art and fashion, the avant-garde and the classical, and timeless luxury and forward-thinking modernity.

Throughout these pages, you'll encounter the very essence of Prada's evolution - from luxurious leather goods and sleek minimalism to the unexpected and sometimes provocative runway collections that have challenged and expanded notions of beauty. More than a visual journey, this book explores the philosophy that drives Prada - a fusion of intellectual curiosity, artistic exploration and a refusal to conform. This book is simultaneously a retrospective and an invitation to further explore the allure of Prada and discover its history, philosophy, cultural impact and undeniable mystique. A creative force not only of fashion but also of vision, artistry, and a relentless pursuit of something truly original.

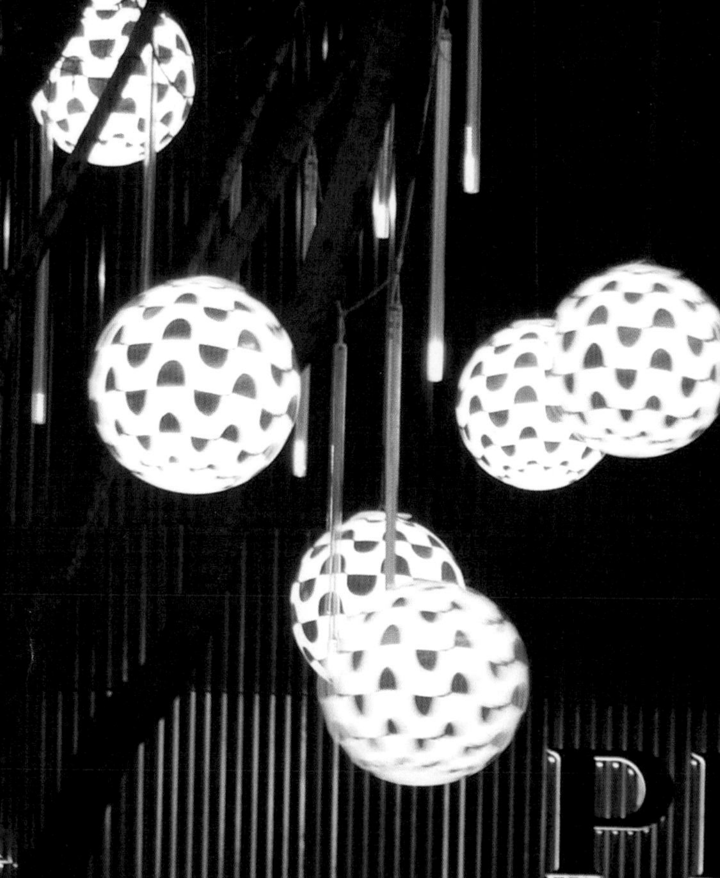

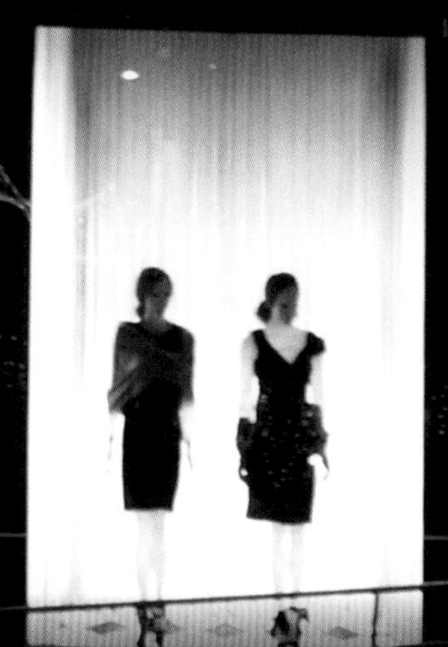

PRADA

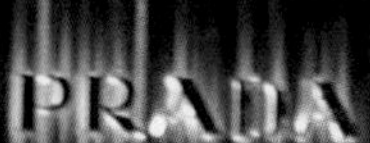

PRADA

PRADA - A HISTORY

"I want the name Prada to be huge"

Miuccia Prada

Prada came into the world – as, indeed, did other iconic Italian fashion labels – as a luxury leather goods company. In Milan, of course. Where else? Over centuries, the city and its environs had been a centre for high-quality leather production – due in no small part to the abundance of tanneries and skilled leatherworkers located throughout northern Italy. Mario Prada was one such skilled leatherworker. It was in his genes. Born in Milan on 17 January 1881, Mario's father Luigi ran his own small leather goods company in the city centre, making leather bags, trunks and luggage of a truly superlative quality. From childhood, Mario spent time in the workshop – absorbing the life of an artisan and eventually becoming his father's apprentice. He had inherited his father's flair, skill and love for leather, becoming a skilled, meticulous and master craftsman with a keen eye for quality and a passion for crafting exquisite goods. As Mario Prada meticulously created leather trunks for the elite, he unknowingly set the stage for a revolution far beyond luggage – a revolution that would redefine fashion itself.

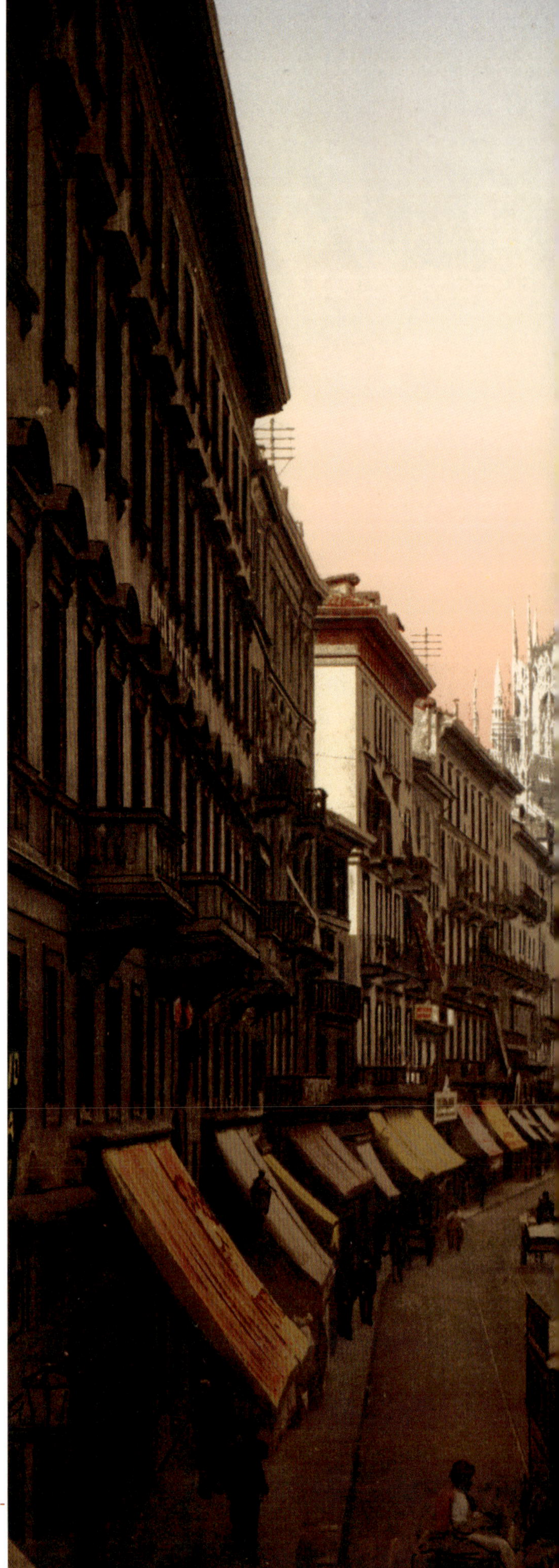

RIGHT: Corso Vittorio Emanuele, Milan, Italy, 1890s

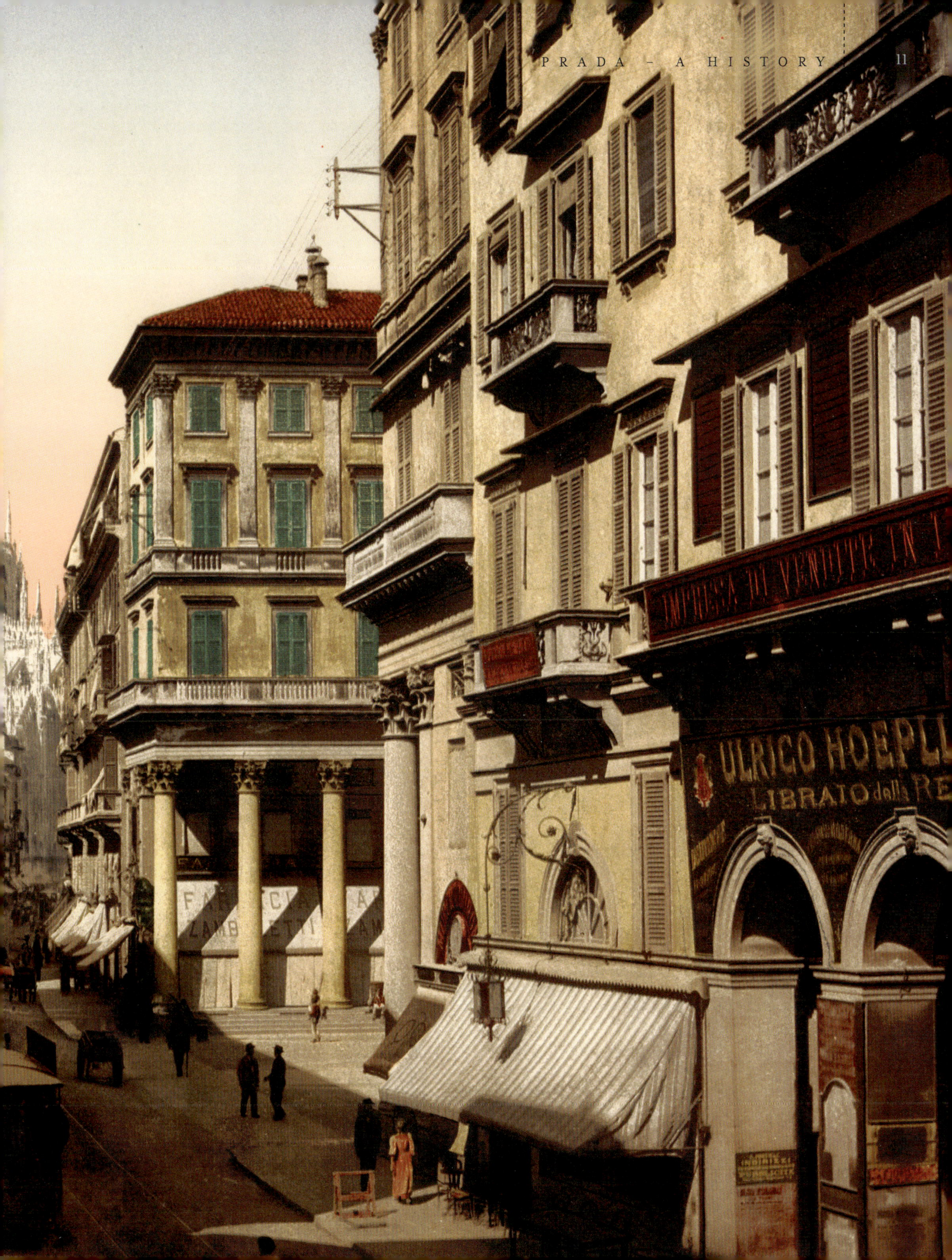
IMPRESA DI VENDITE IN
ULRICO HOEPLI
LIBRAIO della RE

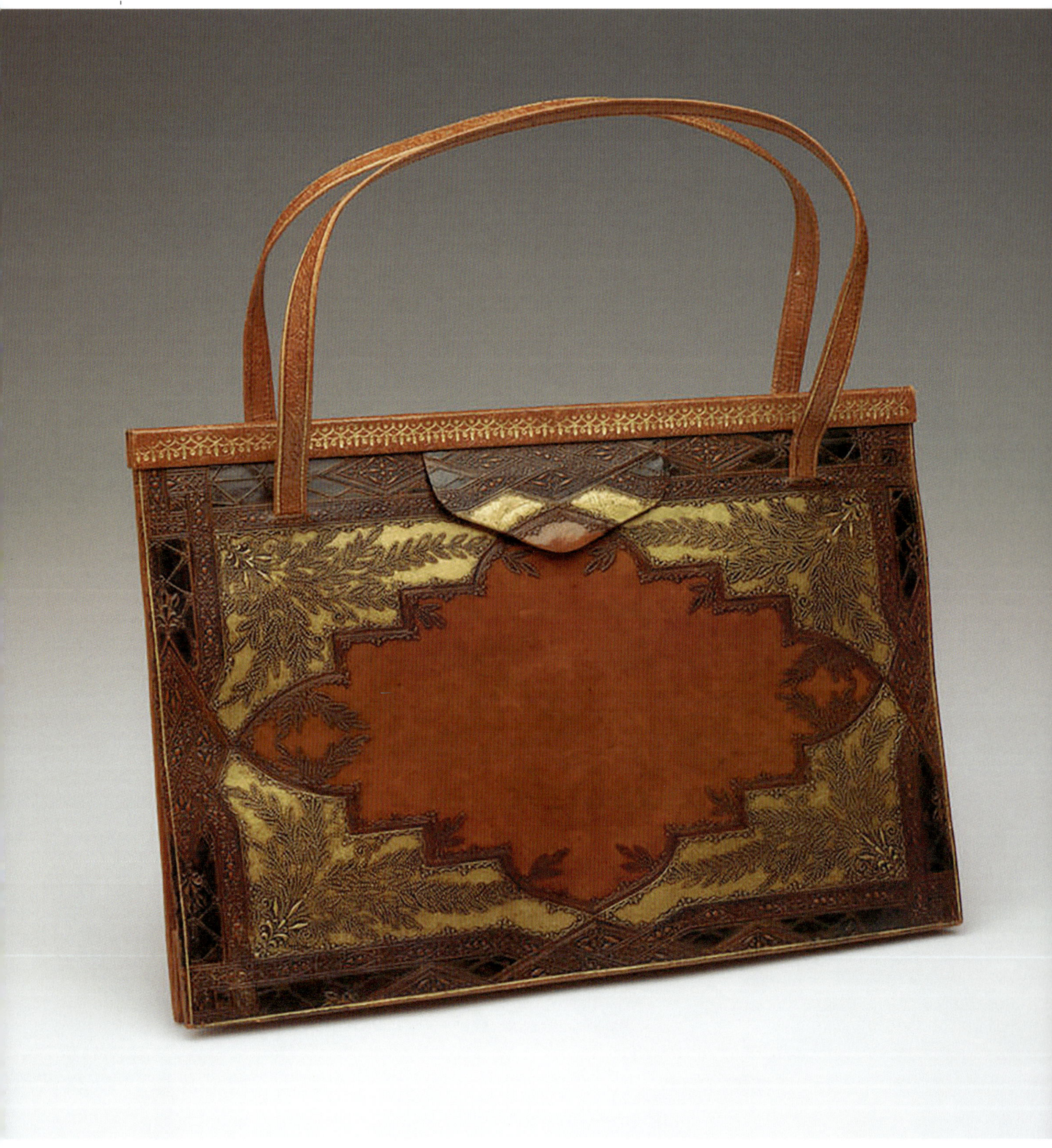

ABOVE: Tooled leather handbag made by Prada, circa
1935–1945, displayed at the Rhode Island School of
Design Museum USA

In 1913 when he was 32, Mario – along with his brother Martino – founded 'Fratelli Prada' (Prada Brothers), a small store located in the prestigious Galleria Vittorio Emanuele II in Milan, one of the world's oldest, most beautiful and most prestigious shopping arcades. It remains a Prada store to this day. This location in the heart of Milan signalled the brand's aspirations from the outset – that is, to cater to a sophisticated clientele and to establish itself as a symbol of Italian luxury. Mario and Martino saw an opportunity to cater to upper class travellers who sought the finer things in life. The Prada brothers specialized in leather bags, trunks, and travel accessories, meticulously crafted from the finest materials. Fratelli Prada rapidly gained a reputation for quality, attracting an elite clientele that included European aristocracy and the Italian royal family. In 1919, the company was named the official supplier to the Italian Royal House. It was a huge honour and this recognition allowed Prada to display the House of Savoy coat of arms and knotted rope design in its trademark logo, which contributed to making the brand a benchmark for luxury and master-craftsmanship. Mario Prada designed this logo himself. Featuring a striking, upside-down triangle in monochrome and emblazoned with 'PRADA' and 'MILANO' written in upper case font, it encapsulated the classically clean lines and minimalism of Prada design. The triangle also had extra significance – the shape being associated with strength and stability.

At some point Martino bowed out of the business, leaving Mario in sole charge. The idea had always been to hand the running of the business down through the male line as was de rigeur at the time. However, Mario's only son had no interest in taking over. This caused a real headache for macho Mario who firmly believed that women had no place in business – to such an extent that he would not even allow female members of the family to work in the shop. But his daughter Luisa was keen to take the reins and, left with no option, Mario turned the business over to her in the 1950s. Mario passed away in 1958, aged 87.

Luisa changed the company name to 'Prada' and, under her steady hand, kept the business stable as they transitioned away from ocean liner travel more towards airline travel. Luisa's management style was relatively conservative as she maintained Prada's traditional product lines and reputation for luxury craftsmanship. Under her leadership, Prada maintained its status as a respected luxury goods retailer, though it remained a relatively small and traditional family-run company. When Luisa decided it was time to look to the next generation to takeover, it was reporting annual sales of $450,000. In 1977, her daughter Miuccia joined the family firm. It was this youngest grandchild of Mario's who would revolutionalise Prada and transform it into the high-fashion powerhouse it is today.

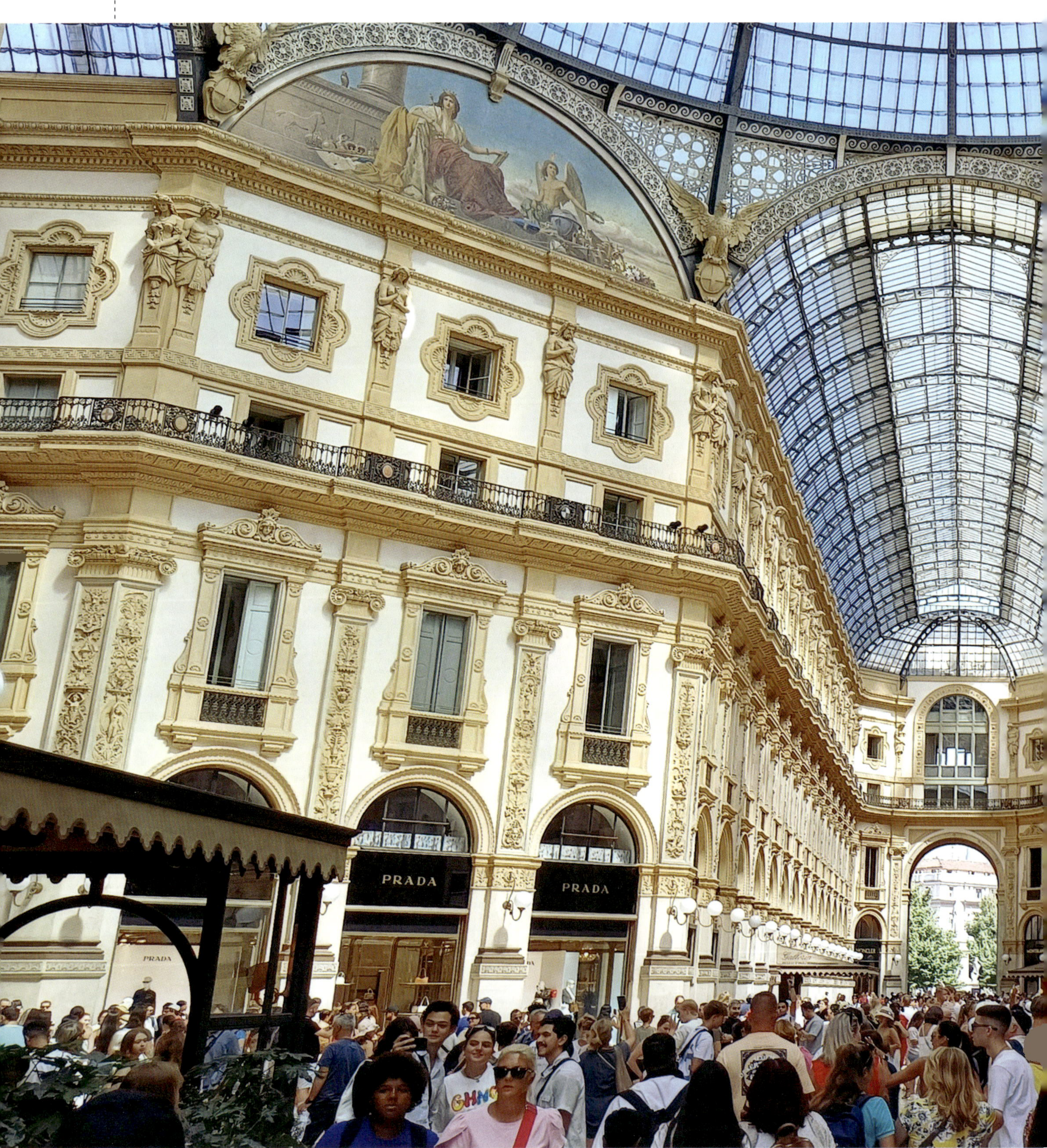

ABOVE: Galleria Vittorio Emanuele II, Italy's oldest active shopping arcade and a major landmark of Milan

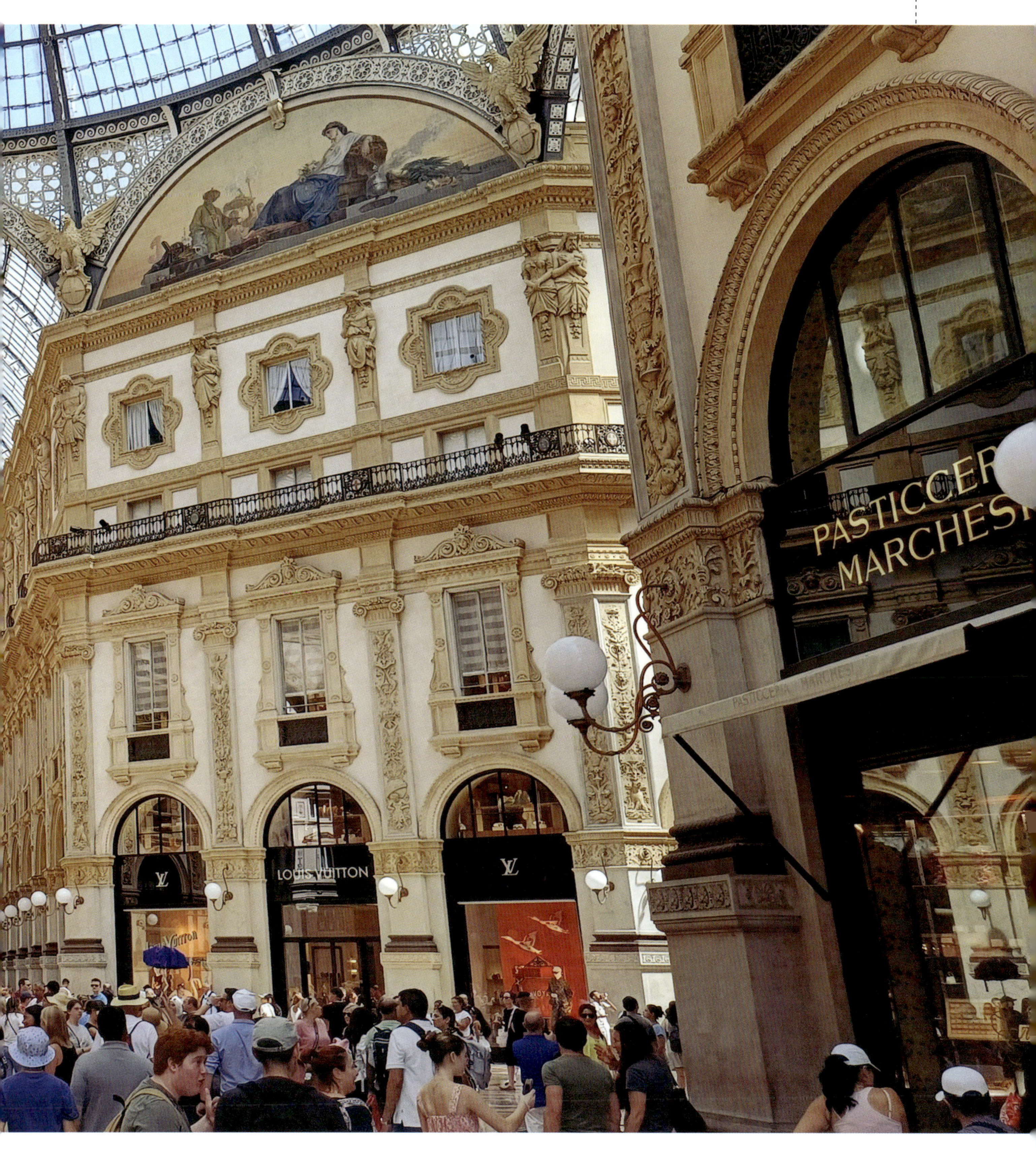
PASTICCERIA
MARCHESI
LOUIS VUITTON

THE LEGEND THAT IS MIUCCIA PRADA

"Creativity is what drives my business; it's always been about that. I believe that for me, this is the only way to do business"
Miuccia Prada

Miuccia Prada, born Maria Bianchi Prada on 10 May 1949 in Milan, was the second of three children born to Luisa Prada Bianchi, heiress to the luxury leather goods company then known as 'Fratelli Prada', and Luigi Bianchi, head of a company that manufactured putting-green mowers. Her parents were traditional and strict with the result that Miuccia was severely bored and felt stifled. Intellectually curious and fiercely independent, she received a classical education at Milan's elite educational institutions but by her mid-teens, she, like so many middle-class kids in the 1960s, had begun to rebel.

'I was always frustrated, because I had to dress so seriously. I was a proper young girl and I was dreaming of pink shoes, red shoes, pink dresses. Anything with colour. Exciting underwear. Everybody had this kind of dull underwear and wore boring striped dresses. I couldn't stand it,' she was later to say.

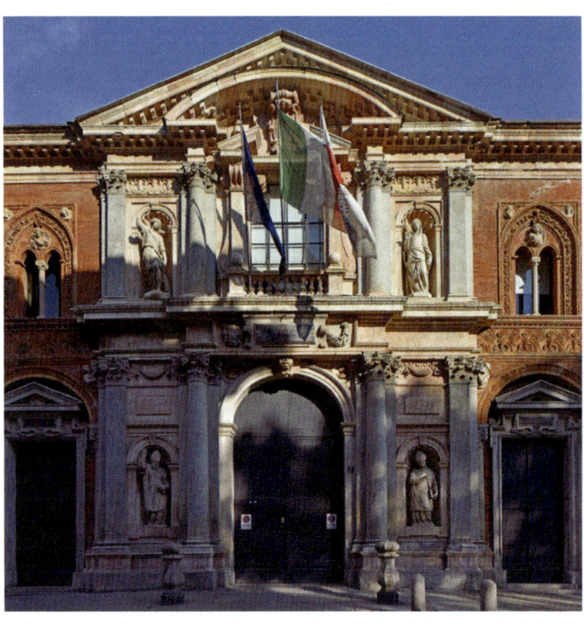

Miuccia enrolled at the University of Milan, where she studied political science and became politically active in the student movements of the late 1960s, aligning herself with left-wing ideologies and feminist causes. Her interest in the arts and theatre was also strong and she even trained as a mime at the Teatro Piccolo in Milan until her disapproving parents put a stop to it. Miuccia's world was filled with political

ABOVE RIGHT: University of Milan main entrance
OPP PAGE: Miuccia Prada walks the runway during the finale of the Miu Miu 2019 Cruise Collection show on 30 June in Paris, France

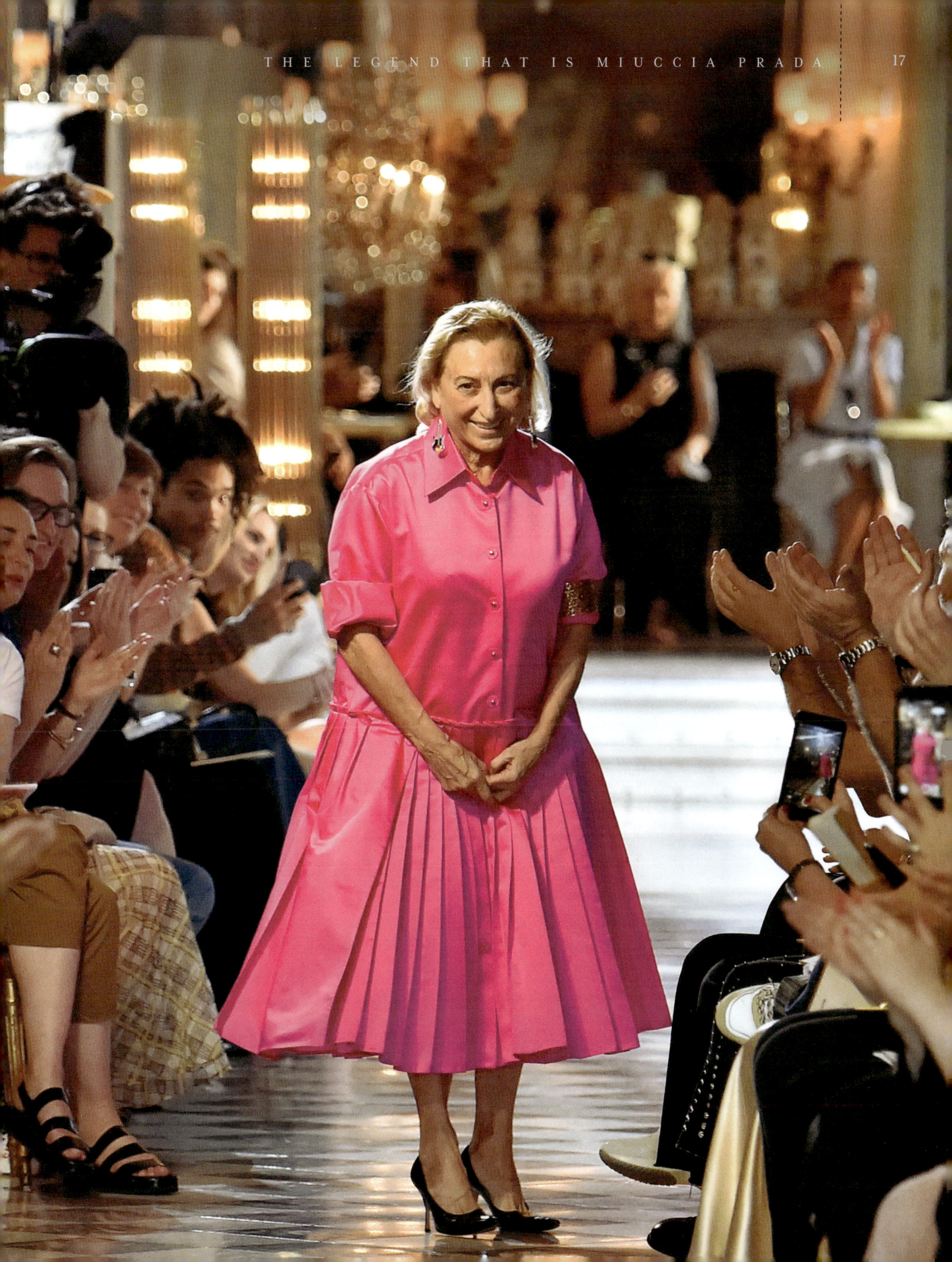

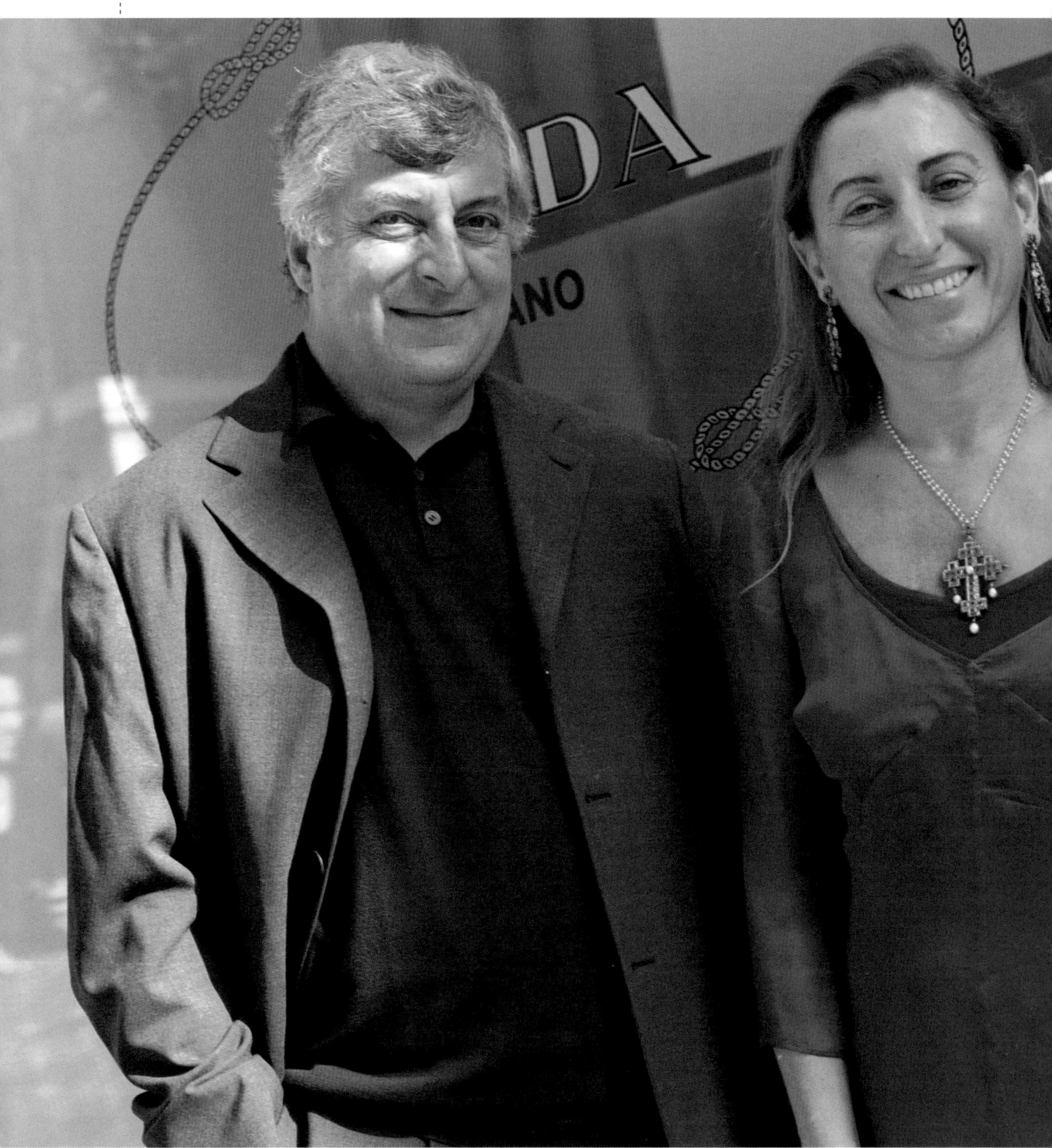

ABOVE: Miuccia Prada and executive Patrizio Bertelli pose for photographs in front of the newly opened Prada flagship store at Madison Avenue and 70th Street in New York City on 28 October, 1996

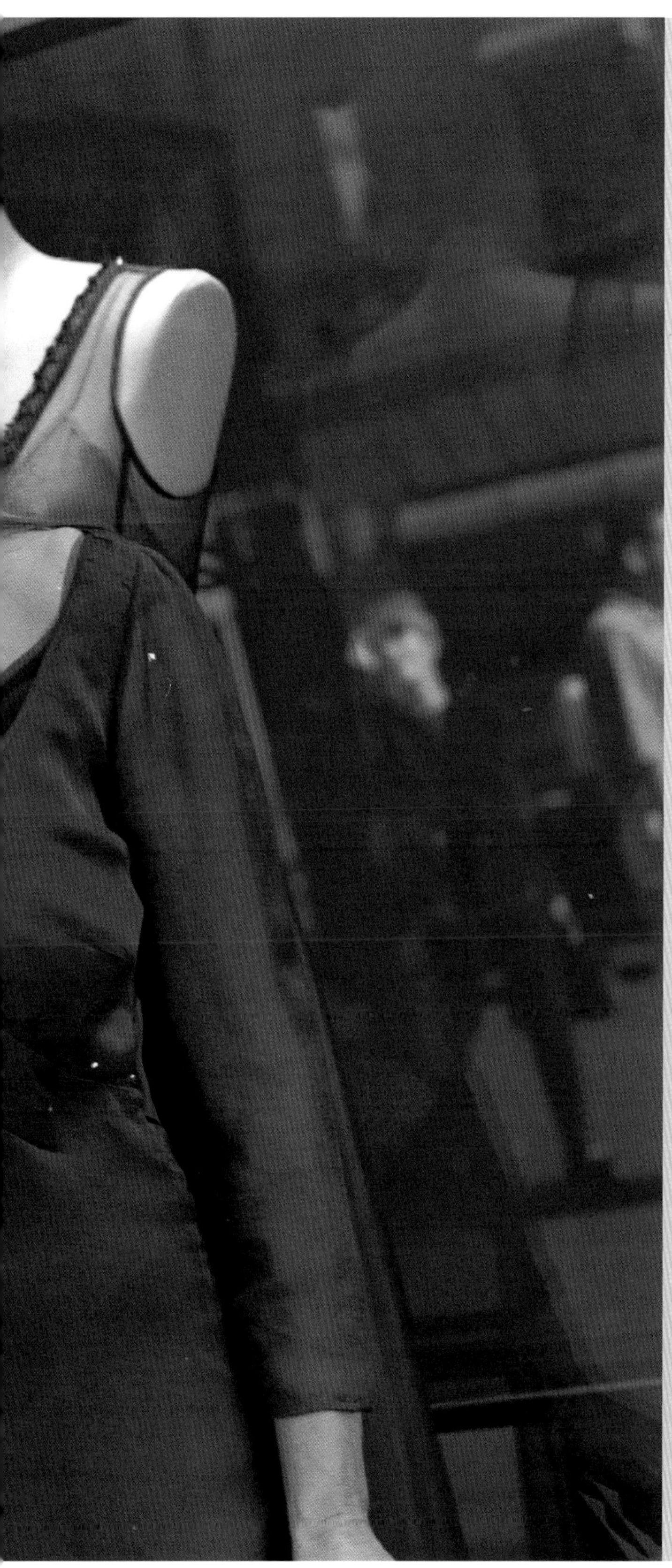

activism and intellectual pursuits, far removed from the glamour of luxury fashion. However, in 1978, she reluctantly joined the family business, feeling a sense of responsibility to her family's legacy rather than a personal passion for fashion. Miuccia's entry into the company came at a time when Prada was struggling to differentiate itself in an increasingly competitive market. The brand was known primarily for its high-quality leather travel bags and accessories and, while it needed to move forward, it lacked the innovation and vision that would eventually make it a powerhouse in the luxury sector. Miuccia's approach to this highly traditional business was unconventional, blending her intellectual inclinations and social consciousness with her avant-garde sensibilities, intellectualism, and unconventional approach to fashion.

One of the most influential events during Miuccia's early years at Prada was her partnership with Patrizio Bertelli, an ambitious entrepreneur who would become both her business partner and her husband. She met him at a trade fair in 1978. Bertelli joined Prada soon after that meeting, bringing with him a strong business acumen and a knack for strategic growth. Bertelli's approach to business complemented Miuccia's creative vision. He understood her need for creative freedom and it was he who took on the challenge of expanding Prada into a global brand. Miuccia and Patrizio laid the foundations for what would become one of the most successful partnerships in fashion. Bertelli encouraged Miuccia to take risks with her designs and pursue her unique vision, while he handled the operational and business aspects of the company. This partnership gave Miuccia the freedom to experiment and innovate without being burdened by the day-to-day business operations. The synergy between Miuccia's creative genius and Bertelli's business pragmatism became a defining element of Prada's early growth and success.

One of Miuccia Prada's first major contributions to the brand was the introduction of nylon bags in the early 1980s – a revolutionary idea at the time. The decision to use nylon, a material typically associated with practicality and durability rather than luxury, was both daring and innovative. While luxury brands were emphasizing opulence and traditionally luxurious materials, Miuccia saw beauty in an industrial fabric that was durable, lightweight, and unassuming. Her black nylon backpack, the Vela, which launched in 1984, was a departure from traditional leather bags that dominated the luxury market. This move was met with scepticism initially. Nylon was considered an odd choice for luxury goods. However, the minimalist and functional aesthetic of the nylon bag resonated with consumers looking for a different kind of luxury — one that was understated and modern rather than ornate and traditional. The success of the nylon bag not only brought Prada into the global spotlight but also redefined the concept of luxury itself. Through this innovation, Miuccia Prada demonstrated

that luxury did not have to be defined by obvious extravagance. It could be subtle, functional and intellectual instead.

Miuccia then began exploring an aesthetic that would become a hallmark of the brand – 'ugly chic'. She was interested in pushing the boundaries of traditional beauty standards, often creating designs that challenged conventional ideas of elegance and luxury. Miuccia was never one to create for the mainstream. She wanted her designs to provoke thought, stimulate conversation and defy the prevailing tastes of the time. Her Spring/ Summer collection of 1996, titled 'Banal Eccentricity' incorporated unconventional colourways such as 1970s inspired avocado greens, mustards, and browns. She combined these with eccentric patterns, unconventional silhouettes and retro-inspired designs. The deliberate use of elements considered unattractive or outdated was a bold move which set Prada apart from other luxury brands that adhered strictly to conventional ideals of beauty and glamour. Miuccia's designs appealed to a sophisticated, intellectual clientele who appreciated fashion as a form of self-expression and cultural commentary. Prada's aesthetic became a breath of fresh air in the industry, appealing to those who sought a luxury brand that was cerebral and thought-provoking. Her early decisions, from the use of nylon to the understated elegance of her ready-to-wear collections, laid the foundation for Prada's reputation as a brand that was ahead of its time,

OPP PAGE: Model Kristen McMenamy backstage at the Prada Spring 1996 Ready to Wear Runway Show on 10 October, 1995

bridging the gap between traditional luxury and modern innovation.

This concept of 'ugly chic' remains a signature of Miuccia's design philosophy, as she continues to blend elements that are seemingly discordant or unconventional. Her willingness to experiment has become one of Prada's defining characteristics. Miuccia Prada's raison d'être has always been to redefine luxury in a modern world. She creates pieces that speak to contemporary women — intellectual, independent women who are not bound by traditional expectations. Her designs often blur the lines between masculinity and femininity, functionality and beauty... and challenge her audience to reconsider their ideas of what luxury means. Miuccia Prada's early years at Prada set the stage for the brand's ascent to one of the most iconic names in fashion. Her intellectual approach to design, her bold choices in materials and aesthetics, and her strategic partnership with Patrizio Bertelli transformed a family-owned leather goods shop into a global fashion empire. Her early contributions not only reimagined the brand but also set a precedent for how fashion could be used as a platform for exploring deeper cultural and intellectual themes. Through her vision, Prada has become more than just a brand. It is a symbol of forward-thinking, progressive luxury.

In 1993, Miuccia founded Miu Miu, named after her own family pet name, a more affordable line

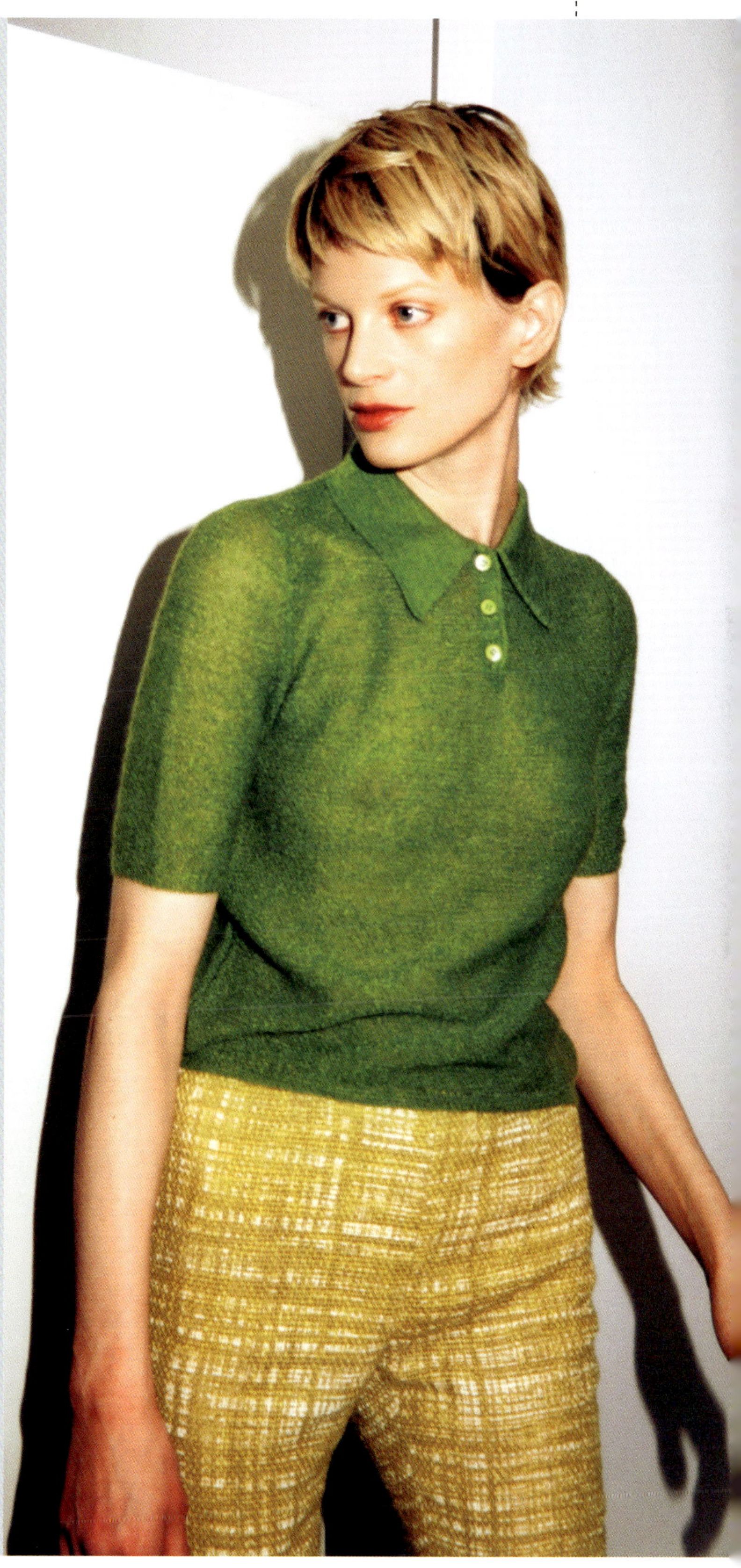

reflecting her personal style and appealing to a younger audience. Under her leadership, Prada has also expanded its product lines and acquired other brands, including Jil Sander and Helmut Lang. In 2013, she was listed as the 75th most powerful woman in the world by Forbes. She has collaborated with such diverse business associates as Adidas, artist Damien Hirst, rugged design label Carhartt, National Geographic, and auction house Sotheby's. In 2020, she appointed Belgian designer Raf Simons – whose career prior to Prada included influential roles at Jil Sander, Dior and Calvin Klein - as Co-Creative Director of Prada, marking a new chapter in the brand's history. This collaboration – referred to by Miuccia as *'a new wind'* has been described as a *'dialogue'* between the two creatives, breathing new life to Prada through explorations of technology, culture, and design. Miuccia's innovative approach and commitment to blending fashion with art and culture have solidified her status as a leading figure in the fashion industry.

As with many other high fashion houses, Prada has branched out into beauty – admittedly coming to it later than most. The brand first ventured into the beauty sector in 2000 with the introduction of single-dose skincare products. Four years later, Prada launched its first fragrance – 'Amber'. In August 2023, Prada re-entered the beauty market with a comprehensive line of makeup and skincare products, developed in partnership with L'Oréal. A year earlier Prada introduced its first fine jewellery collection 'Eternal Gold' crafted entirely from recycled gold, demonstrating Prada's commitment to sustainability. The brand offer a diverse range of jewellery for women, including bracelets, necklaces, earrings, rings, and brooches.

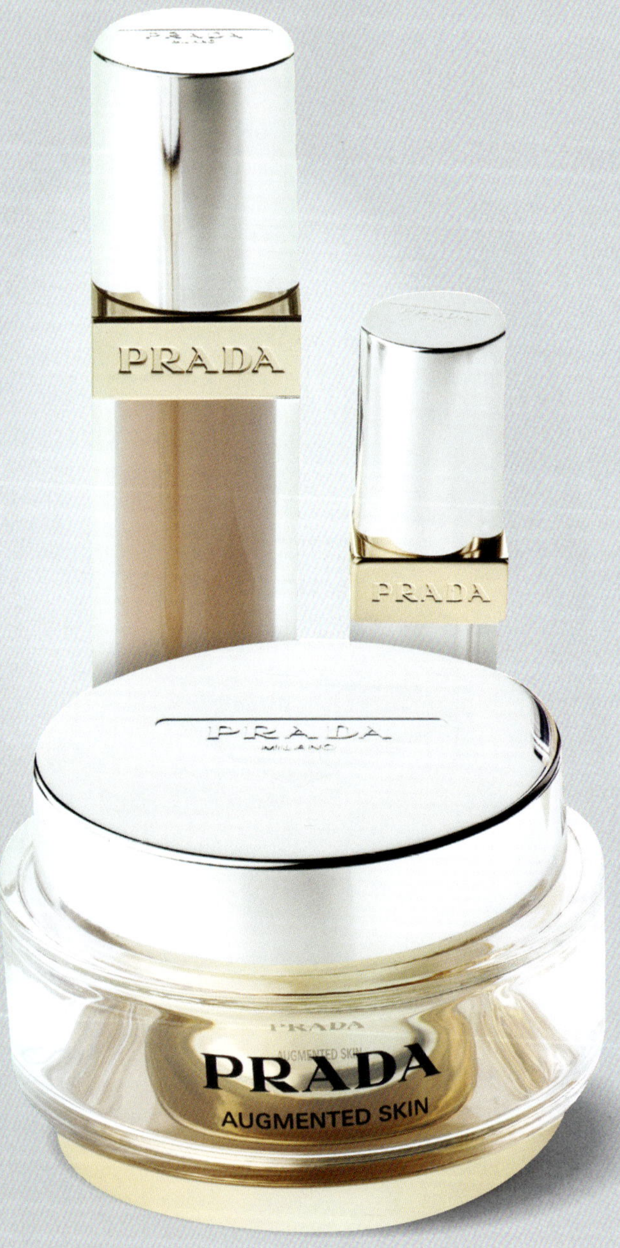

ABOVE: Prada skincare products
OPP PAGE: Prada's 'Eternal Gold' final jewellery collection, as seen in Lifestyle and Fashion Magazine, November 2022

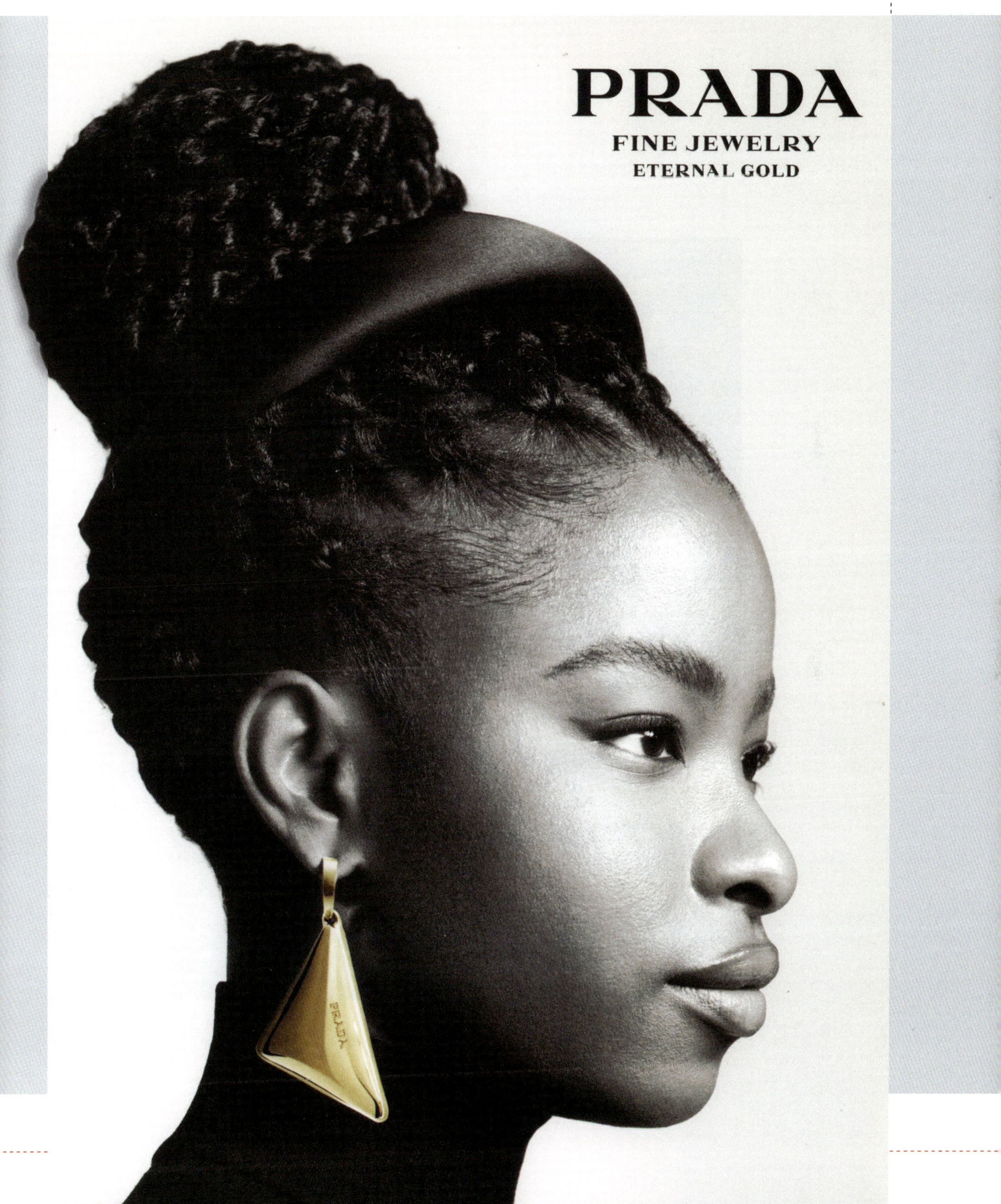

PRADA
FINE JEWELRY
ETERNAL GOLD

Their collections feature both fashion jewellery and fine pieces crafted from materials like 925 sterling silver and certified recycled gold. And a year before jewellery – in 2021 - Prada ventured into the homeware sector in November 2021 by opening its first dedicated home collection boutique at Harrods in London. This permanent space on the department store's third floor is fully dedicated to *'homeware and sophisticated accessories'*. The collection includes handmade objects, fine porcelain plates, bowls, and trays adorned with geometric patterns and iconic Prada motifs. Scented candles, decorative objects, and games designed to enhance living spaces with a modern and sophisticated touch also feature.

Beyond the brand, Miuccia is a passionate supporter of the arts. In 1993, she co-founded the Prada Foundation (Fondazione Prada) with husband, Patrizio, to promote contemporary art and culture. The foundation has hosted exhibitions featuring prominent artists and has become a significant cultural institution. She and Patrizio have two sons, Lorenzo (born 1988) and Giulio (born 1990). Keen rally driver Lorenzo joined Prada in 2017, initially overseeing digital communication. In May 2021, he was appointed as an executive director of the company. Giulio, however, is not involved in the running of the family business, preferring a quiet life away from high-end fashion.

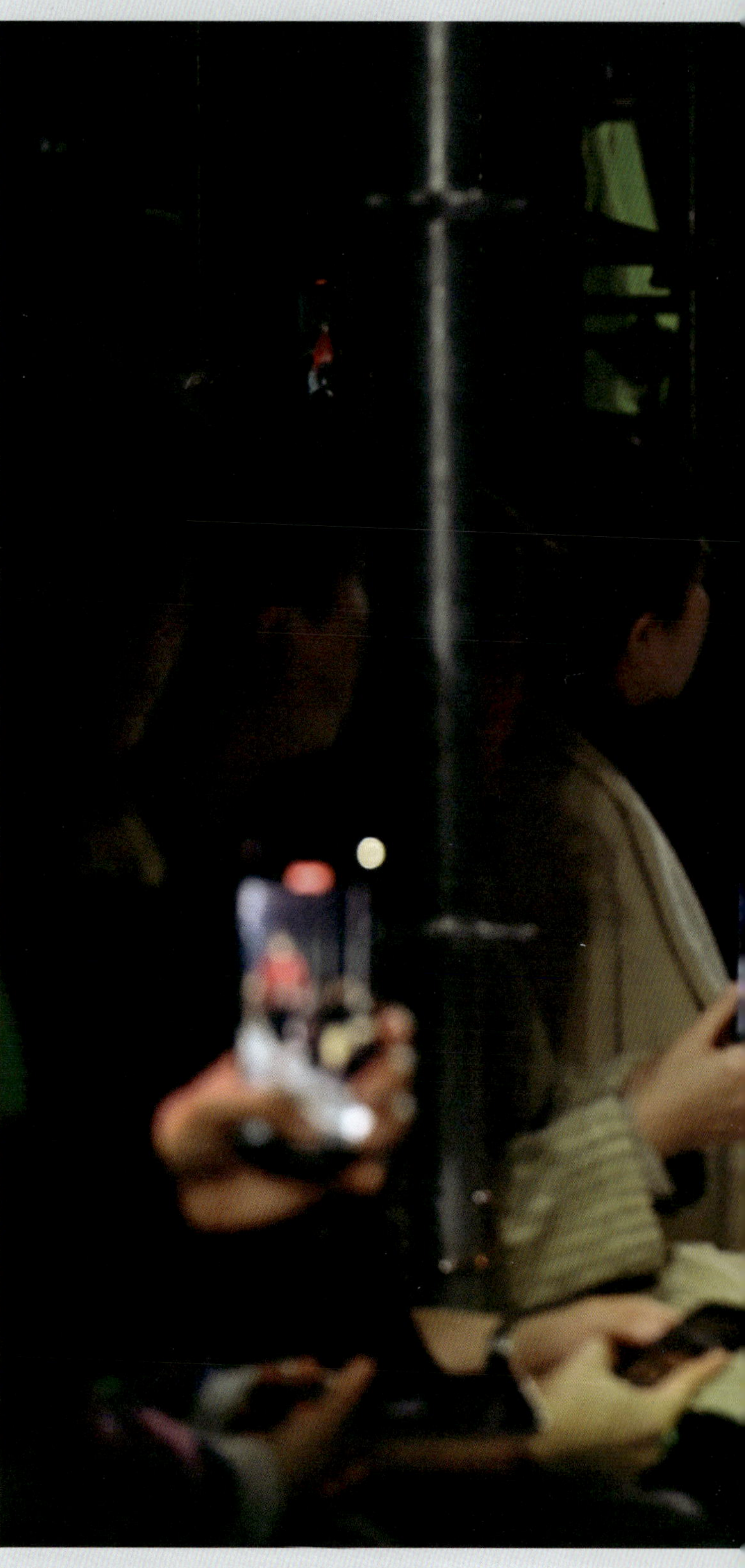

RIGHT: A model wears a creation by Prada for the Womenswear Ready-to-wear Fall-Winter 2025/26 collection as part of the Milan Fashion Week, at Fondazione Prada, in Milan on 27 February, 2025

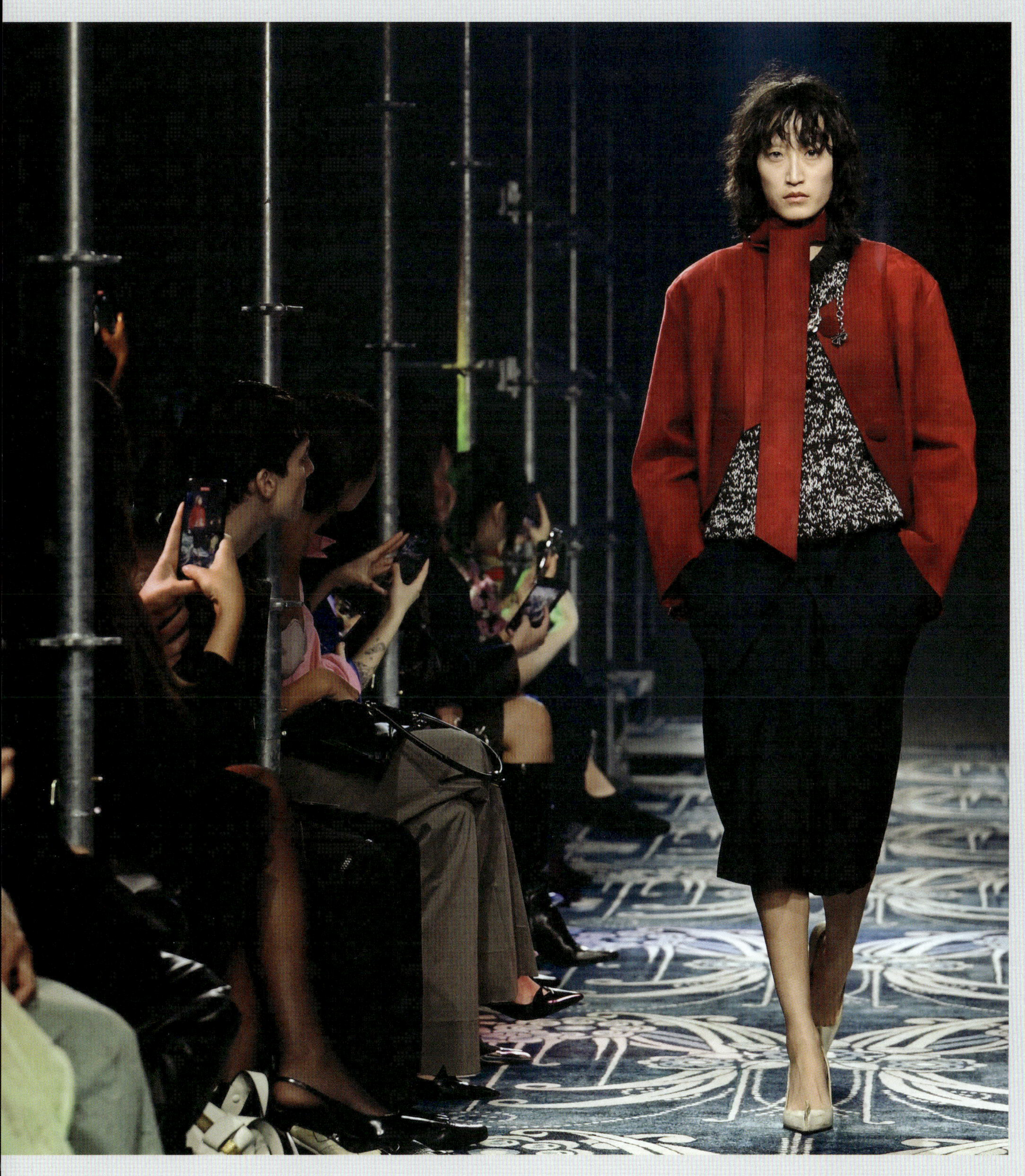

LA CUCINA PRADA

Prada does fashion but the brand also does food! The label has branched out into hospitality with a few high-profile restaurants and cafes which reflect the same elegance, sophistication, and innovative design for which it is sartorially renowned.

MARCHESI 1824 (MILAN, ITALY AND LONDON, UK)

In 2014, Prada acquired a majority stake in the historic Milanese patisserie, Pasticceria Marchesi, which was originally founded in 1824. Prada's involvement with Marchesi 1824 has helped the brand expand its presence in the culinary world while preserving the patisserie's traditional craftsmanship. Marchesi, known for its artisanal pastries, chocolates, and coffee, serves traditional Milanese panettone, delicate sweets, and elegant cakes along with a carefully curated menu of light meals. The three Milanese Pasticceria Marchesi offer an elegant yet relaxed atmosphere for breakfast, lunch, or afternoon tea. The Via Santa Maria alla Porta – the original Marchesi location - is a charming, traditional space that retains its historic feel; the Galleria Vittorio Emanuele II – this elegant, pastel-perfect branch complete with

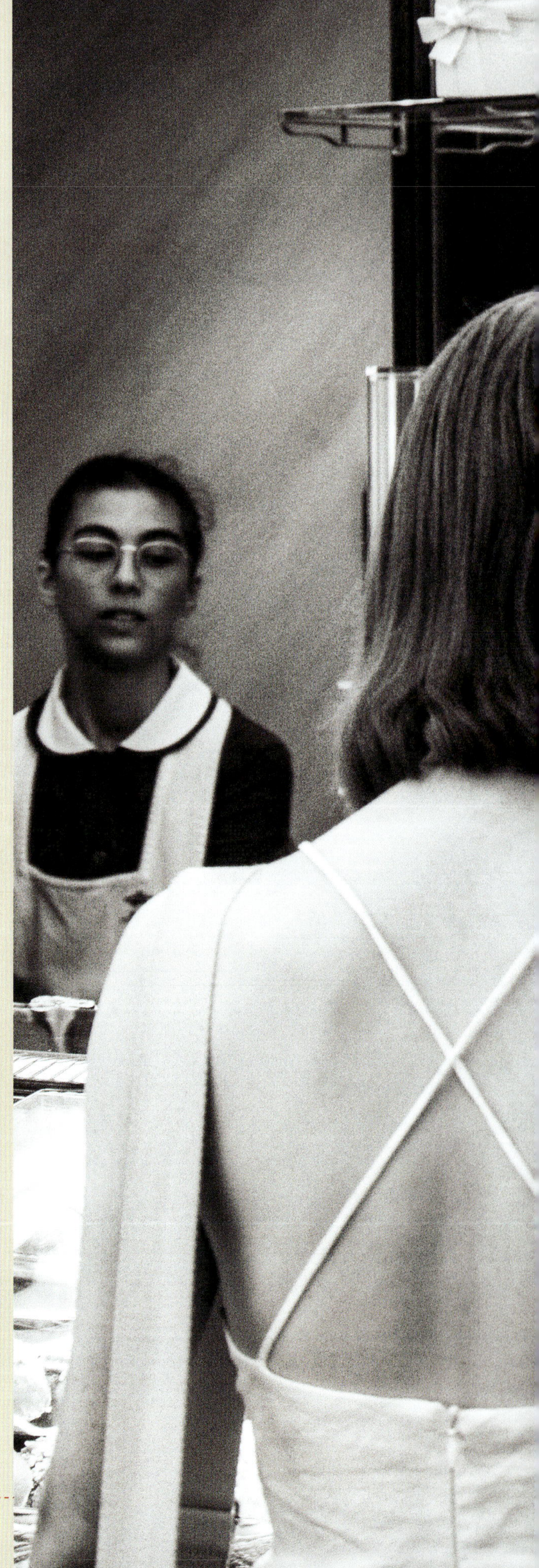

RIGHT: The historical Pasticceria Marchesi 1824 at Galleria Vittorio Emanuele II, Milano

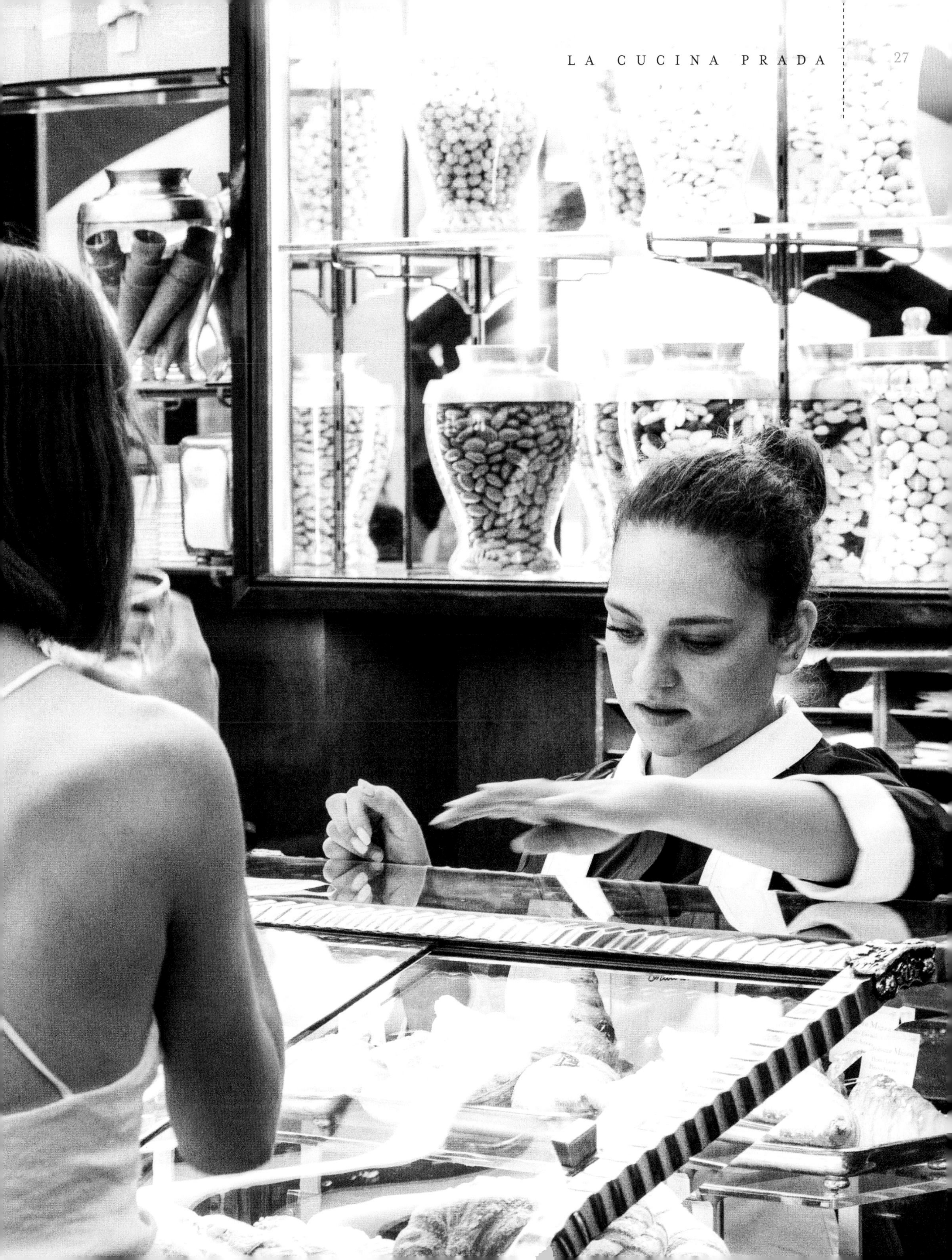

brass details and marble counters is located in one of Milan's most iconic shopping galleries and reflects Prada's sleek design aesthetic where modernity meets heritage; the Via Monte Napoleone - another chic location in Milan's luxury shopping district. London's Mayfair also became home to a branch of Marchesi in 2019 – 117 Mount Street to be exact.

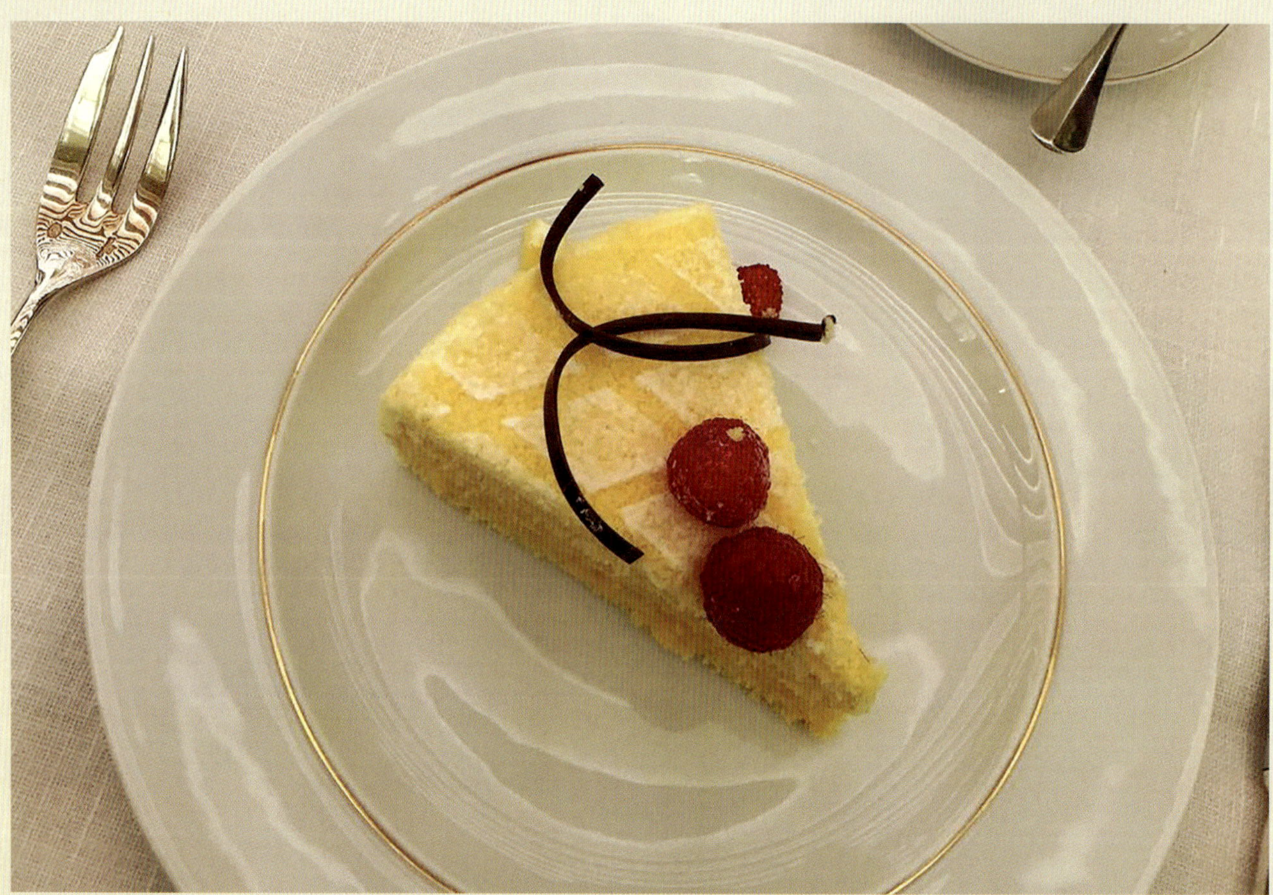

PRADA CAFFÈ AT HARRODS (LONDON, UK)

In 2023, Prada opened Prada Caffè inside famous luxury London department store Harrods. This is a temporary pop-up café designed to provide a full Prada experience in the context of dining. The menu features a mix of Italian classics - from coffee and pastries to a range of lunch items – all echoing the elegantly unique Prada touch. As do the décor and design. The café's interior is inspired by Prada's signature aesthetic, with bold use of its recognizable green colour palette, checkerboard floors (reminiscent of Prada's historic flagship stores), and sleek, contemporary furnishings.

ABOVE: A beautiful dessert at Pasticceria Marchesi
OPP PAGE: Entrance to the Prada Caffè at Harrods in Knightsbridge, London

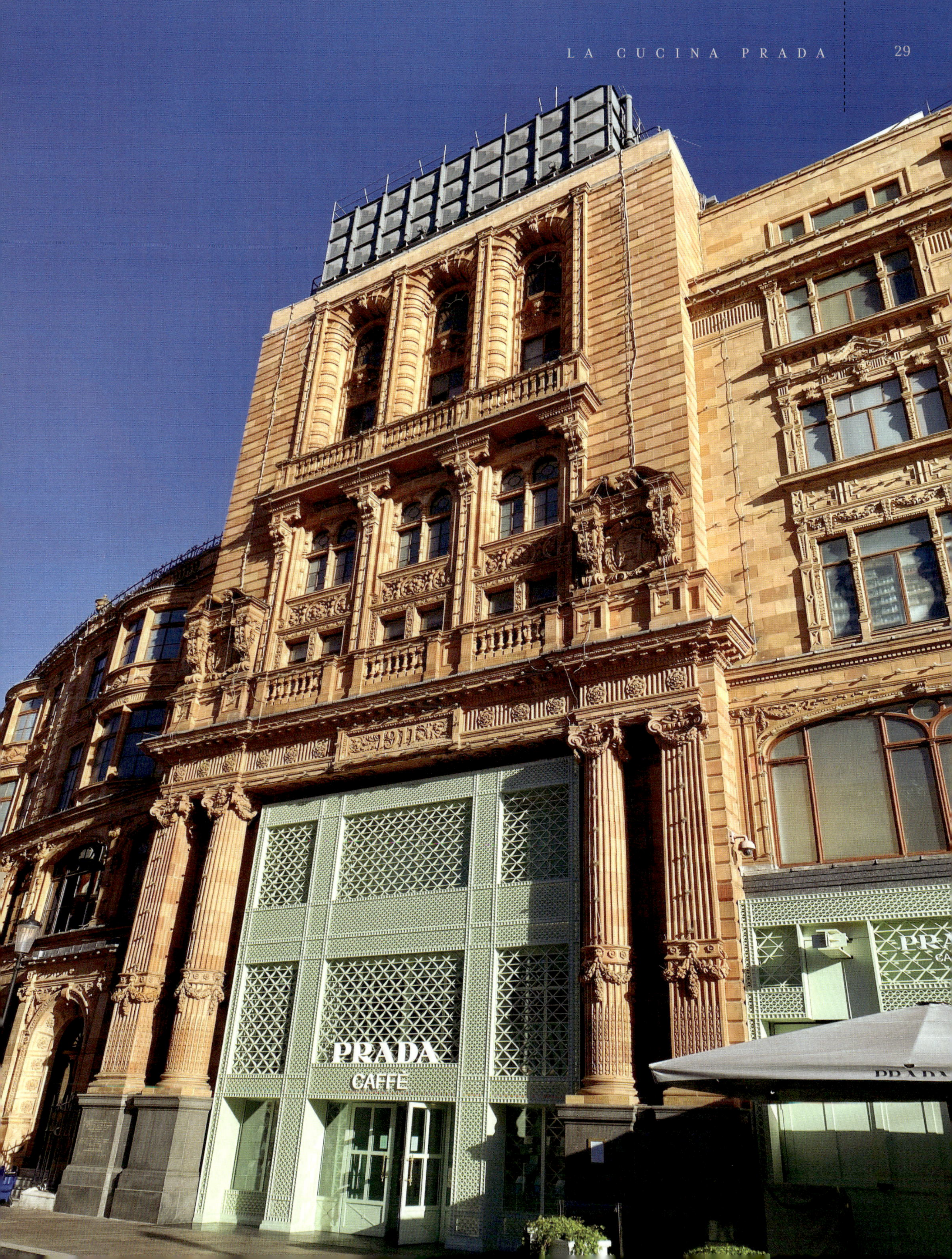
PRADA
CAFFÈ
1911

TORRE RESTAURANT AT FONDAZIONE PRADA (MILAN, ITALY)

Torre is a fine-dining restaurant located at the Fondazione Prada, the contemporary art and cultural centre founded by Miuccia Prada and her husband Patrizio Bertelli in Milan. The restaurant occupies the sixth and seventh floors of the complex's iconic Torre or Tower building, which was designed by architect Rem Koolhaas. The restaurant offers a stylish, art-filled dining experience with floor-to-ceiling windows that provide stunning panoramic views of the city. The space is decorated with vintage furniture from the 1950s and 1960s, and the ambiance is elevated with art pieces from the Prada collection. The menu combines Italian and international flavours, with an emphasis on modern Italian cuisine.

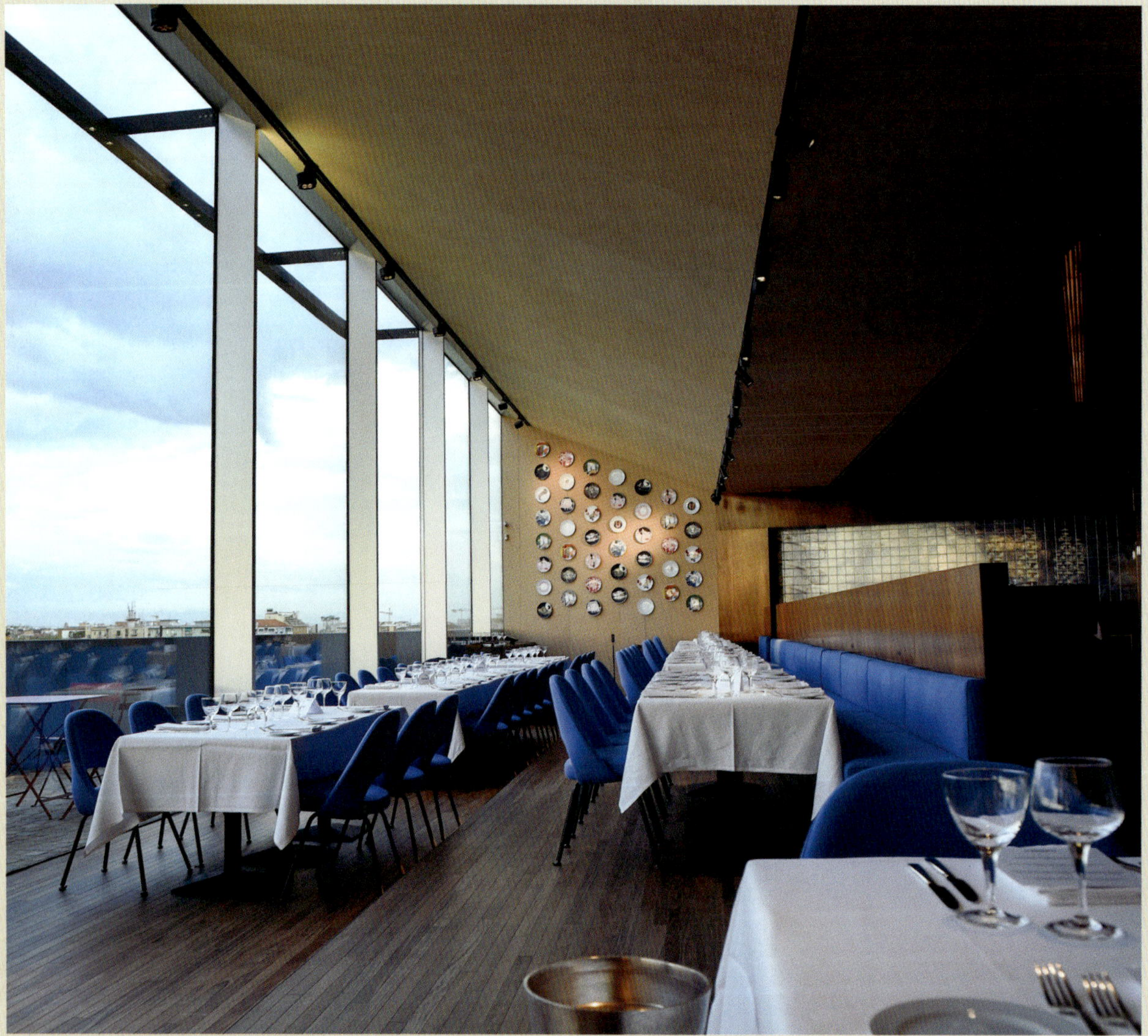

ABOVE: Torre restaurant at the Fondazione Prada
OPP PAGE: Bar Luce in Milan, Italy and one of their beautiful Aperol Spritz cocktails

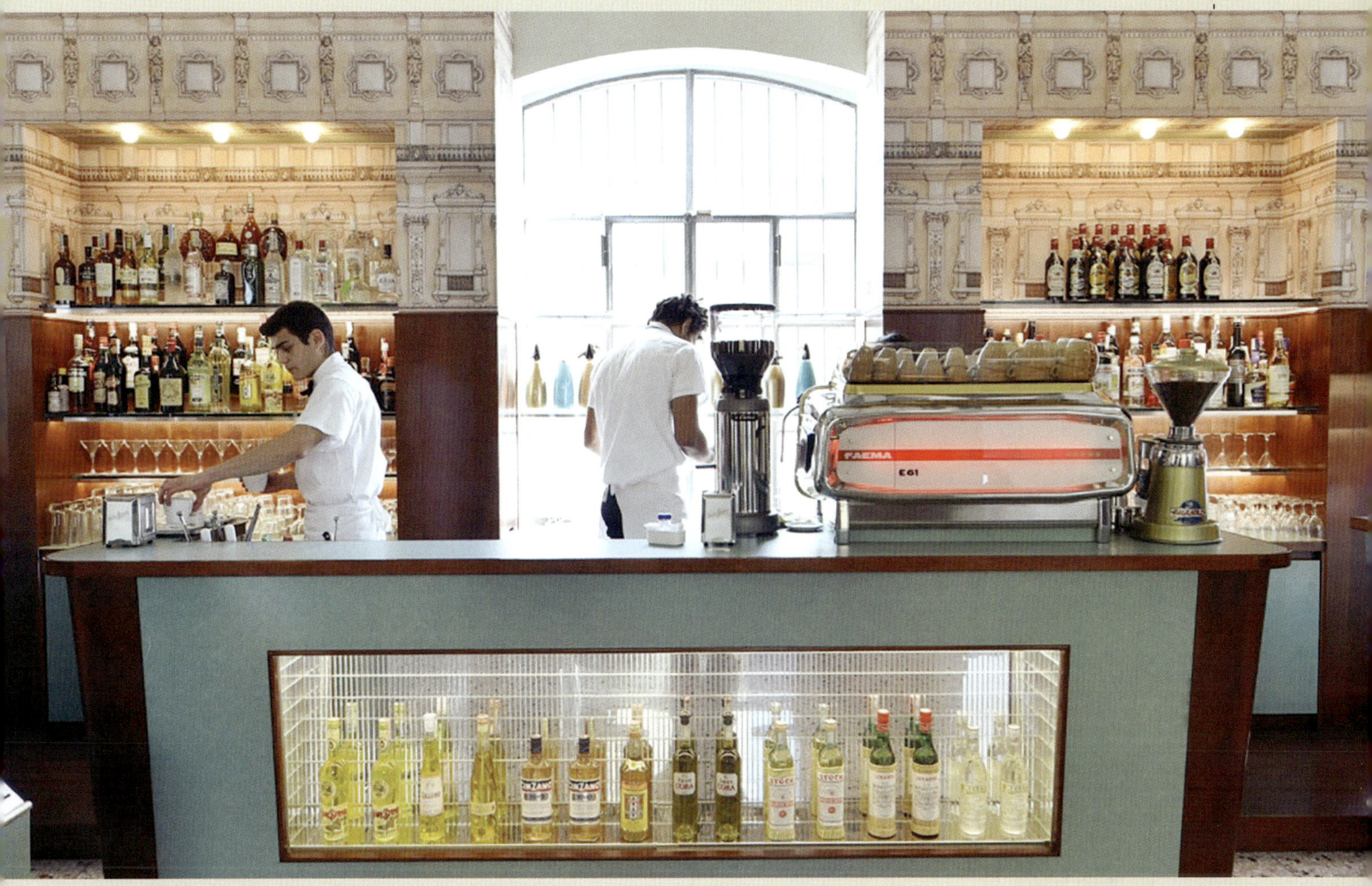

BAR LUCE AT FONDAZIONE PRADA (MILAN, ITALY)

Bar Luce is another eaterie located within the Fondazione Prada. Designed by film director Wes Anderson, Bar Luce evokes the atmosphere of a typical 1950s or 1960s Milanese café, with pastel colours, retro furnishings and a distinctly nostalgic ambience. The space features colourful Formica furniture, pinball machines, and a whimsical, cinematic vibe. Think stepping onto a vintage film set. The menu includes a variety of Italian coffees, pastries, and light snacks.

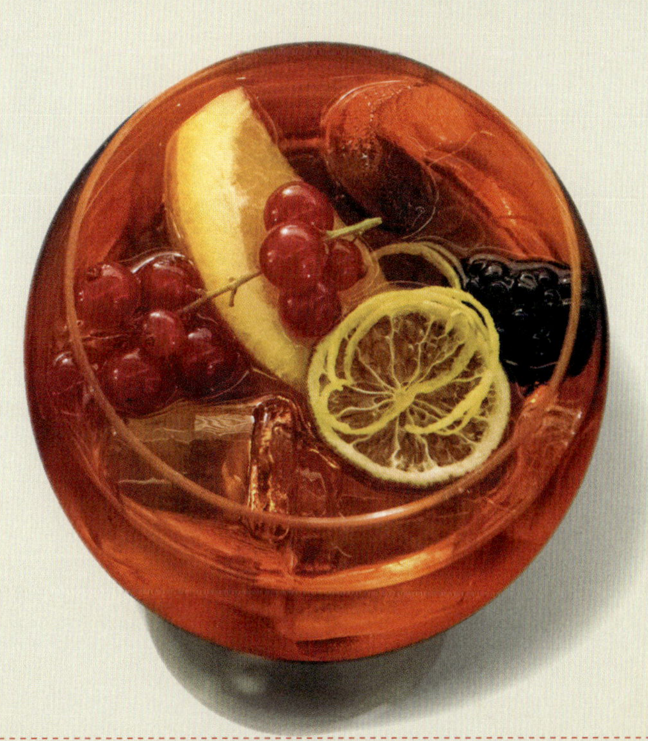

PRADA MODE (POP-UP CLUB CONCEPT)

Prada Mode is an exclusive travelling social club concept launched by Prada in 2018. It offers a unique fusion of art, culture, and food, transforming temporary spaces around the world into cultural hubs which blend fine dining, curated music, and exhibitions. It typically coincides with major cultural events like Art Basel or international film festivals. Each 'Prada Mode' features a tailored menu by renowned chefs, offering high-end culinary experiences in a Prada-designed space.

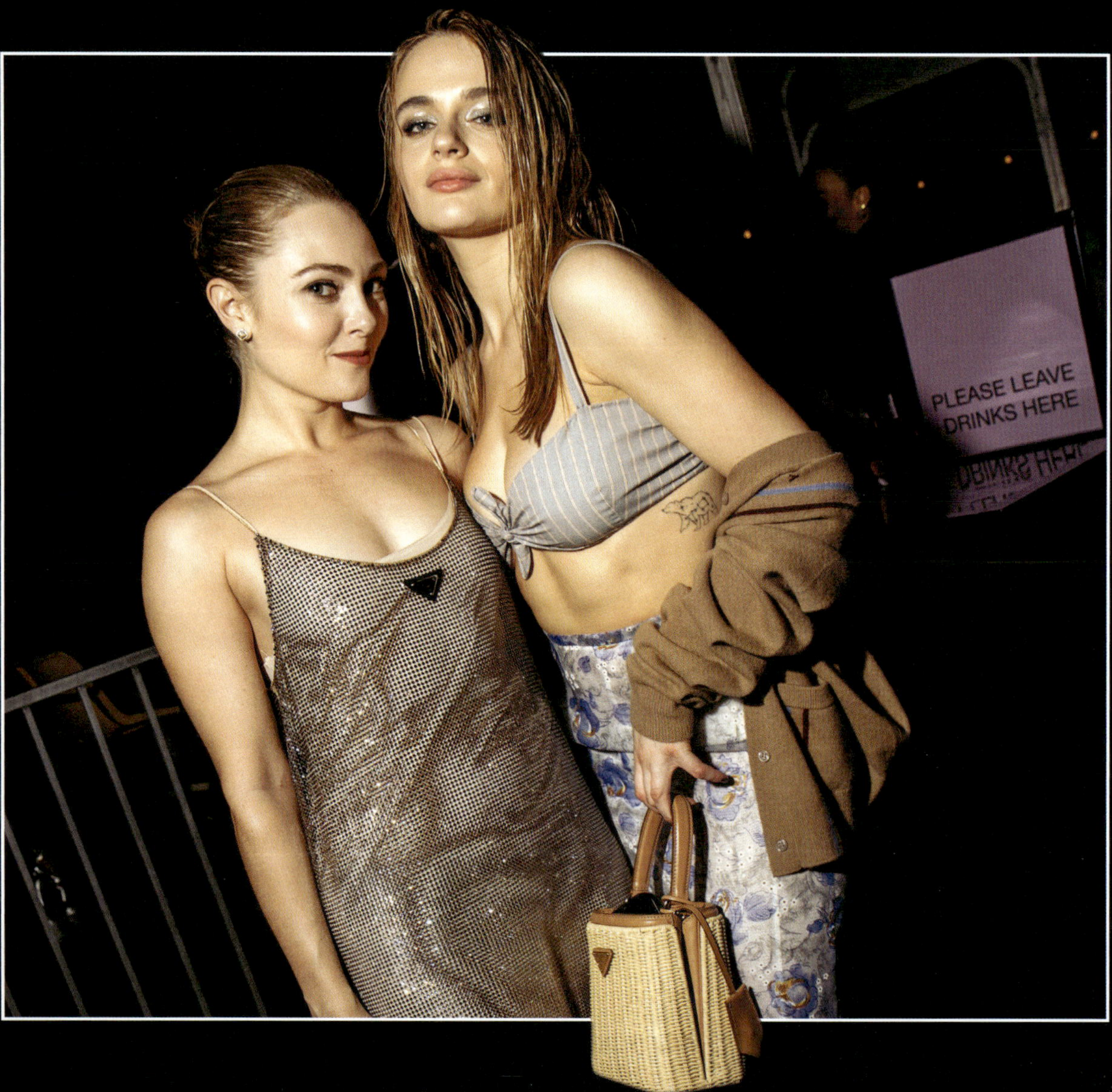

IMAGES: AnnaSophia Robb and Joey King (Inset) and Aja Naomi King (Right) at The Double Club Los Angeles, presented by Prada Mode, held at Luna Luna on 8 March, 2024 in Los Angeles, California

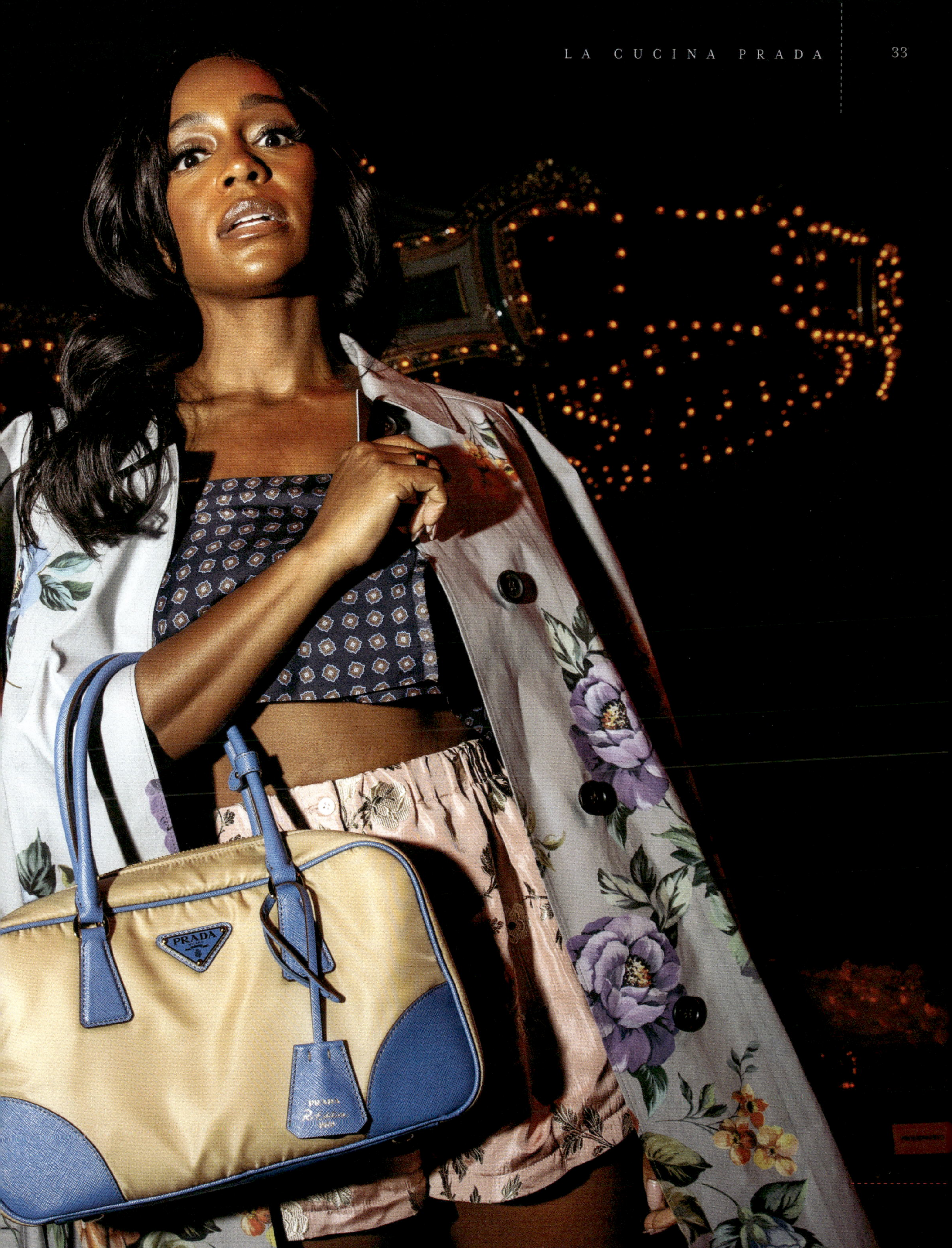
PRADA
MILANO

PRADA SHOES

"Shoes are the quickest way for women to achieve instant metamorphosis"

Miuccia Prada

On taking control of the family business in the late 1970s, Miuccia wanted to expand Prada's appeal beyond its traditional range of high-quality leather goods – and where better to start than with shoes? She first launched footwear bearing the famous Prada triangle logo in the '80s. In the years since – from sleek formal footwear through sartorially sexy high heels to bold, fashion-forward sneakers – Prada shoes have become synonymous with luxury, craftsmanship, and innovation. The brand is known for using the finest Italian leather for its shoes, ensuring durability and comfort in addition to good looks. Classic styles combined with that unique Prada avant-garde design. For the technically minded, approximately 250 manual processes and eight weeks of manufacturing are necessary to create a single pair of Prada shoes.

ABOVE: Burgundy Prada leather high heel shoe
OPP PAGE: Classic hand-made Italian designer Prada shoes

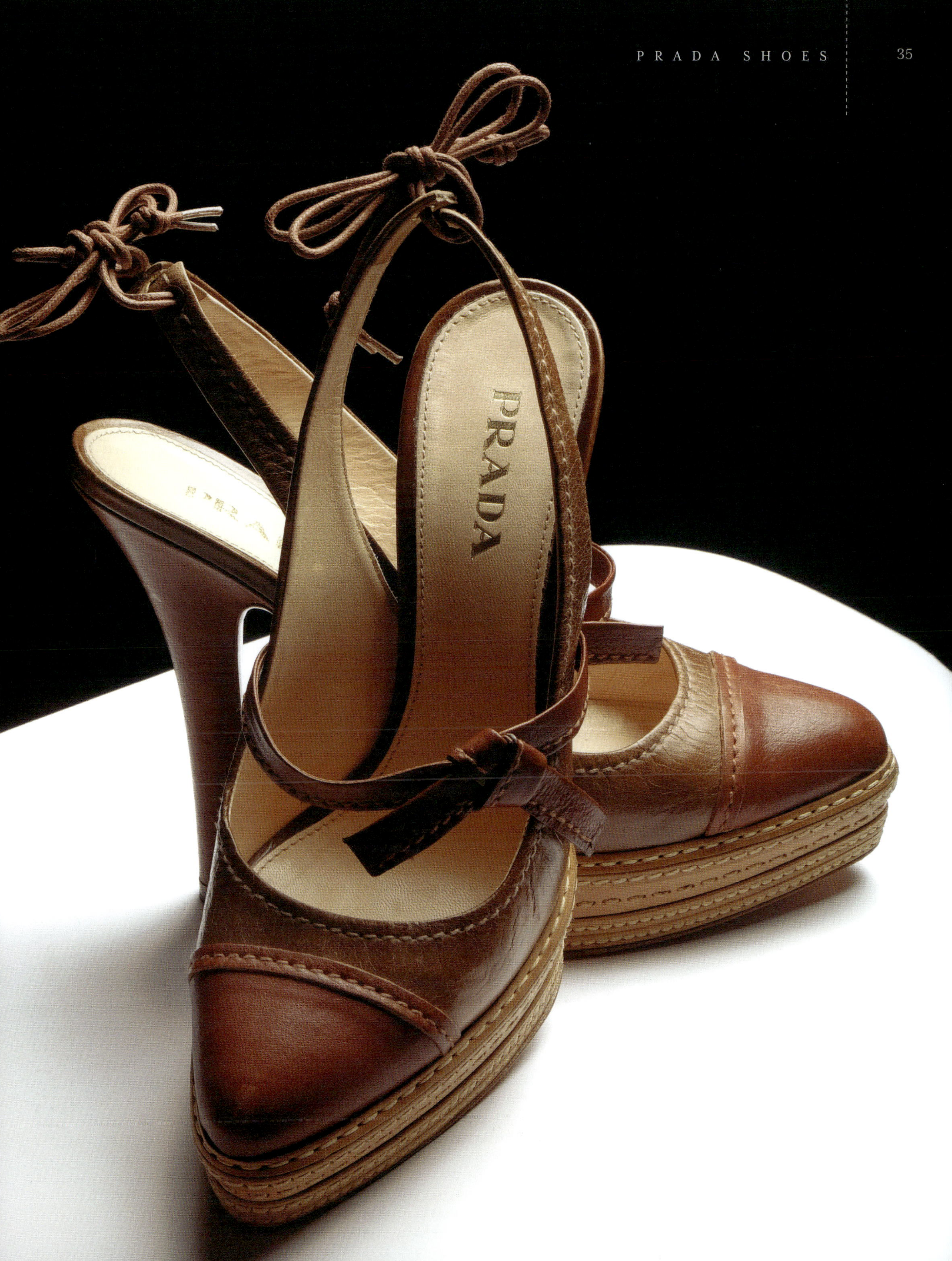

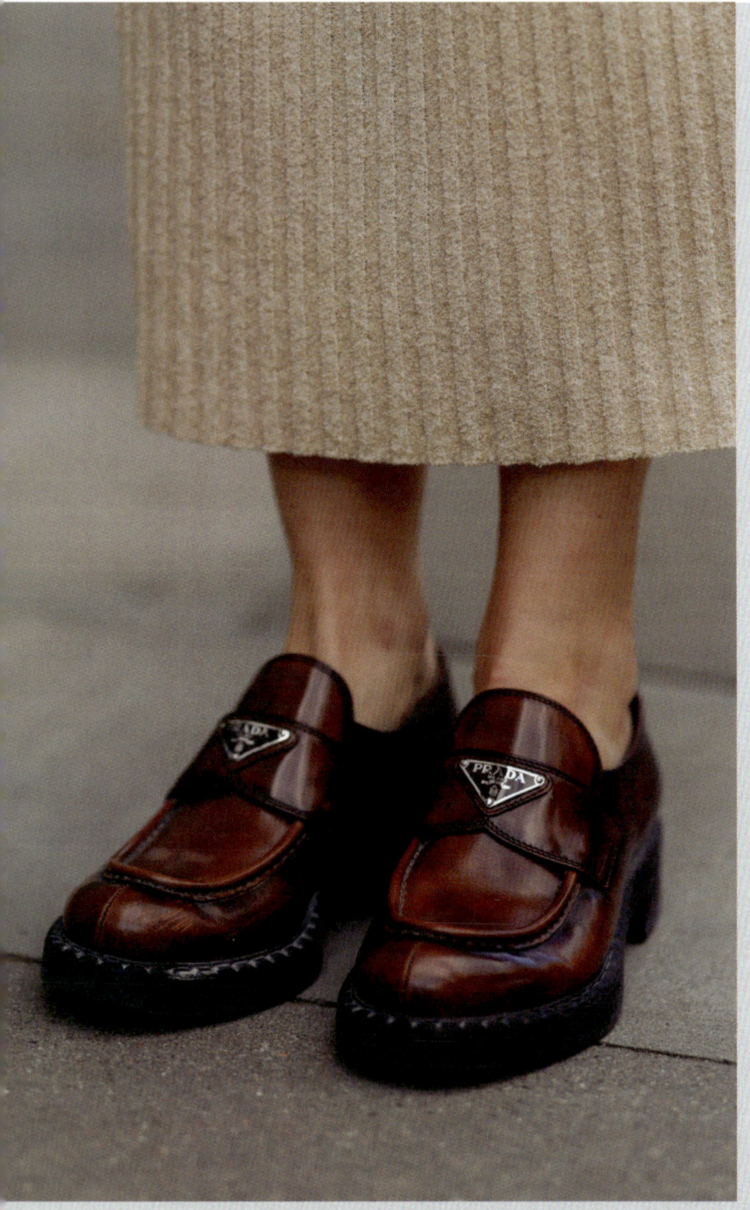

PRADA LOAFERS

Prada first introduced its iconic loafer in 1996. The shoe quickly gained popularity due to its minimalist, streamlined and timeless design, which contrasted sharply with more ornate styles of the 1990s. The Prada loafer, often crafted in premium black or patent leather with a chunky or classic sole and Prada's triangle logo, has become a staple in the brand's collections. Its timeless appeal and versatility have allowed it to remain a classic, influencing numerous iterations and cementing it as the ultimate symbol of luxury and sophistication in footwear. Popular styles include Prada brushed leather loafers and Prada Monolith platform loafers which feature chunky soles for an edgier aesthetic.

PRADA SNEAKERS

Prada launched its first line of sneakers in 1996, marking its initial foray into the luxury sportswear market. The collection ranges from minimalist leather designs to bold, futuristic styles with the sneakers crafted in premium materials, distinctive colour combinations, and often featuring the Prada logo. Popular styles include the Prada Cloudbust Thunder sneakers – a futuristic design with chunky soles, and Prada America's Cup sneakers – classic, sleek and inspired by sailing.

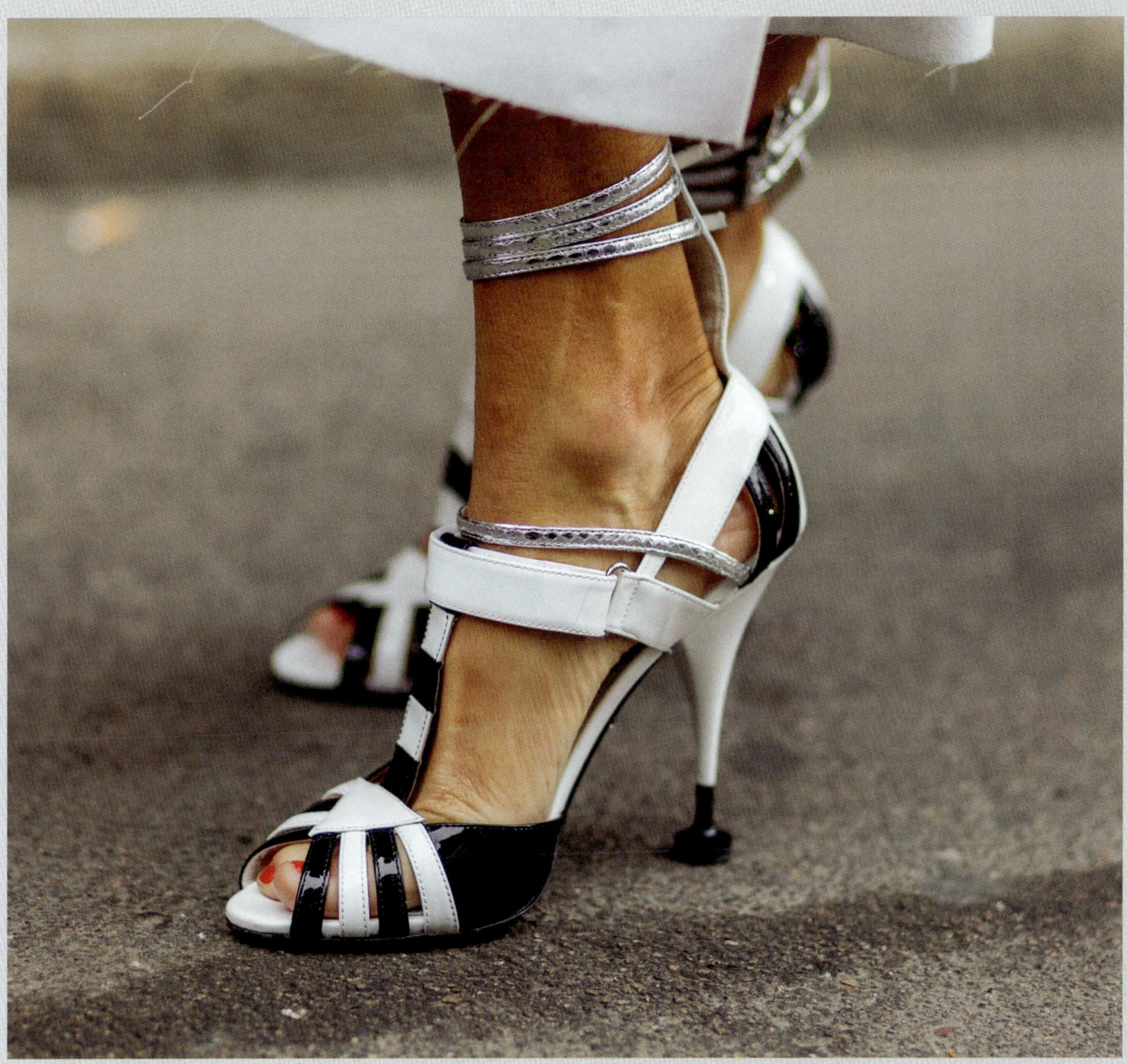

PRADA HEELS AND SANDALS – WOMEN

Prada launched its first women's shoe collection in 1984. Elegant, modern, and luxurious, Prada's women's shoes have become iconic in the world of high-end fashion, and are known for their innovation, quality, and timeless appeal. Prada offers a variety of styles, from classic heels to contemporary sneakers, and is known for blending elegance with the label's signature avant-garde design. Popular styles include Mary Janes, satin slingback high heels – often in vibrant colours, embellished sandals, platform sandals and classic leather high-heeled pumps.

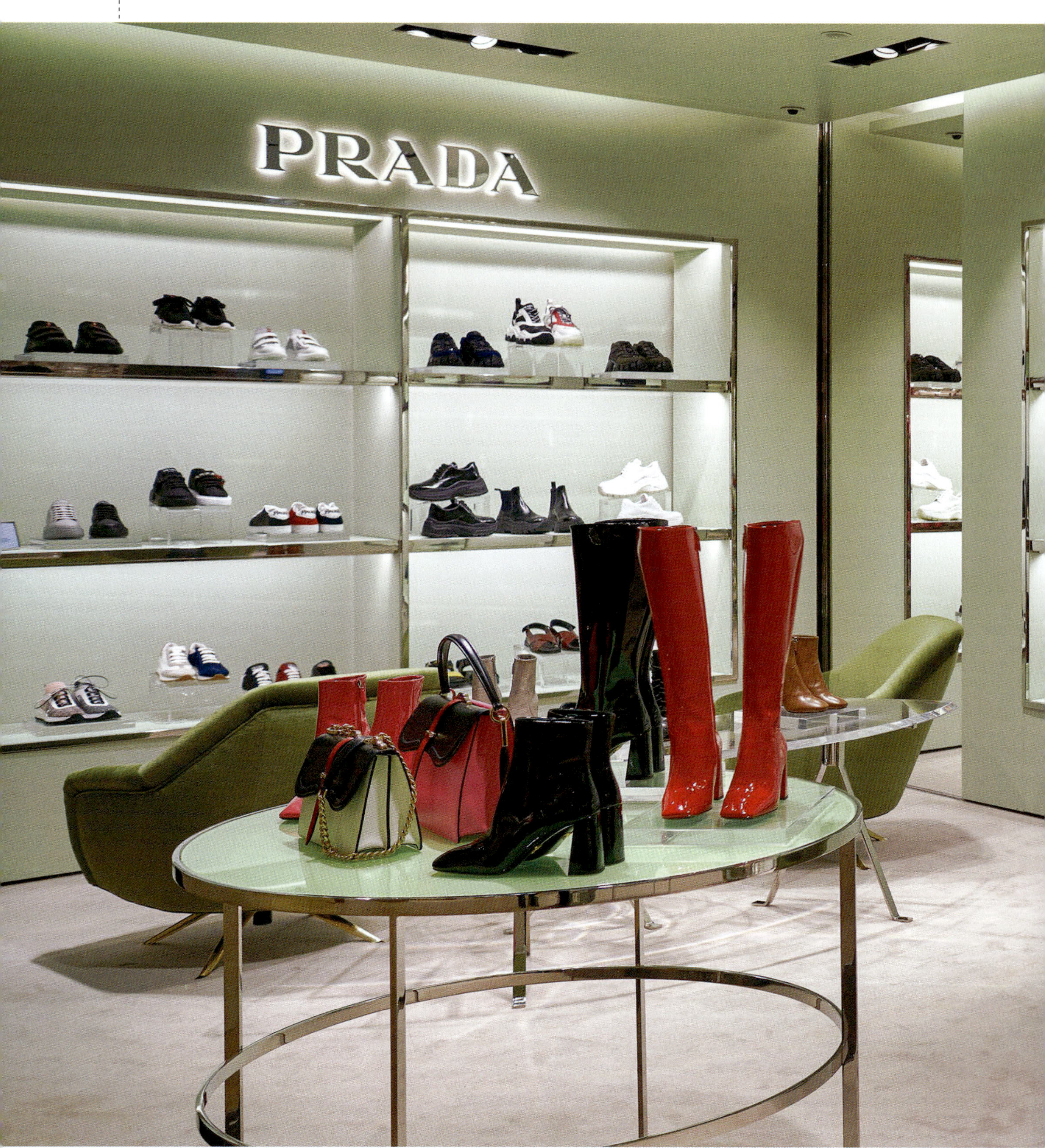

ABOVE: A fabulous selection of Prada shoes on display at the Kaufhaus des Westens (KaDeWe) department store in Berlin

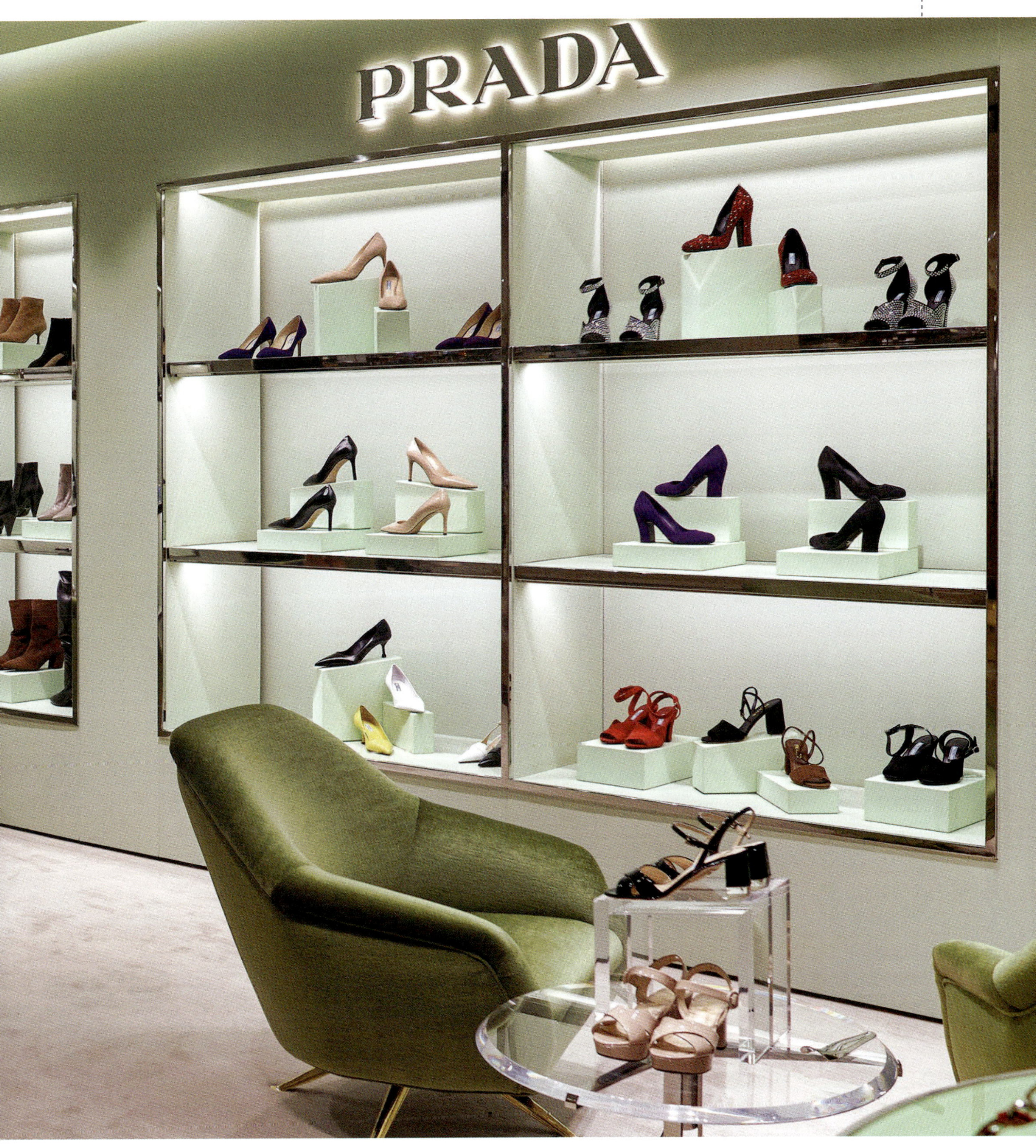

PRADA COMBAT BOOTS

Launched in the late '90s, Prada Combats aligned with the brand's growing exploration of edgy, utilitarian fashion. These initial designs leaned into a grunge-inspired aesthetic that blended luxury with a tough, practical look, marking a departure from Prada's more traditional offerings. Introduced in the 2010s, the Monolith boots were a standout from the start – featuring chunky platform soles, rugged designs, and details like detachable pouches. Boots that balance practicality with bold fashion.

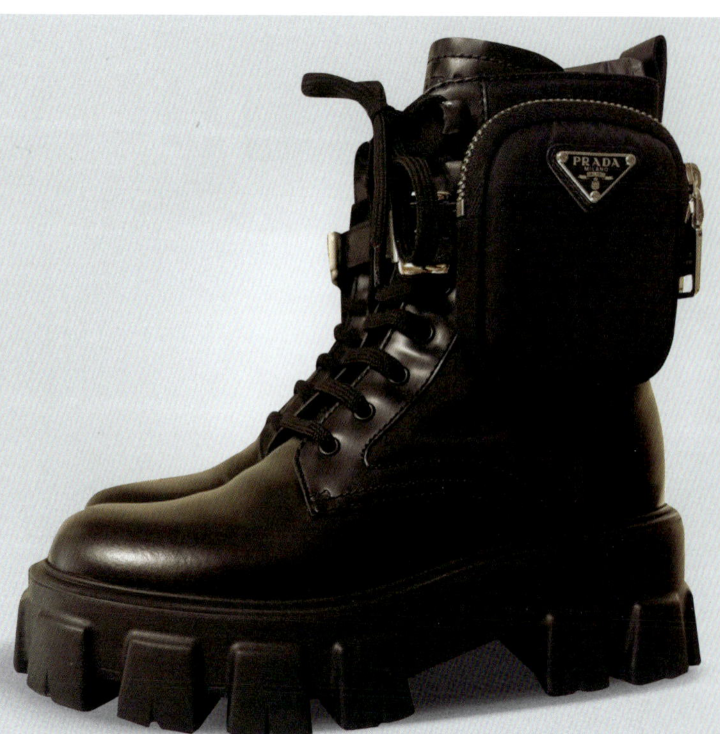

PRADA ESPADRILLES AND MULES – WOMEN

Around 2011/12, Prada introduced espadrilles for women during a time when luxury brands were beginning to revisit and elevate traditional, casual footwear styles. Prada's version featured premium materials, such as high-quality canvas, leather, and jute, and often included embellishments or unique design twists that set them apart from traditional espadrilles.

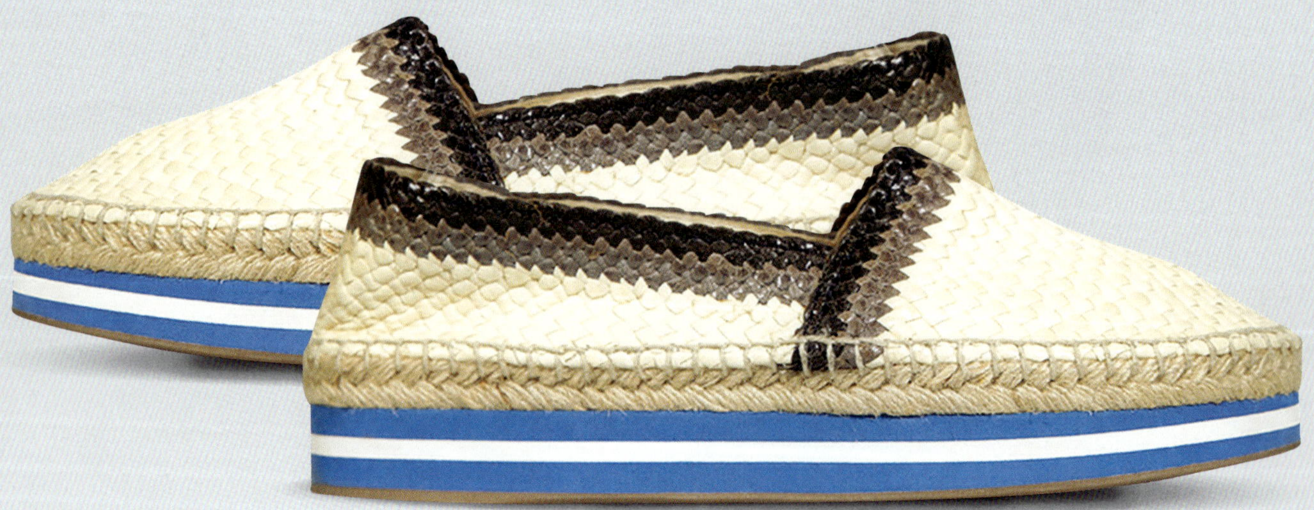

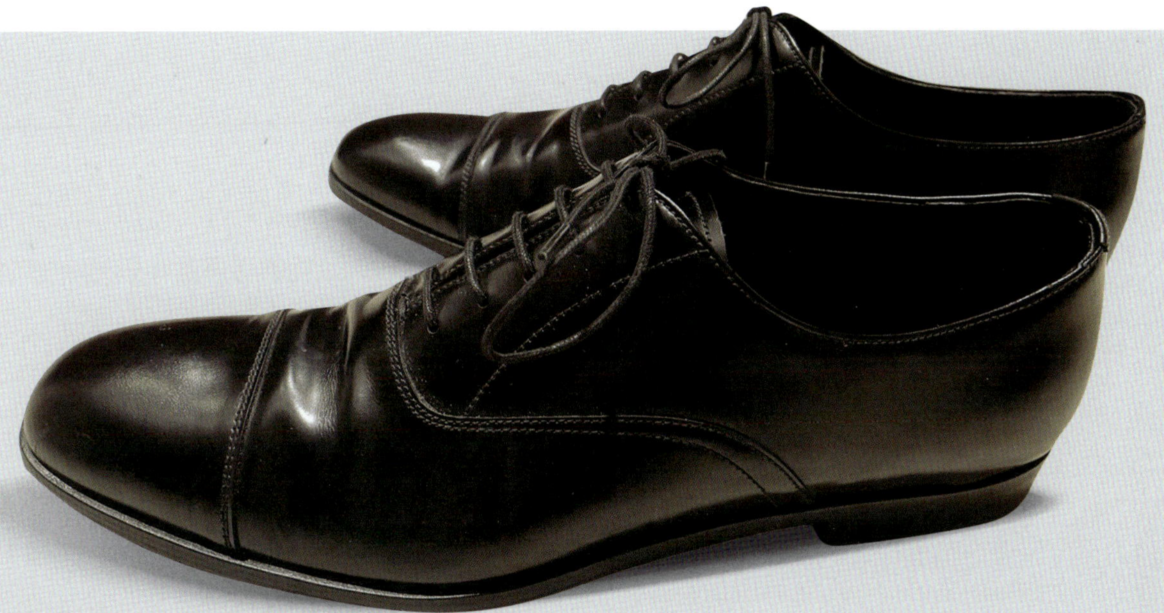

PRADA FORMAL SHOES – MEN

Launched in the late 1980s, Prada men's shoes quickly became known for their classic Italian design and meticulous attention to detail with styles ranging from elegant loafers to polished Oxfords and Derby shoes crafted from premium leather. Over time, Prada has continued to innovate within the men's formal footwear line, introducing distinctive modern elements such as sleek silhouettes, unique materials, and unexpected detailing while maintaining the brand's luxurious aesthetic. Prada acquired Church's, the renowned British luxury shoe brand, in 1999. This acquisition was part of Prada's strategy to expand its footprint in the luxury footwear market and diversify its portfolio with a brand known for traditional British craftsmanship and classic, high-quality men's shoes. Church's, established in 1873 in Northampton, England, brought a heritage of shoemaking expertise that complemented Prada's modern Italian luxury image.

PRADA SANDALS – MEN

Launched in the late 1990s, men's sandals from Prada emphasized technical details, like adjustable straps and durable soles, often blending luxury with a sporty look that made them stand out in the world of high fashion. They quickly became iconic, especially for their clean lines and use of high-quality materials. This launch helped to pave the way for the popularity of designer sandals and sport-luxury footwear in men's fashion.

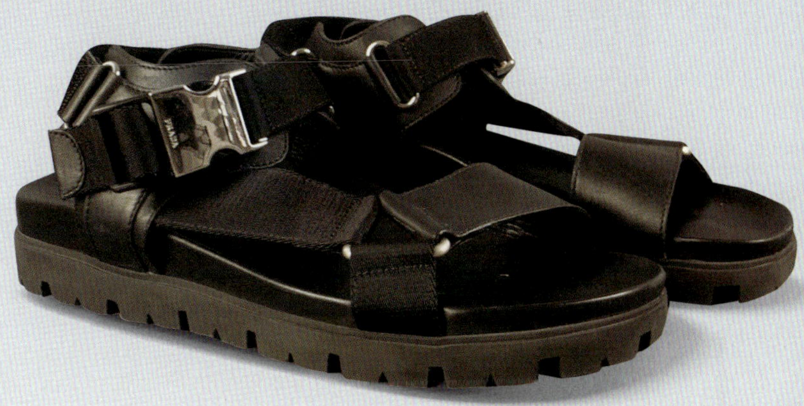

PRADA BAGS

"What I like is when the handbag is a bit of a contradiction. It has to be beautiful and at the same time it has to be practical"
Miuccia Prada

Prada's relationship with handbags began in the early 1980s when Miuccia Prada introduced innovative styles that would soon define the brand. Prada's first major handbag success was the nylon backpack, initially introduced in 1984. Known as the Prada Vela backpack, it was made from durable black nylon, setting it apart from the traditional leather bags of the time. This item established Prada as a modern luxury brand, blending practicality with high fashion. By the 1990s, Prada's sleek, understated handbags were gaining popularity which grew in the noughties with the introduction of the 'Saffiano' leather bags, featuring the textured, durable leather – originally 'discovered' by founder Mario Prada many years earlier - that is now a brand staple. Gold or silver-tone hardware was often used, with the iconic Prada triangle logo featuring on most bags. This period marked the beginning of Prada's reputation for creating minimalist yet elegant and sophisticated bags that were sartorial status symbols. Blending practical functionality with high fashion. Prada's classic bags are timeless investments.

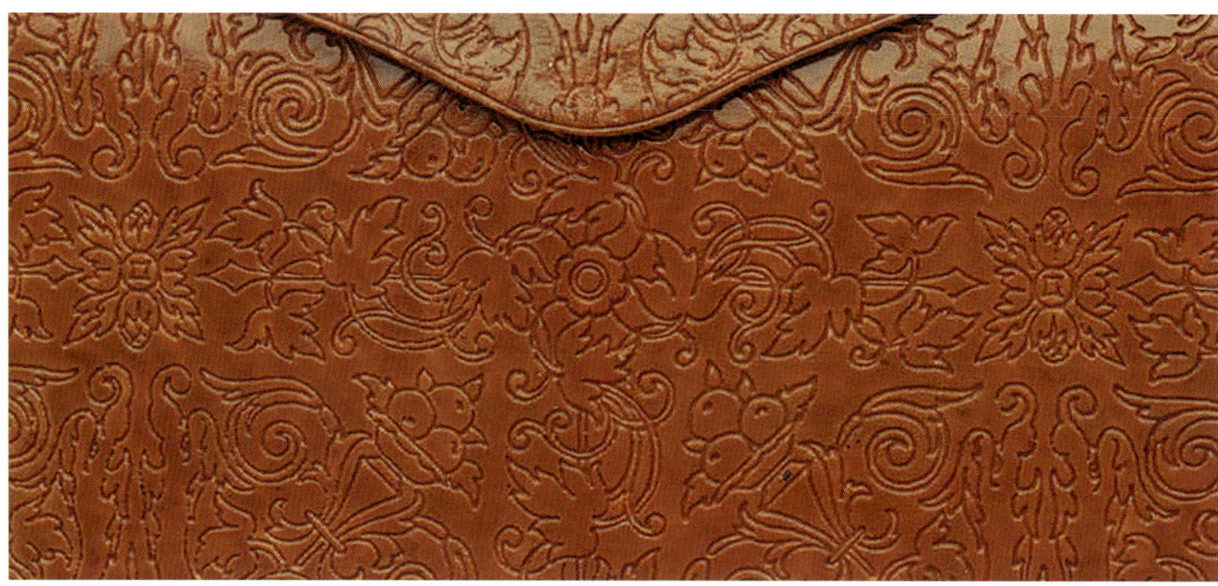

ABOVE: Hand tooled and gilded leather detail on a Prada handbag, circa 1935-45
OPP PAGE: Prada Supernova handbag in shop window display in Florence, Italy

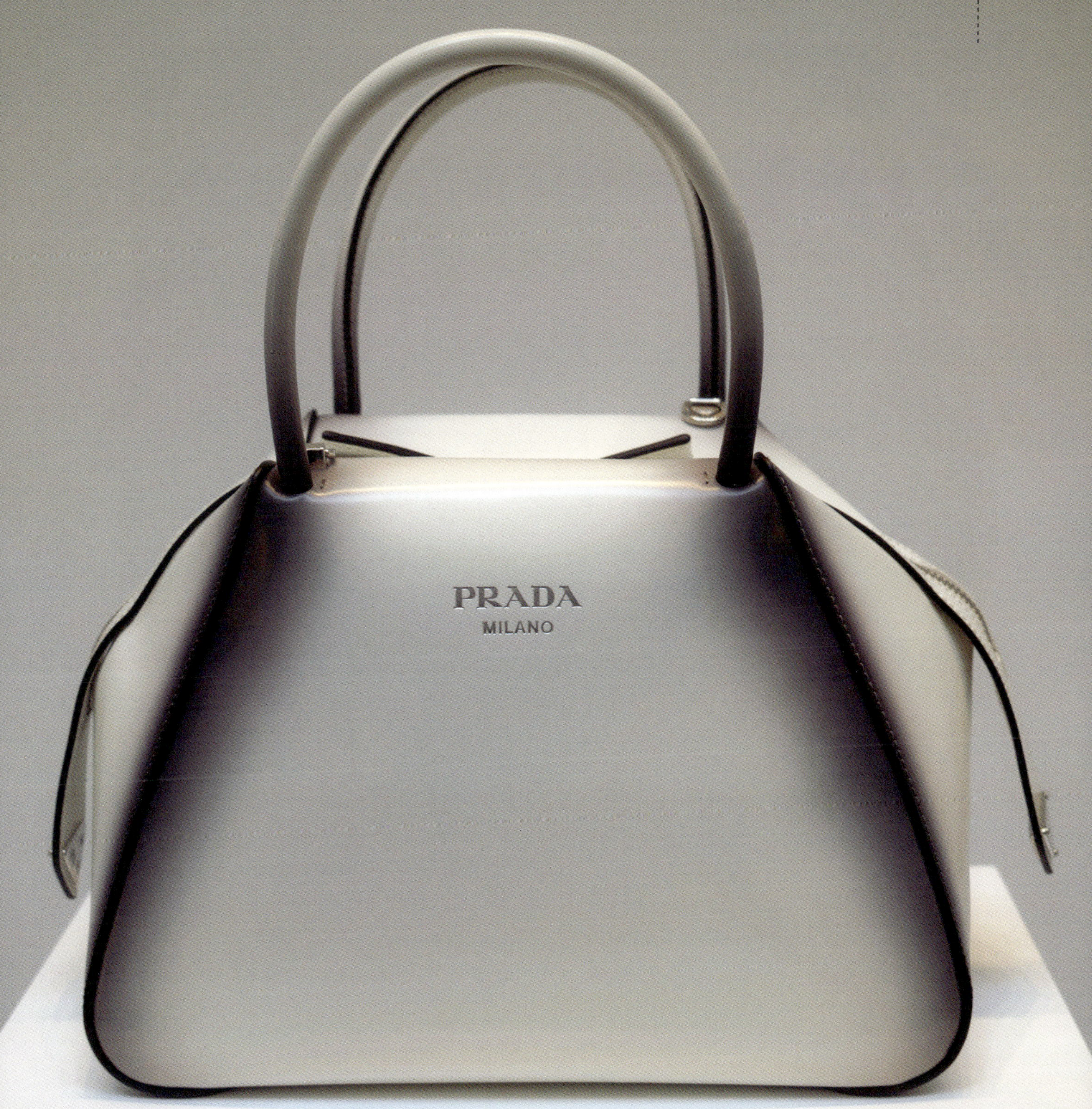

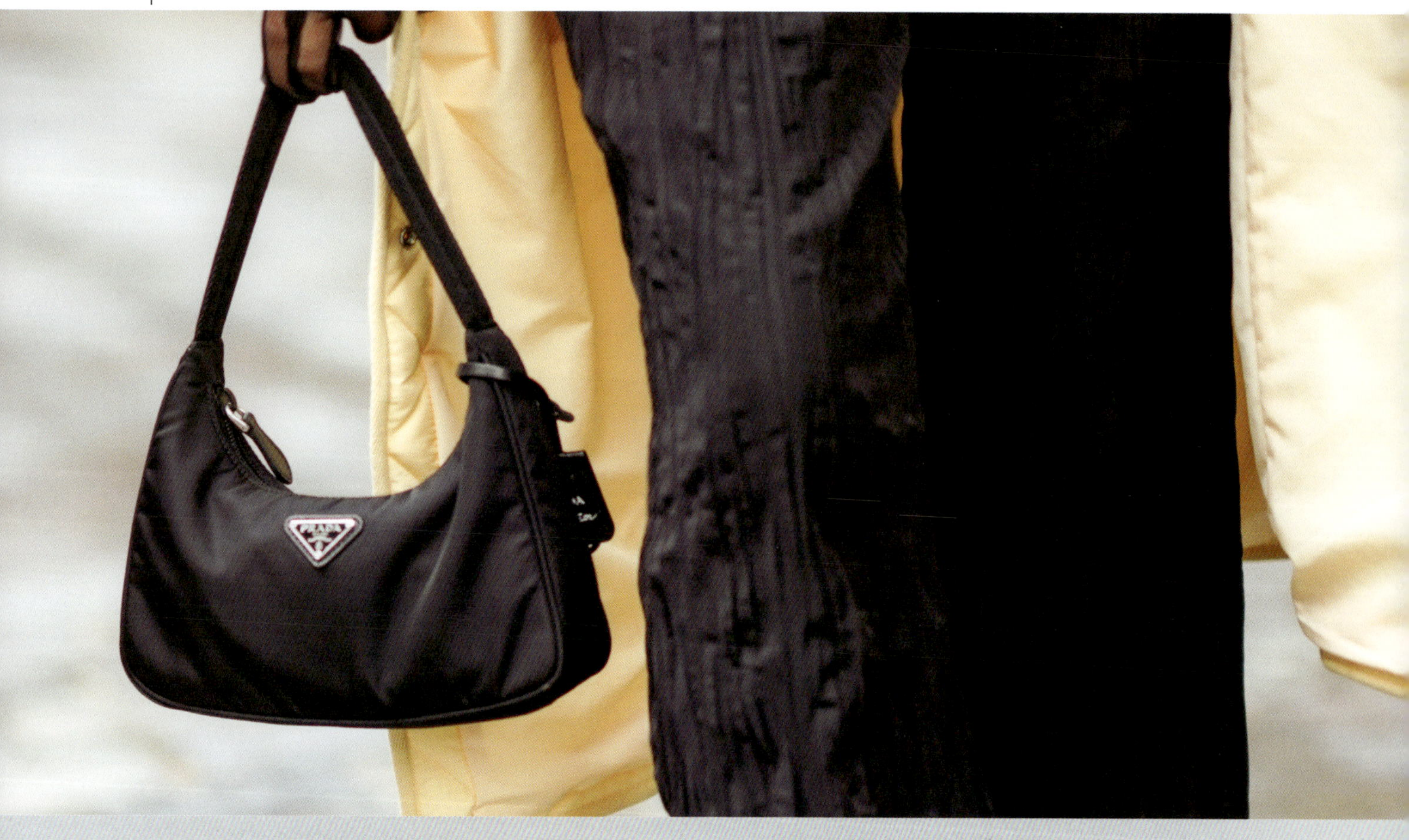

PRADA NYLON BAG

In the late 1970s, newly appointed head of Prada, Miuccia Prada, began experimenting with industrial materials like nylon. Her vision was to create luxury bags from this durable, water-resistant material. In 1984, Prada released its first nylon bag, the Vela Backpack. Made from a durable, lightweight, black nylon called Pocono nylon, the bag had a minimalist design that set it apart from more ornate luxury bags of the time. It became a statement piece and helped redefine luxury as understated and modern. By the 1990s, nylon bags had become a Prada signature item, aligning with the minimalist fashion trends of the decade. Celebrities and fashion insiders embraced the brand's understated style, making Prada nylon bags status symbols. The Re-Edition 2000 and 2005 are re-releases of the Vela, complete with detachable chains and mini pouches. Also crafted in nylon are the Nylon Tote, the Nylon Belt Bag and the Re-Nylon Shoulder Bag. Prada Re-Nylon is a sustainable line of products made from recycled nylon and launched by the brand in 2019. It builds on Prada's legacy with nylon but this time with an eco-conscious approach. Using Econyl – a regenerated nylon fabric produced from ocean plastic, fishing nets, textile waste, and industrial plastics – Re-Nylon aims to reduce the brand's environmental footprint.

ABOVE: A guest holds a black Re-Nylon Re-edition 2000 Prada handbag during Paris Fashion Week, 2021

PRADA GALLERIA BAG

The Prada Galleria bag, also known as the Prada
Saffiano Lux tote, was launched in 2007. Named after
the historic Galleria Vittorio Emanuele II in Milan,
where Prada opened its first store in 1913, the bag
reflects the brand's heritage and sophistication.
Made from the brand's signature Saffiano leather (a
textured, cross-hatched leather), the Galleria bag –
available in mini, small, medium and large - quickly
became an iconic piece. Its structured shape, double
handles, and classic aesthetic have made it one of
Prada's most popular and enduring designs.

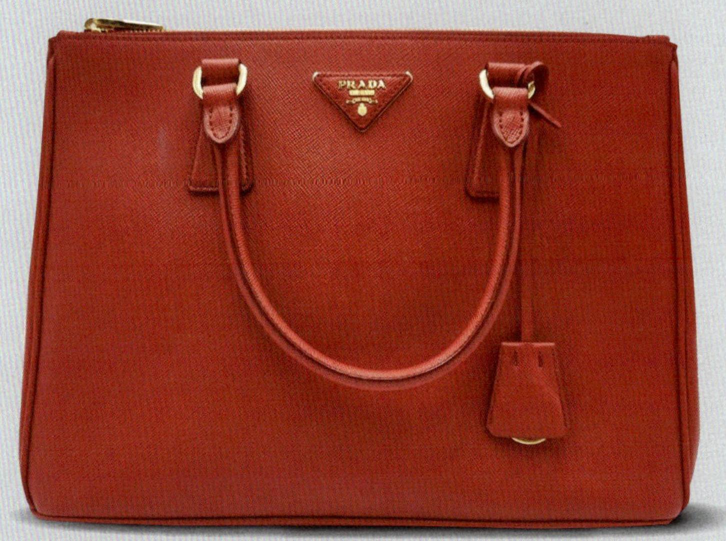

PRADA CAHIER BAG

The Prada Cahier bag was introduced in 2016 and
quickly became one of Prada's standout designs.
Its name, 'Cahier' means 'notebook' in French, and
the bag's design was inspired by antique books and
vintage journals. The bag features distinctive details
like metallic corner reinforcements, bold hardware,
and structured leather panels, which all give it a
timeless, vintage look reminiscent of old-school book
bindings. Made from Prada's luxurious Saffiano leather
or smooth calf leather, the Cahier bag is known for its
durability and high craftsmanship. It comes in various
styles and sizes, including crossbody and shoulder
versions, and is available in a range of colours and
materials. The Cahier's unique, old-world charm mixed
with modern elegance has made it a favourite among
fashion enthusiasts and collectors.

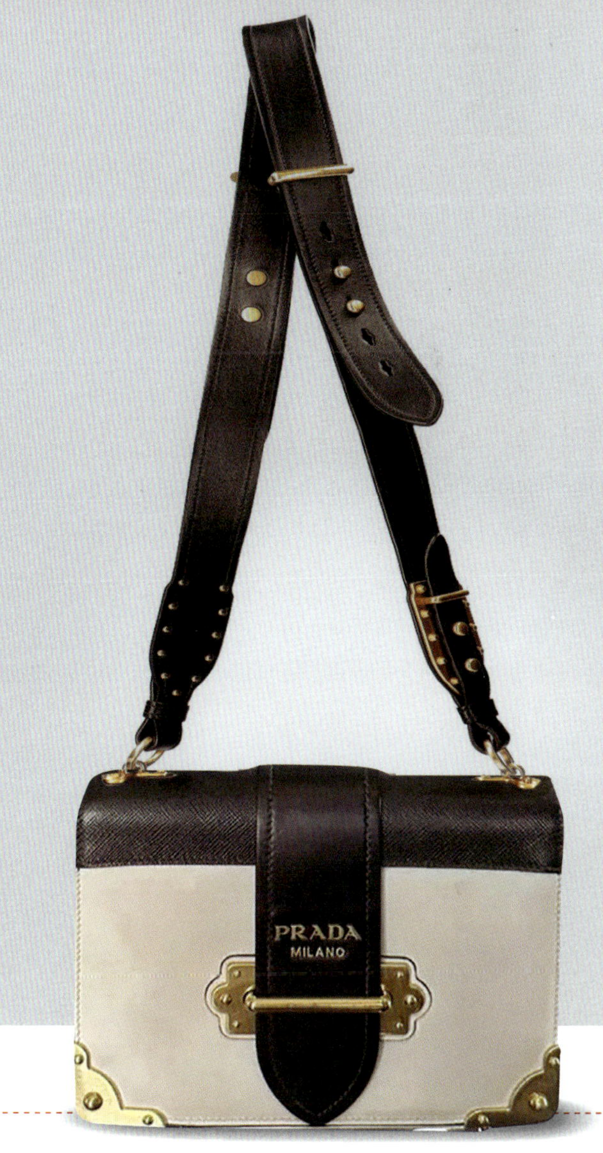

PRADA DIAGRAMME BAG

The Prada Diagramme Bag debuted as part of Prada's Fall/Winter 2024 collection, which was presented by Miuccia Prada and Raf Simons. It features a structured silhouette crafted from premium leather, with refined details like subtle logo placement and sleek hardware, giving it an elegant yet modern appeal. The Diagramme bag is versatile, fitting both day and evening wear, with options for shoulder or crossbody carry. Modern, quilted, and uber chic.

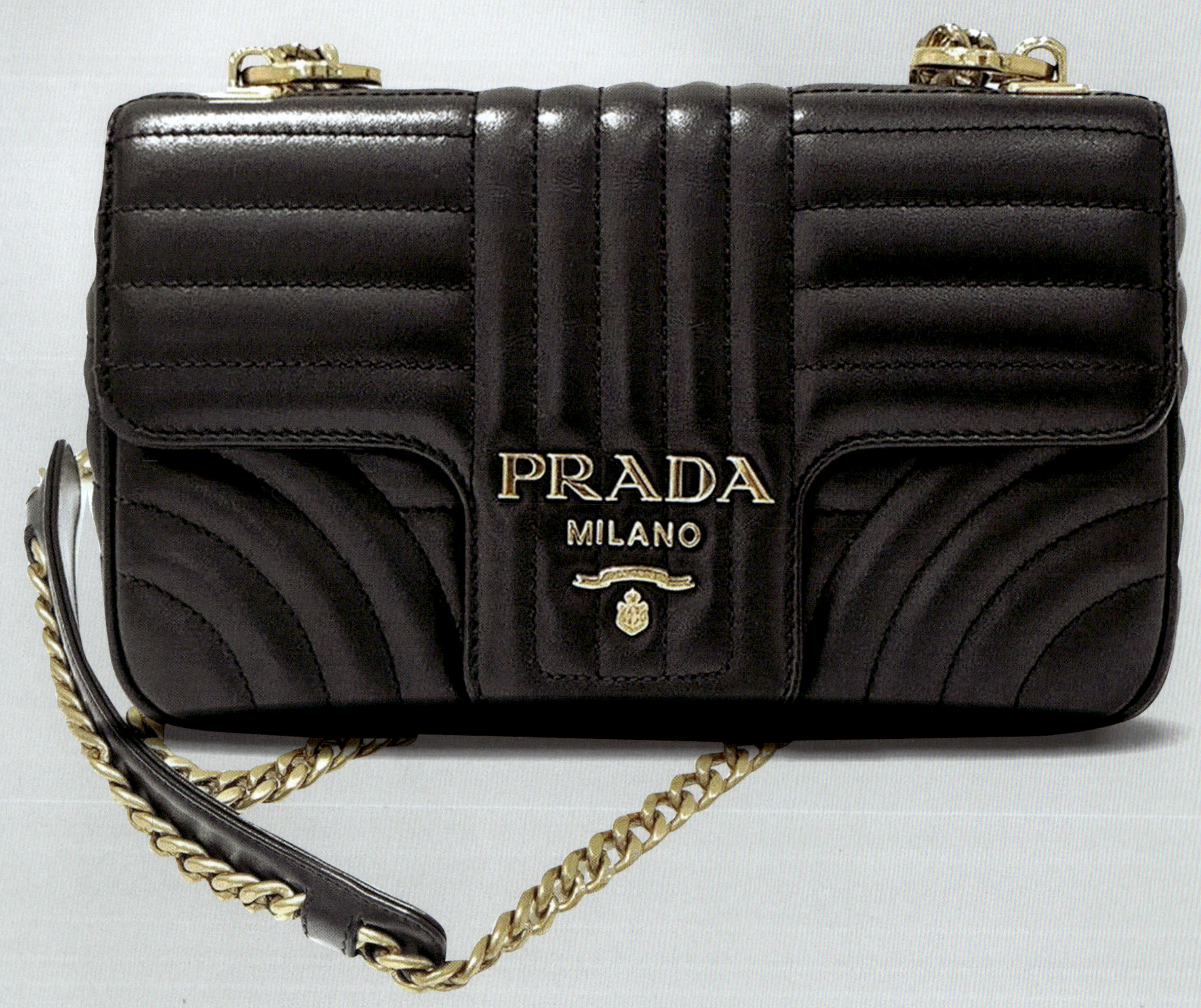

PRADA ETIQUETTE BAG

The Prada Etiquette Bag, launched in 2017, marks a departure from Prada's traditional structured bags. Crafted from soft calfskin leather, which adds a casual yet luxurious feel, the Etiquette has a more relaxed, worn-in look. The most distinctive feature is the external label in powder blue leather, inspired by Prada's interior garment tags, blending the brand's ready-to-wear aesthetic with classic handbag design. Available in several styles and colours - including a shoulder bag, tote, and a small crossbody – and often adorned with metal stud detailing for a subtle edge, the design features adjustable straps and a suede-lined interior, providing both functionality and versatility. Its understated elegance and distinctive branding align with Prada's modern, fashion-forward approach.

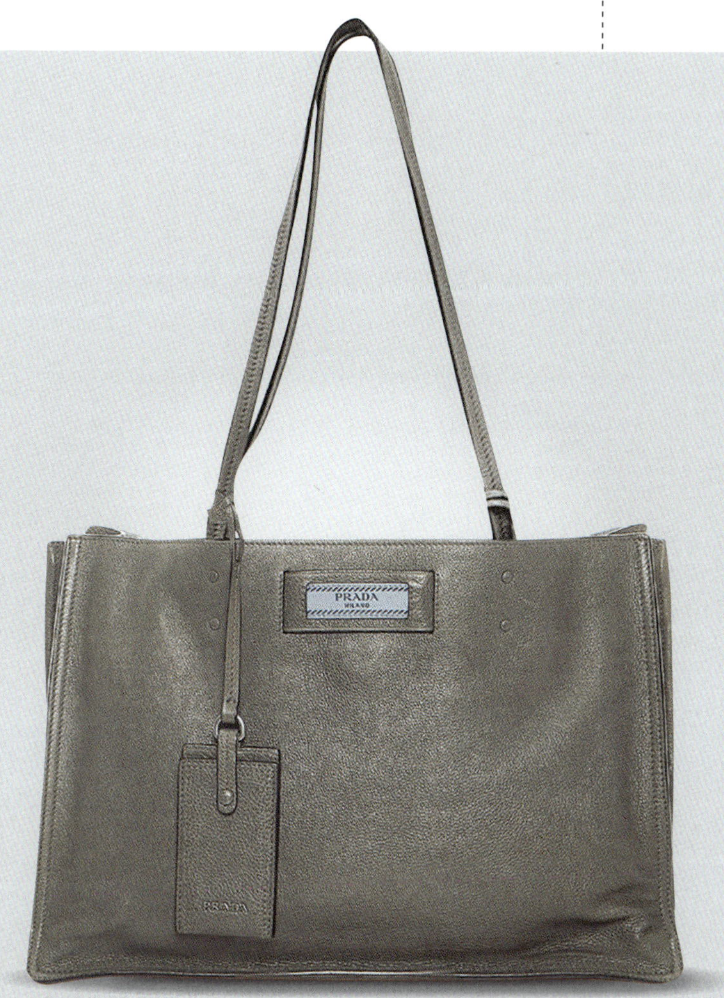

PRADA DOUBLE TOTE

The Prada Double Tote was introduced around 2014 as part of Prada's aim to create a versatile, structured bag that could appeal to both fashion-conscious consumers and those looking for practical luxury. Its minimalist design, manufactured from iconic Saffiano leather or calf leather, and ample interior space quickly became popular and helped cement its status as one of Prada's modern classics.

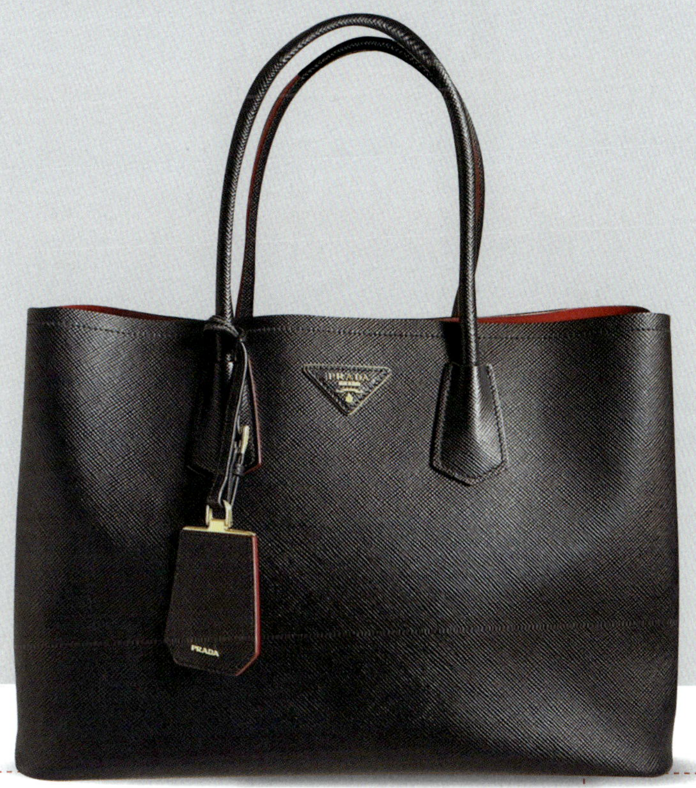

PRADA SIDONIE BAG

The Prada Sidonie bag, introduced in Prada's 2018/2019 collection, is a sculptural design known for its curvy silhouette and distinctive flap closure. The Sidonie is versatile in its style offerings, available as a crossbody, shoulder bag, and belt bag, often featuring rich leather or textured Saffiano leather finishes. It is available in a spectrum of colours – from classic neutrals to bolder hues. Its ergonomic shape and compact size make it both functional and fashionable – housing daily essentials while being versatile enough to dress up or down. The Sidonie bag quickly became iconic, catching the attention of celebrities and influencers.

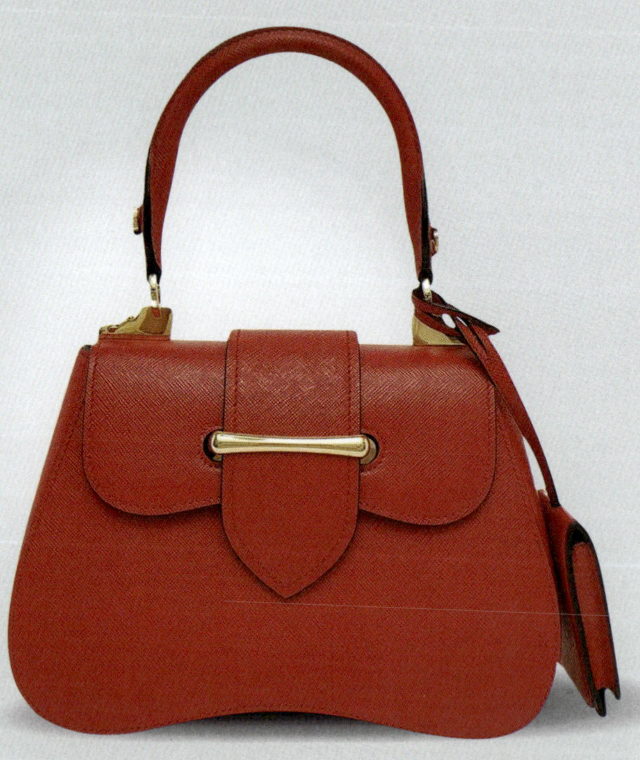

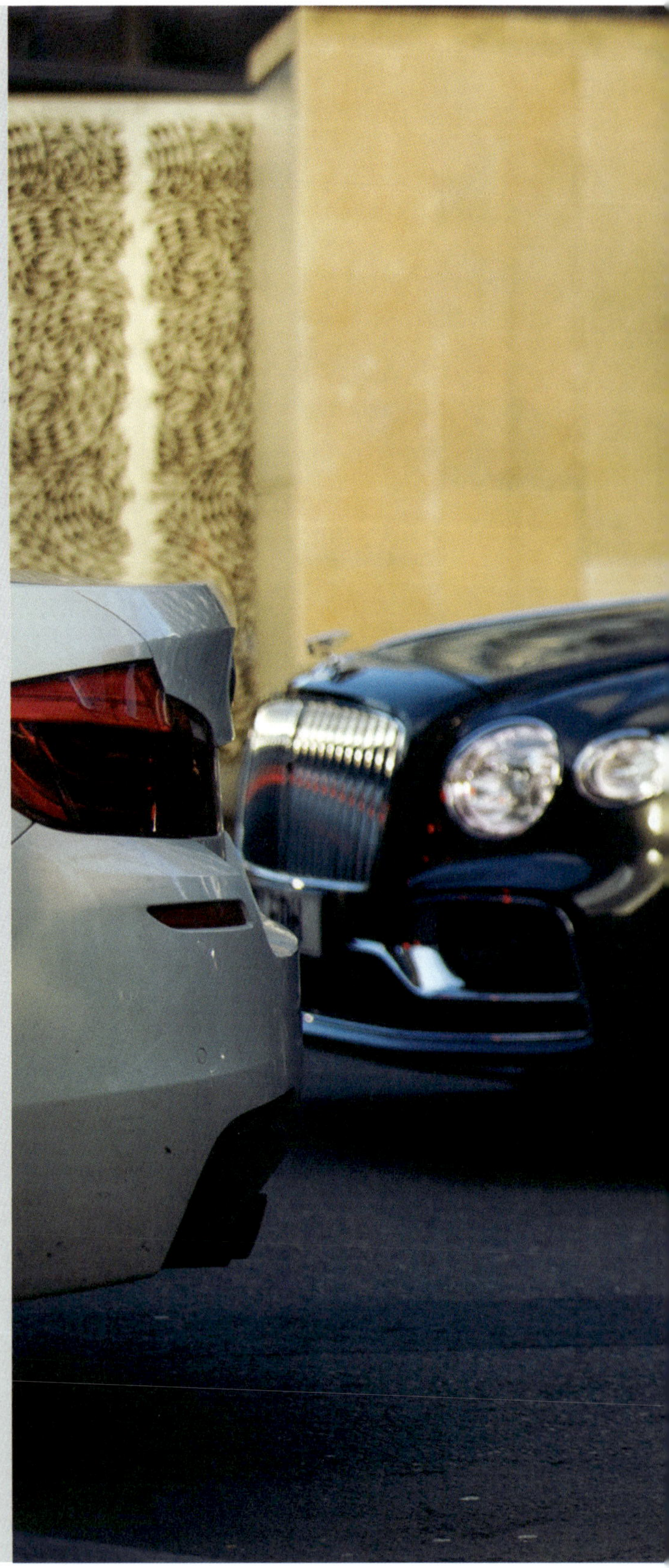

ABOVE: Red leather Prada Sidonie handbag
RIGHT: Model Maxim Magnus with a blue Prada Sidonie shoulder bag during London Fashion Week, 17 February, 2020 in London, England

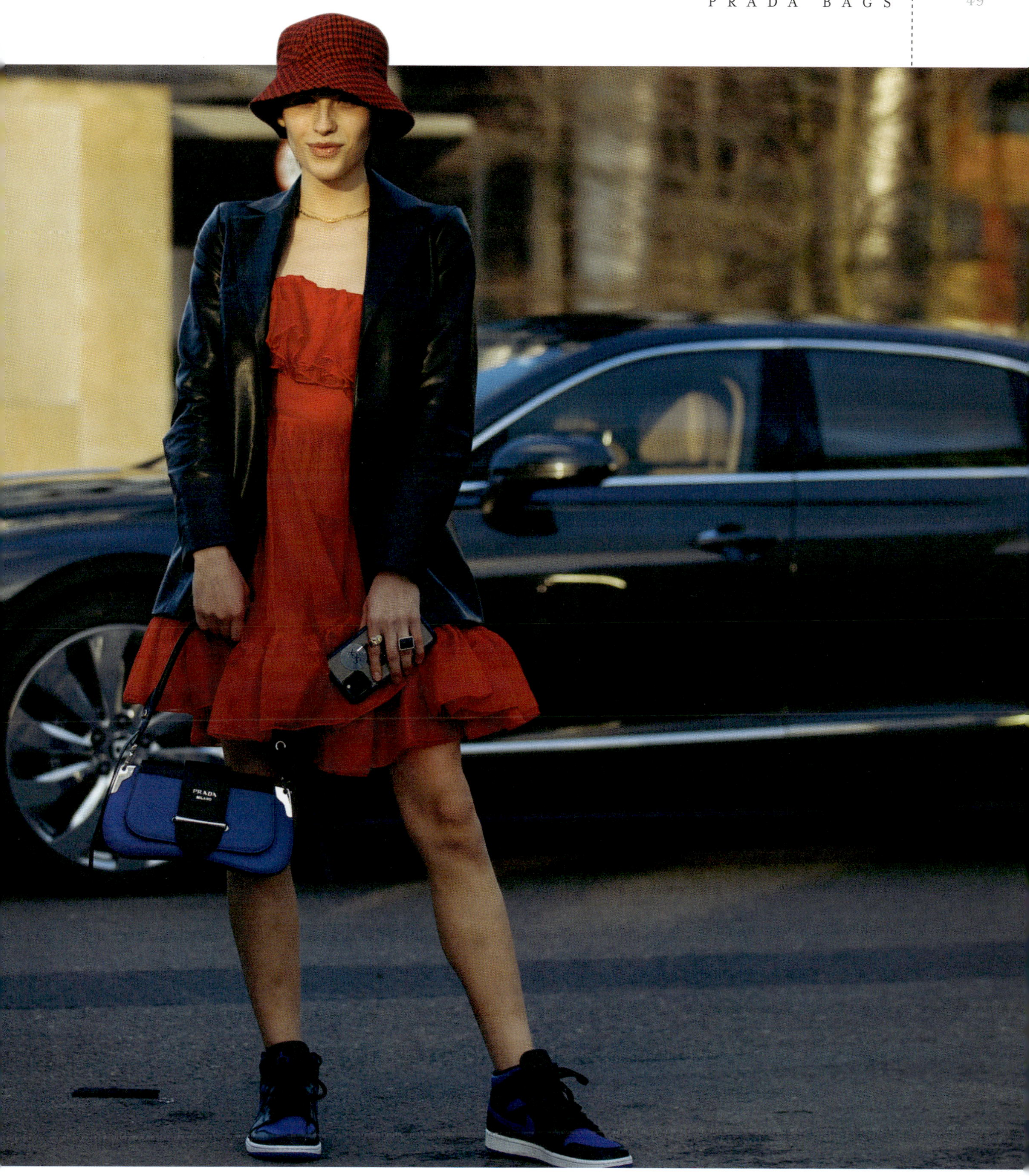

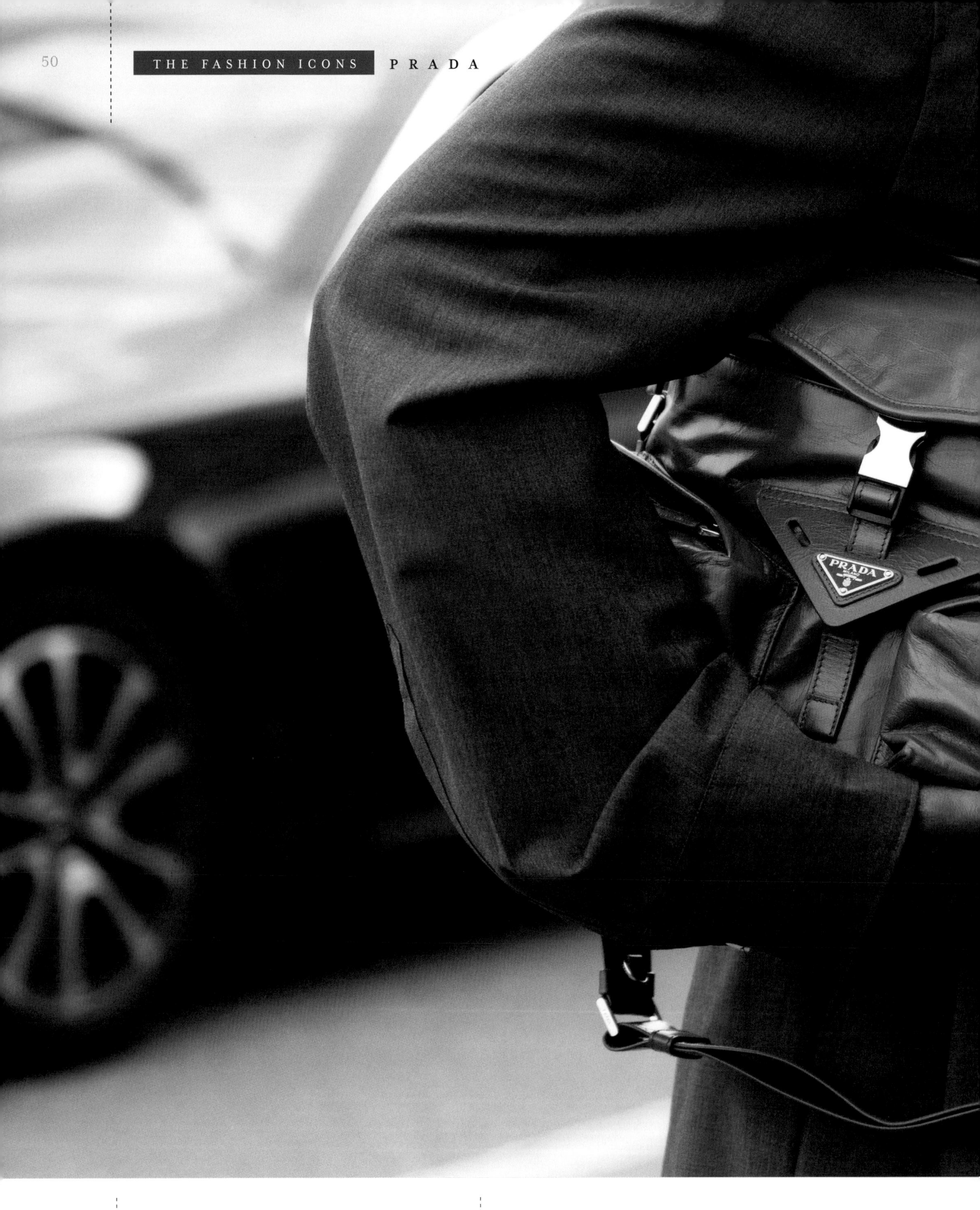

ABOVE: A model carries the green Prada Re-Nylon
leather shoulder strap bag

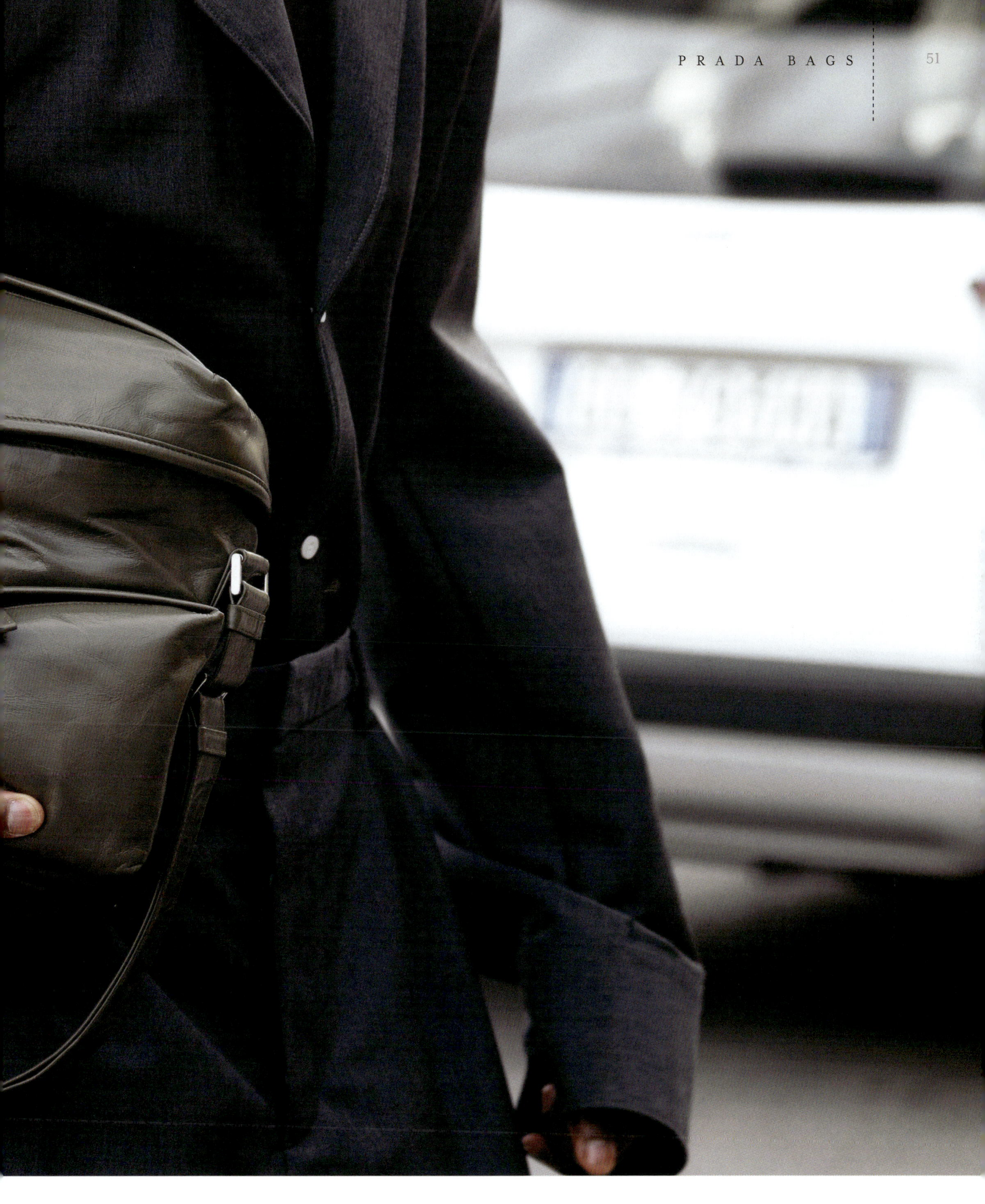

PRADA WOMEN

"When I started doing ready-to-wear, I wanted to make clothes for real women, clothes that they could live in and move in, but that also had a sense of beauty and craftsmanship. I never wanted to be constrained by trends or by what people expected"

Miuccia Prada

Since Miuccia's first foray into RTW in 1988, Prada's ready-to-wear collections have been celebrated not only for their aesthetic appeal but also for the narratives, cultural insights, and bold ideas they convey. From 'ugly chic' to feminist art statements, Miuccia Prada has redefined luxury and modern femininity through her fashion. Each season brings something unexpected and intellectually stimulating, cementing Prada's place as the brand that continually pushes the boundaries of what fashion can represent. Here are some of Prada's best and most influential ready-to-wear collections, showcasing Miuccia signature blend of intellect, innovation, and fearless style.

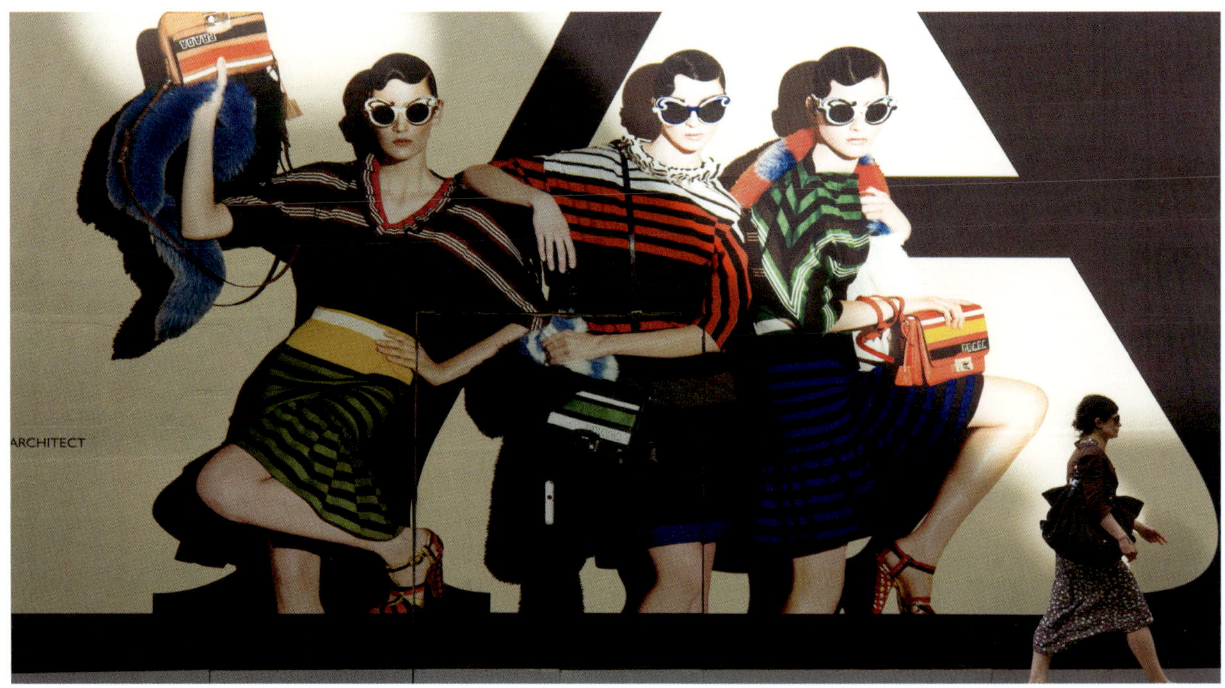

ABOVE: Prada advertisement outside their boutique at 6 Rue Fbg St Honoré, Paris, France
OPP PAGE: Prada Runway, Milan Fashion Week, Womenswear Spring/Summer 2023

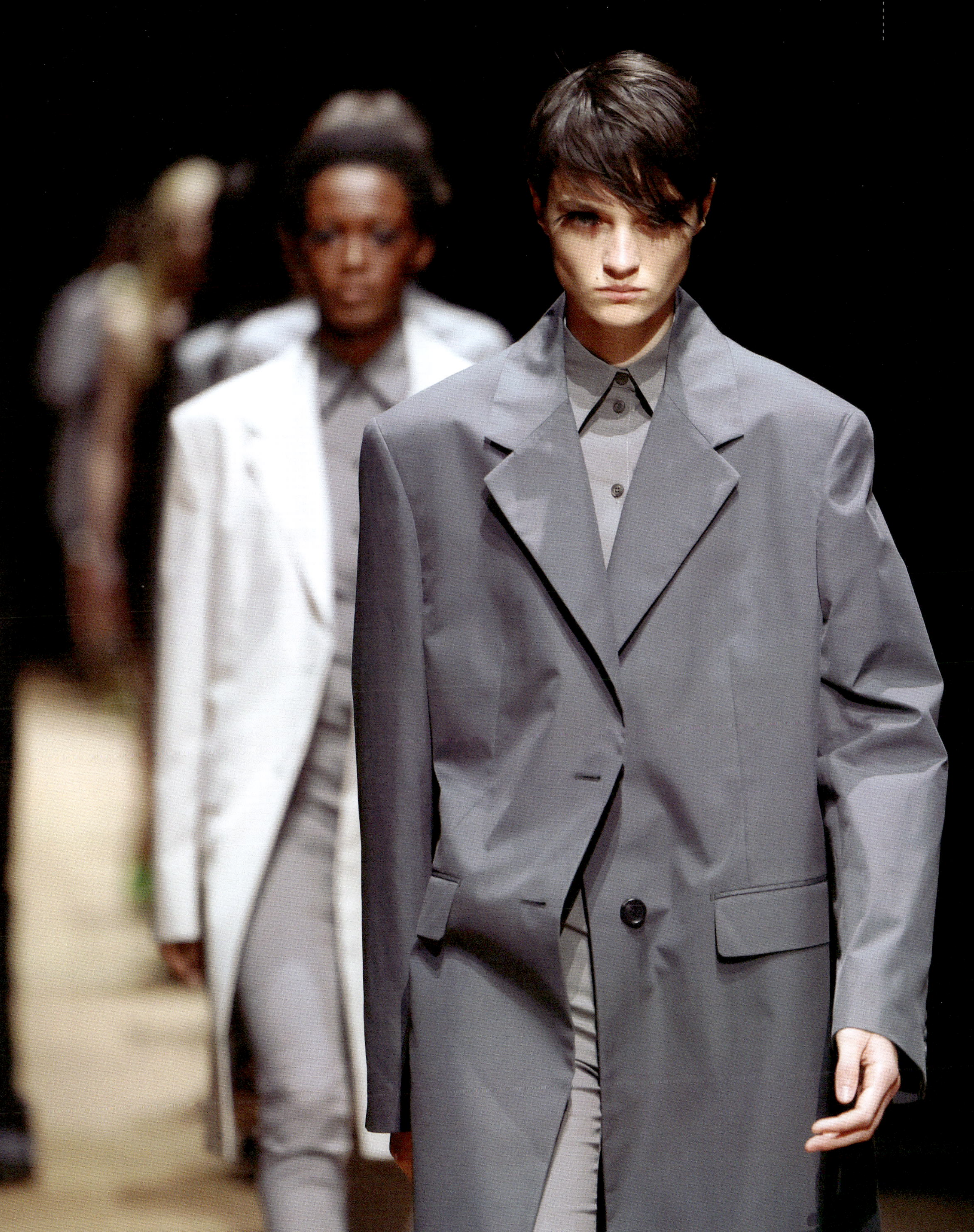

FALL/WINTER 1988 - PRADA'S FIRST OFFICIAL ENTRY INTO THE FASHION WORLD.

The first collection was understated, minimalist, and modern, reflecting Miuccia's desire to create a new kind of luxury. Unlike many other designers of the time, who favoured bold prints and flamboyant designs, Miuccia opted for clean lines and a neutral colour palette. Her work appealed to women who wanted sophistication and practicality rather than just flash and glamour. The success of her first collection validated Miuccia's vision and gave Prada the foundation to build a full-fledged fashion brand. Her early designs set the foundation for what would become the brand's signature aesthetic - a refined, functional elegance blended with subversive and unexpected elements.

SPRING/SUMMER 1996 - THE RISE OF 'UGLY CHIC'

The Spring/Summer 1996 collection is often credited with defining Prada's signature aesthetic of 'ugly chic'. This collection was a radical departure from traditional luxury fashion, embracing as it did muted colours, vintage-inspired silhouettes, and unconventional prints that challenged conventional ideas of beauty. Miuccia Prada used mismatched patterns, quirky florals, and earthy tones which were highly unusual for luxury fashion at the time - oversized cardigans, knee-length skirts in muted

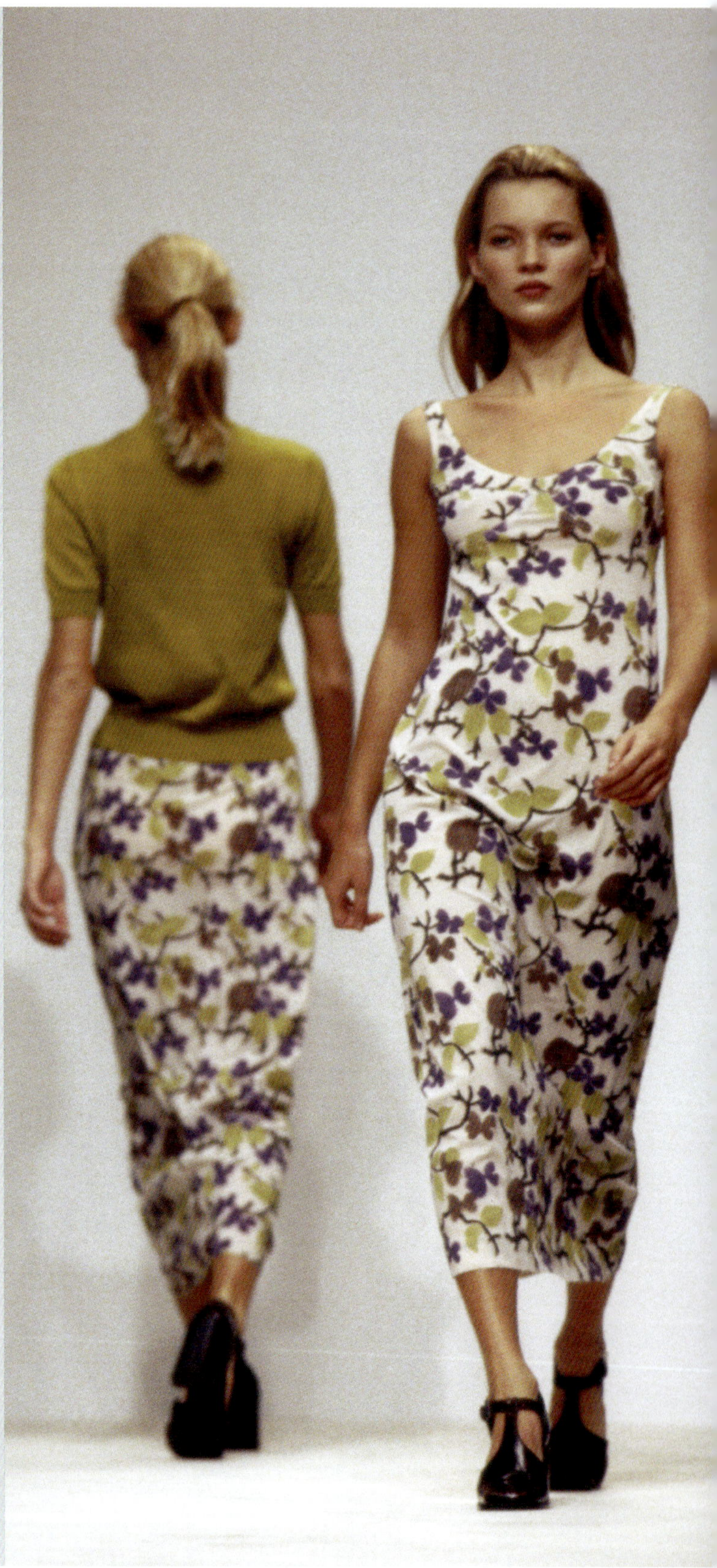

patterns, and quirky accessories in mustard, green, and brown tones. This collection introduced a cerebral approach to femininity, mixing elements that appeared frumpy or plain but were ultimately elegant. By making 'ugly' desirable, Prada redefined fashion's aesthetics and opened the door for other designers to explore unconventional ideas of glamour and beauty.

FALL/WINTER 2008 - GOTHIC ROMANCE AND DARK FEMININITY

For Fall/Winter 2008 collection, Miuccia explored themes of darkness, sensuality, and femininity. The collection was heavy on black lace, velvet, and brocade, evoking a Gothic and almost haunted elegance. It combined traditional romantic elements with a subversive edge, making it one of Prada's most memorable and dramatic collections. This collection highlighted Miuccia's ability to create depth and narrative through clothing, offering a wardrobe that felt mysterious and luxurious, yet strong and empowering. The collection's dark romanticism resonated with audiences and set a trend for Gothic-inspired fashion across the industry. Key pieces included black lace dresses, velvet skirts, and accessories with rich textures and brocade details.

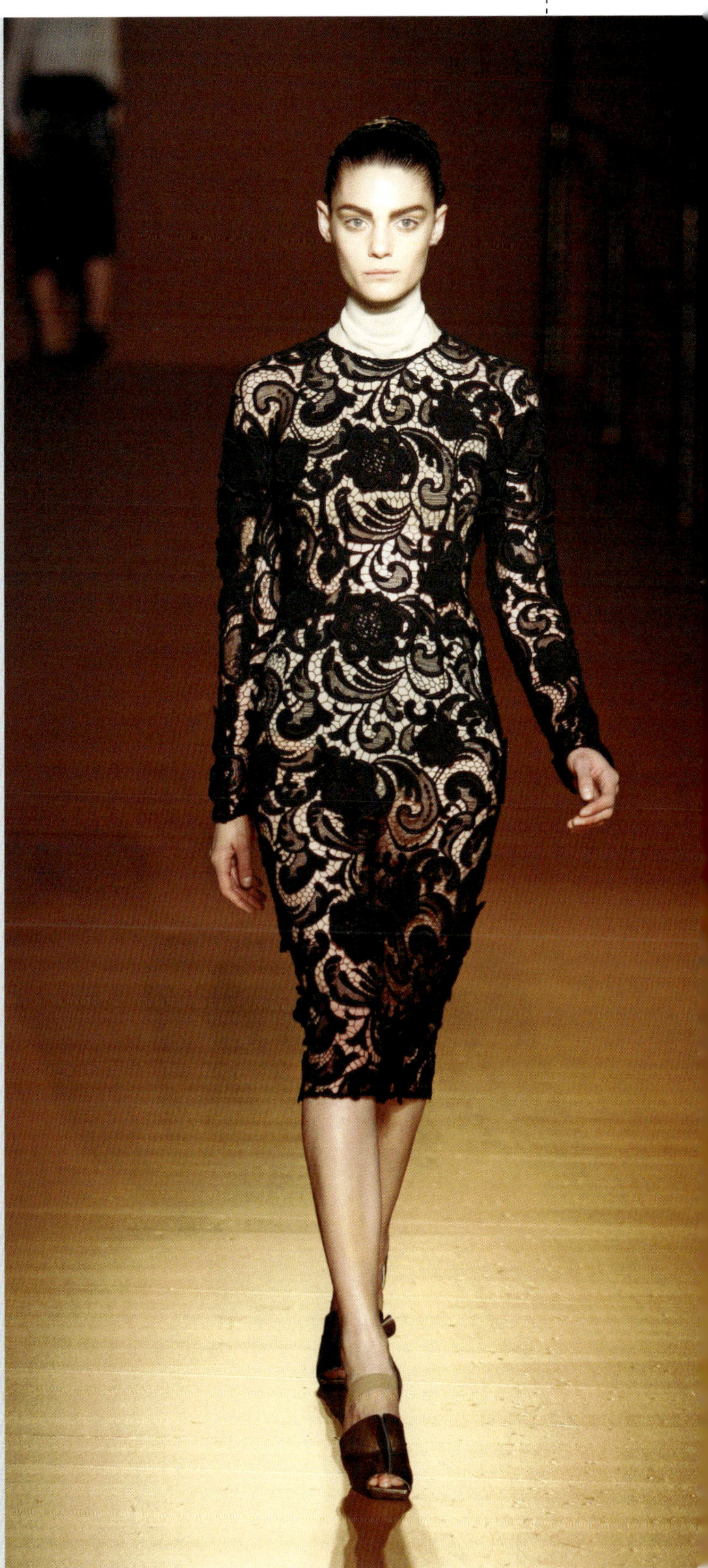

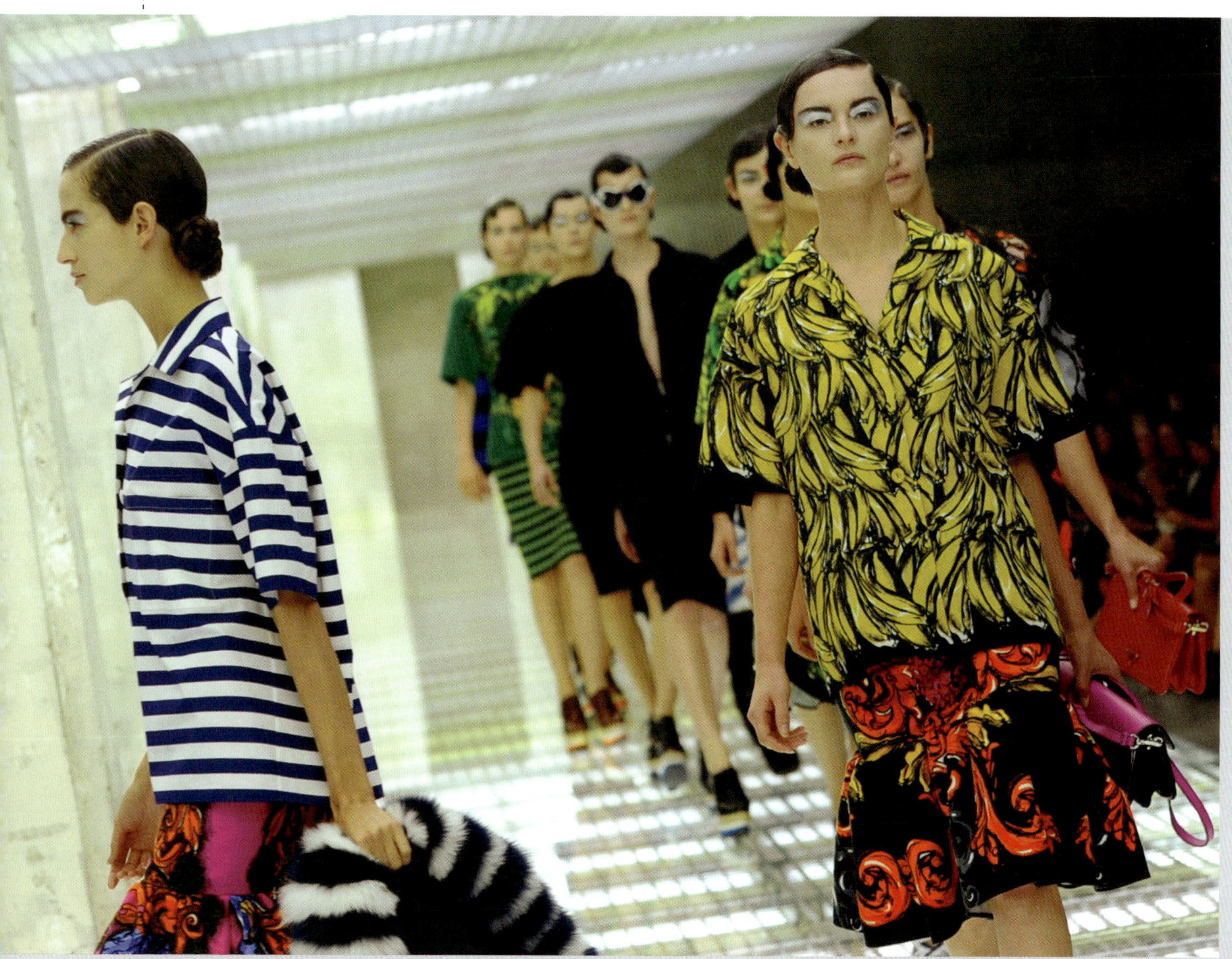

SPRING/SUMMER 2011 - POP ART EXTRAVAGANZA

Prada's Spring/Summer 2011 collection was a riot of colour, fun, and playfulness. Known for its pop art-inspired prints, vibrant colour blocking, and bold stripes, this collection departed from Prada's usual minimalist tones and embraced a joyful aesthetic. The standout pieces featured prints of bananas and monkeys, striped skirts and statement accessories in neon colours captured a whimsical side of Prada rarely seen before. This collection was a commercial success and became an instant classic with celebrities and fashion influencers embracing the quirky and colourful designs. It showcased Miuccia Prada's ability to surprise her audience while staying true to her brand's intellectual spirit.

FALL/WINTER 2012 - MILITARY MEETS RETRO FUTURISM

For the Fall/Winter 2012 collection, Prada drew from military and retro influences, mixing bold geometric patterns with tailored, structured pieces. The collection featured a colour palette dominated by mustard, burnt orange, and maroon, and utilized heavy materials like wool and tweed. The silhouettes were structured yet feminine, offering a futuristic take on vintage aesthetics. This collection is particularly notable for its intricate patterns and optical illusions, as well as its sophisticated, empowering silhouettes. It resonated with women who were drawn to both elegance and strength, making it one of Prada's most powerful statements on femininity. Key pieces included double-breasted coats with bold patterns, knee-length skirts with geometric prints, and embellished Mary Jane shoes.

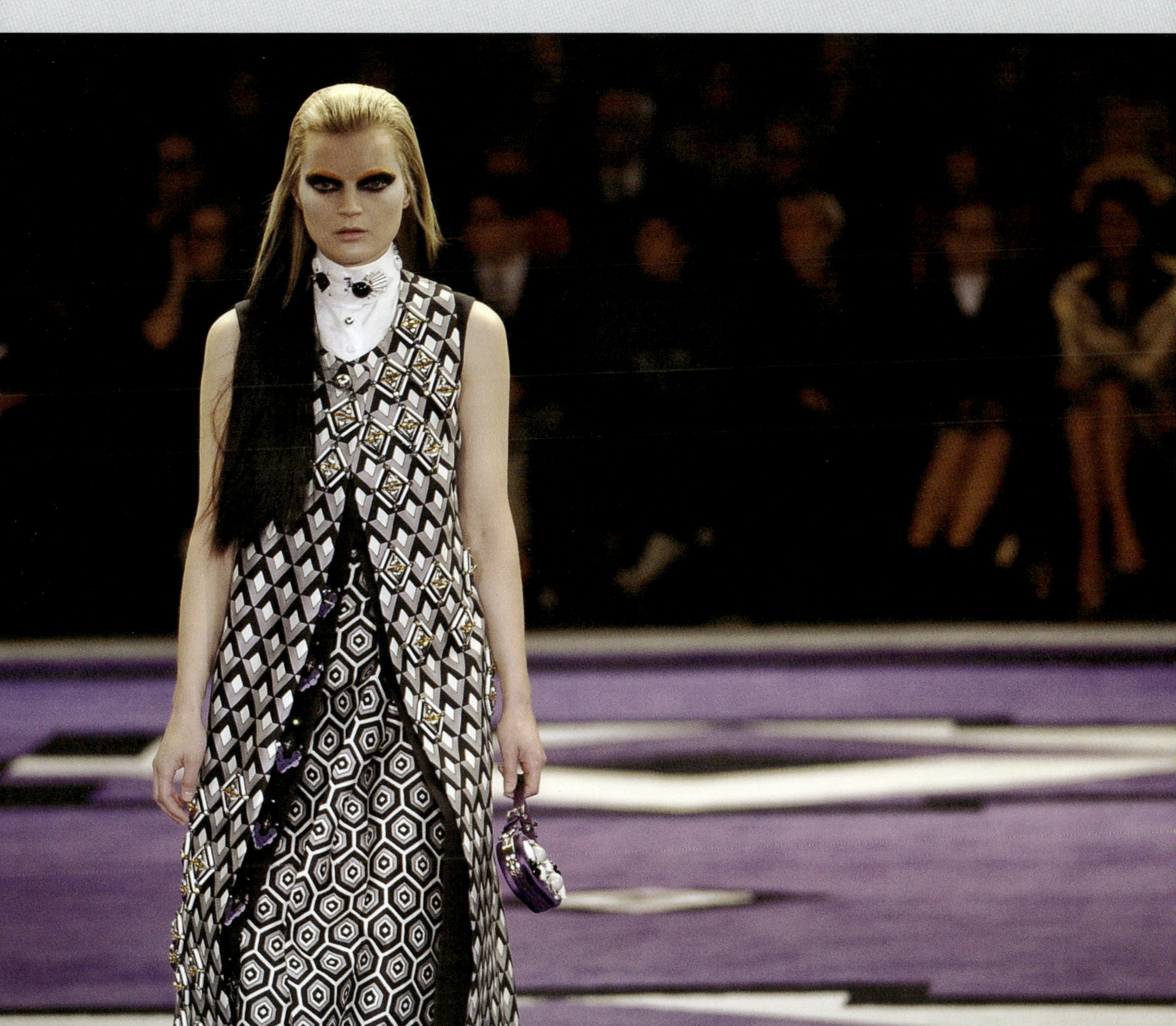

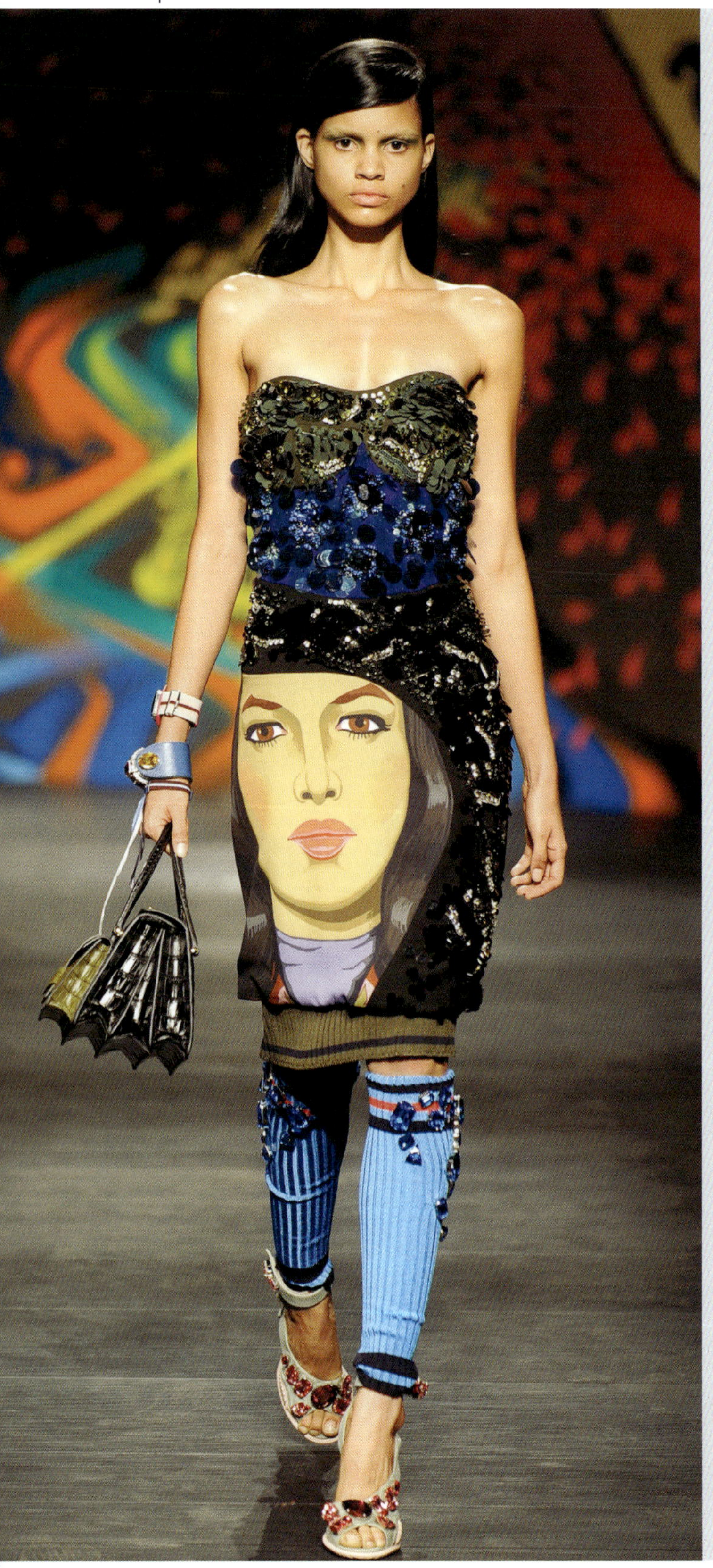

SPRING/SUMMER 2014 - FEMINIST ART AND POLITICAL EDGE

In Spring/Summer 2014, Prada made a powerful statement by incorporating feminist art and political themes into the collection. The runway featured murals of women's faces, painted by contemporary female artists, and the clothes themselves were bold and powerful. The collection included vibrant colours, sportswear influences, and embellishments like crystals, bringing a sense of opulence to the overall look. This collection was widely acclaimed for its bold messaging and its celebration of female strength. It captured the cultural climate, resonating deeply with the fashion world and beyond.

FALL/WINTER 2015 - PASTELS, POWER SUITS, AND GENDER FLUIDITY

In the Fall/Winter 2015 collection, Prada explored themes of gender fluidity and power. This collection was notable for its soft pastel colour palette, juxtaposed with strong, tailored silhouettes. Miuccia Prada played with traditional gender codes, designing power suits and military-inspired coats in traditionally 'feminine' hues such as pale pink, mint and powder blue, and thus blurring the lines between masculine and feminine aesthetics.

ABOVE: On the runway at Prada's Spring 2014 show
OPP PAGE: (Left) Fall/Winter 2015 Collection (Right) Prada Spring 2016 Ready-to-Wear Collection

SPRING/SUMMER 2016 - INDUSTRIAL GLAMOUR

The Spring/Summer 2016 collection brought an industrial edge to Prada's classic aesthetic. The collection featured metallics, sheer layers, and PVC accents, combining elements of glamour with a utilitarian sensibility. Prada showcased skirts and dresses with see-through panels creating a futuristic, almost dystopian aesthetic. The collection was emblematic of Prada's ability to blend high fashion with industrial design elements. It felt experimental yet wearable, merging bold, futuristic details with classic silhouettes. This approach offered a fresh take on luxury - highlighting Miuccia Prada's unique ability to make even the most unconventional materials feel elegant.

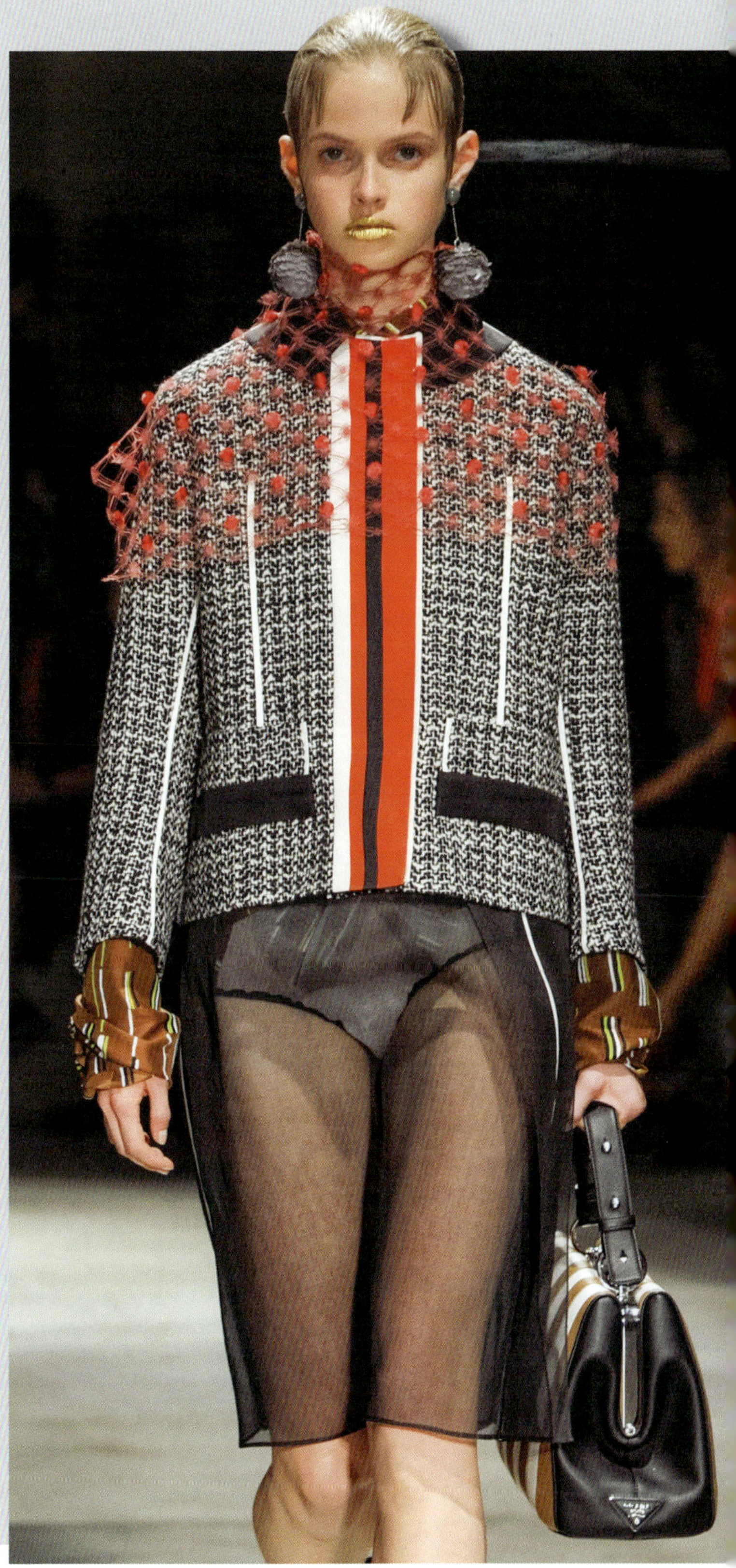

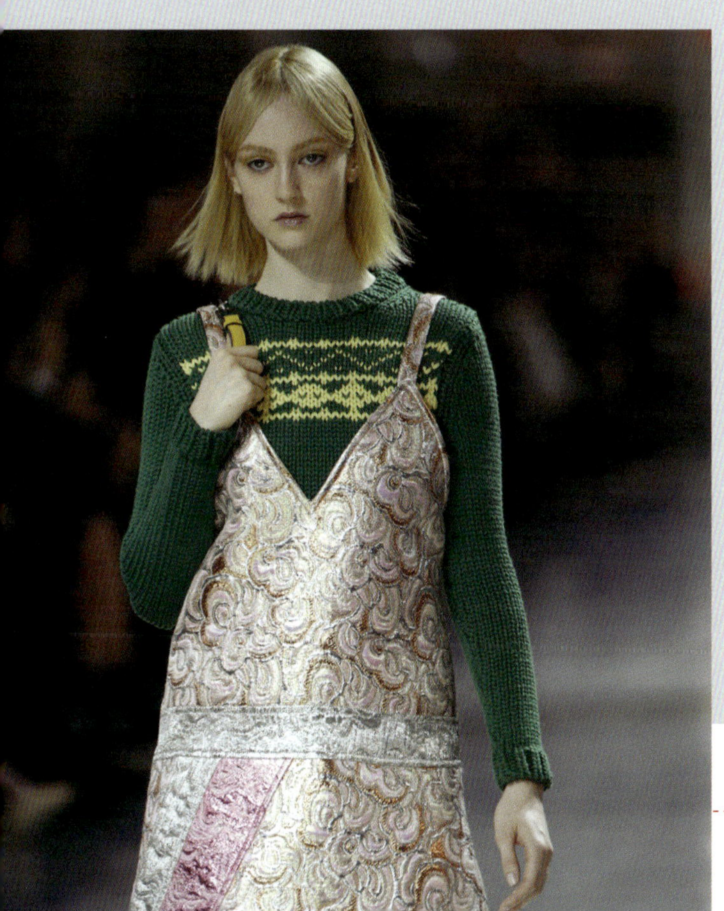

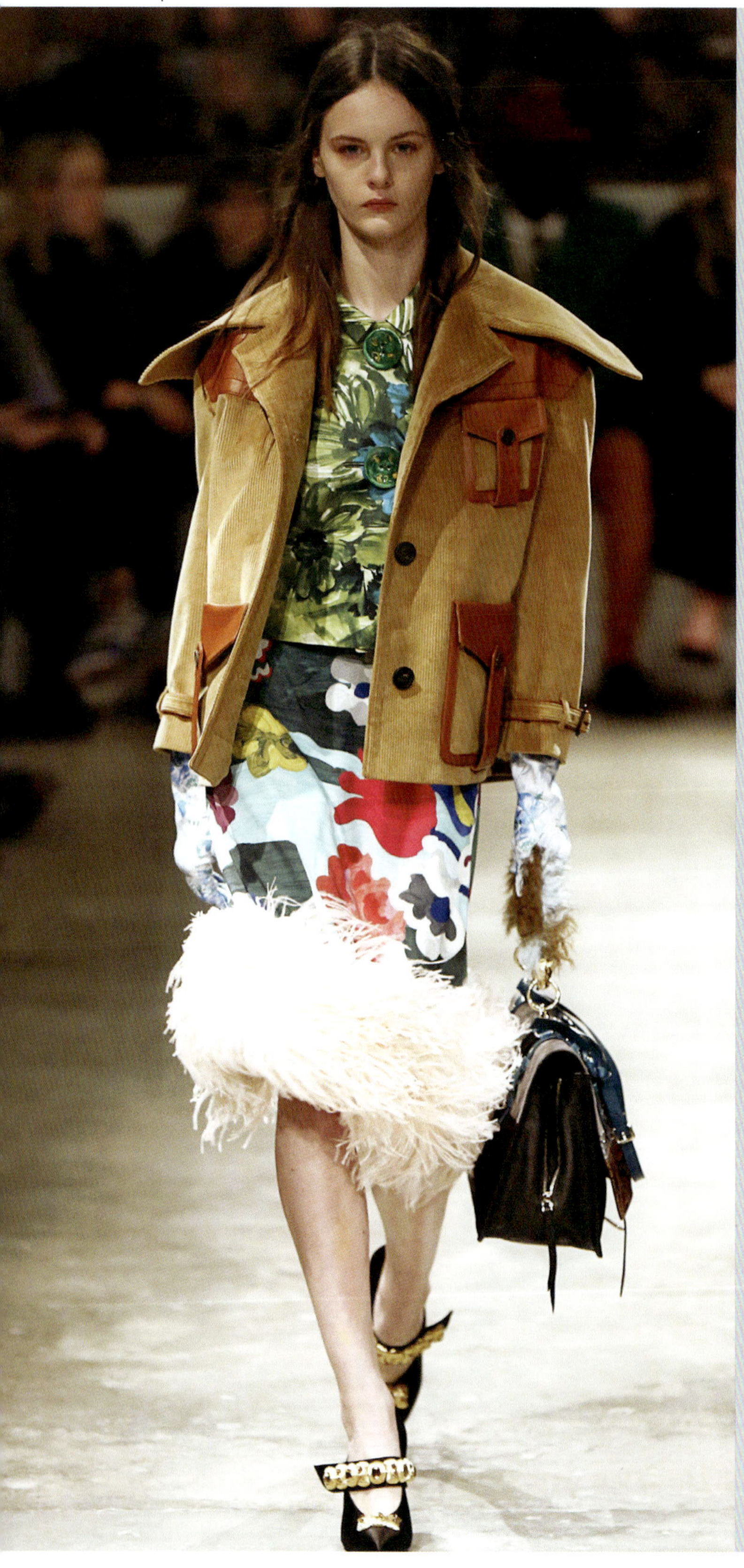

ABOVE: Prada's Fall/Winter 2017 collection
OPP PAGE: Models walk the runway at the Prada fashion
show during Milan Fashion Week, Spring/Summer
2019 in Milan, Italy

FALL/WINTER 2017 - A TRIBUTE TO 1970s FEMINISM

Prada's Fall/Winter 2017 collection was inspired by the 1970s, specifically focusing on themes of women's liberation and empowerment. Miuccia Prada drew from the era's aesthetics - combining corduroy, fur, and patchwork patterns with earthy colours. The collection featured platform shoes, flared trousers and feathered accessories, capturing the spirit of 1970s rebellion and independence. This collection resonated with audiences who appreciated Prada's nod to feminist history and the era's bold, individualistic style. It felt nostalgic yet modern, offering a reinterpretation of 1970s fashion through Prada's distinctive and 21st century lens.

SPRING/SUMMER 2019 - MINIMALIST ELEGANCE

Spring/Summer 2019 saw Prada return to minimalist, understated elegance, focusing on simple silhouettes and clean lines. The collection was defined by muted tones—beige, black, navy—with occasional pops of neon. Dresses and skirts were structured, often cinched with leather belts or adorned with classic bows. The collection was refined, sophisticated, and strikingly modern, embodying a new era of subtle luxury. It reinforced Prada's reputation for intellectual, luxurious fashion without ostentation.

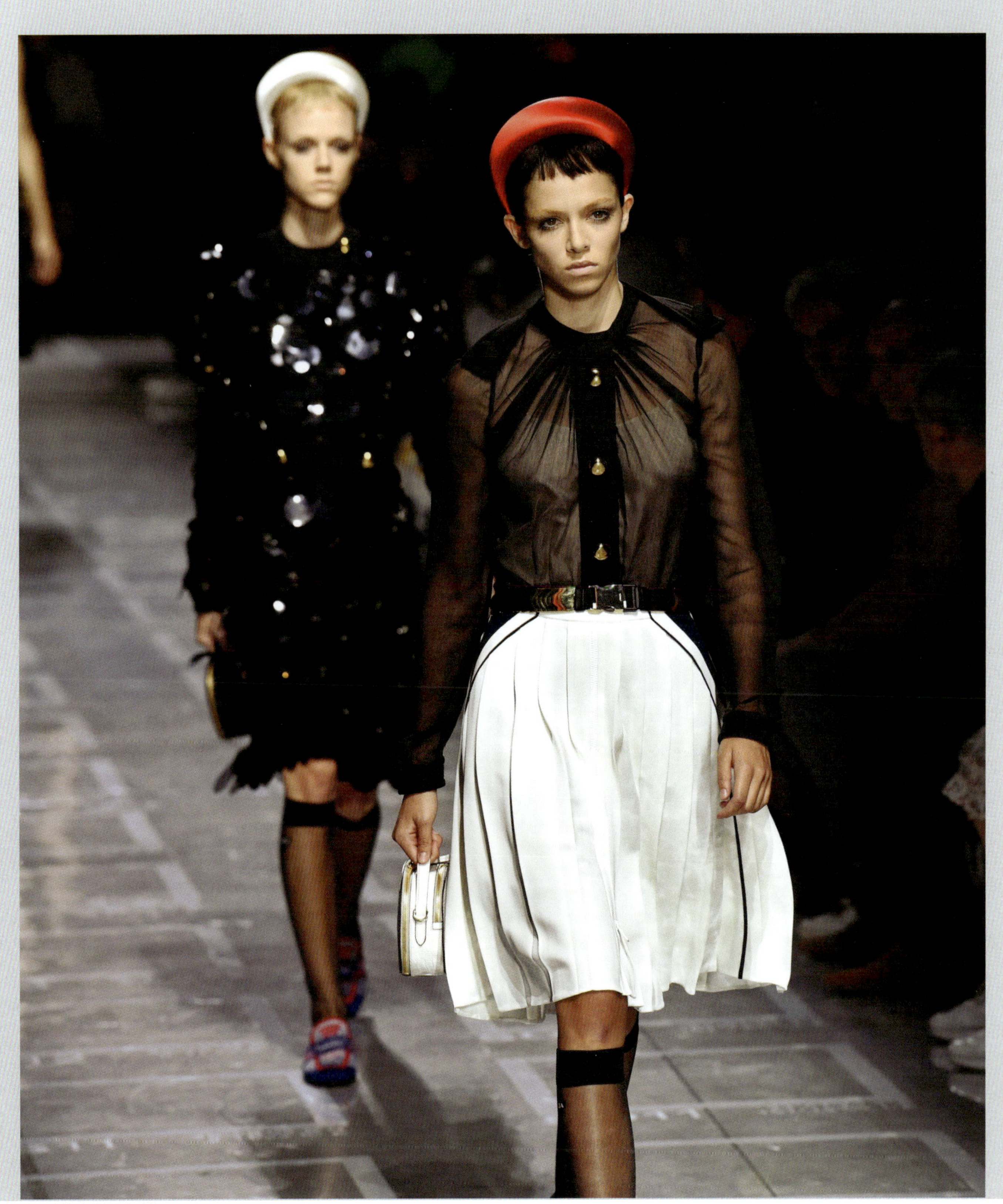

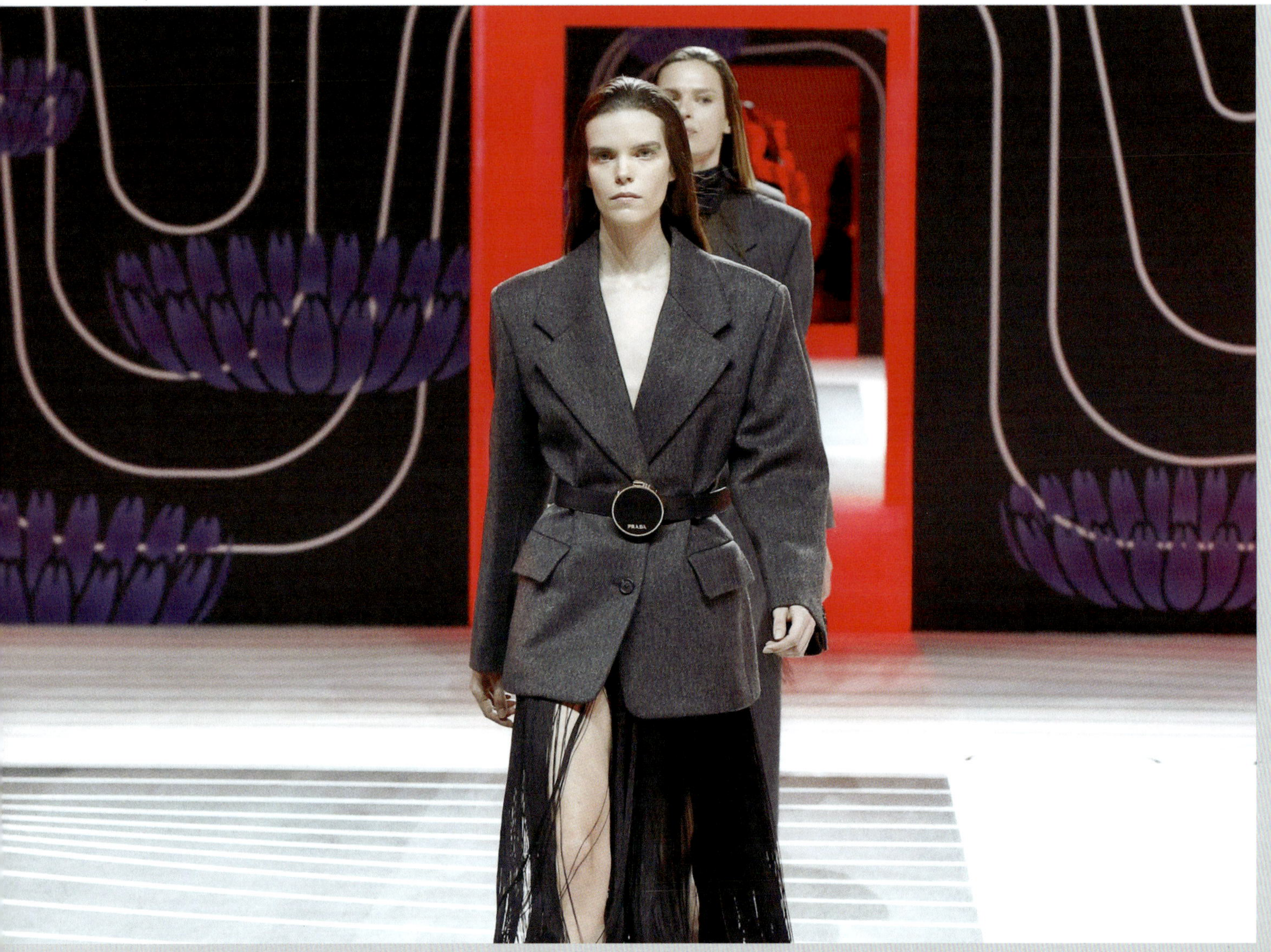

FALL/WINTER 2020 - THE NEW ERA WITH RAF SIMONS

The Fall/Winter 2020 collection marked the beginning of a new chapter for Prada as Miuccia Prada collaborated with Belgian designer Raf Simons for the first time. This collection blended Simons' edgy minimalism with Prada's classic intellectual style, resulting in a collection that focused on empowerment, functionality, and luxury. With utilitarian jackets, oversized blazers, and vibrant gloves, the collection emphasized contrasts and power dressing for the modern woman. This collection was a commercial and critical success, demonstrating that Prada could innovate while respecting its heritage. It set the stage for the future with Raf Simons bringing a new perspective to Prada's rich legacy.

ABOVE: Prada fashion show during Fall/Winter 2020 Milan Fashion Week
OPP PAGE: Prada Spring/Summer 2025 runway during Milan Fashion Week

SPRING/SUMMER 2025

Prada's Spring/Summer 2025 collections showcased a blend of innovation and nostalgia. Skirts reigned supreme. Pencil skirts took on new forms - from minimalist leather versions and loud-print pieces to sportier iterations in Prada's signature nylon.

Some were suspended from belts; others, stiff and shiny in metallic silver, featured decorative hole cutouts. Colours were bright, with macs and jackets in a variety of hues plus the notion of the superhero was explored in accessories like oversized sunglasses and topless hats with tinted viewing panels.

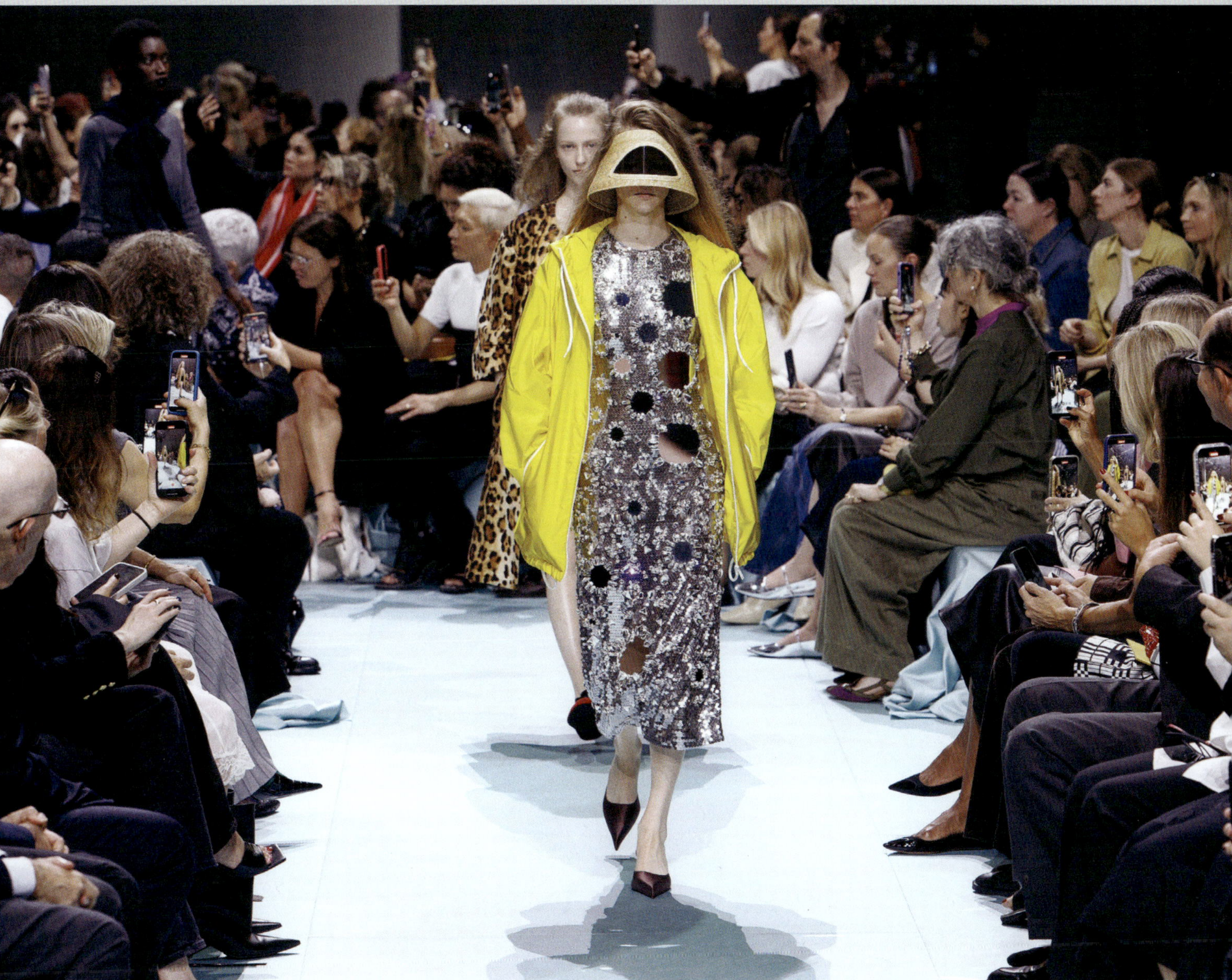

THE A-LIST WEAR PRADA

ON THE RED CARPET

RIHANNA

Ri-Ri rocks a Prada ensemble consisting of a beaded satin bra paired with a high-waisted pencil skirt, trimmed at the hemline with darker hued feathers at the 2017 movie premier of *Valerian City of a Thousand Planets* in Paris.

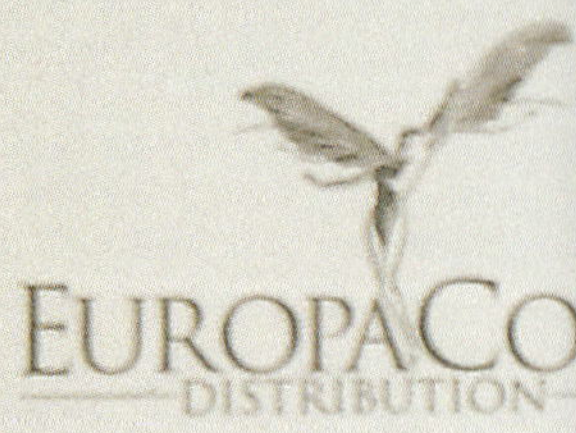

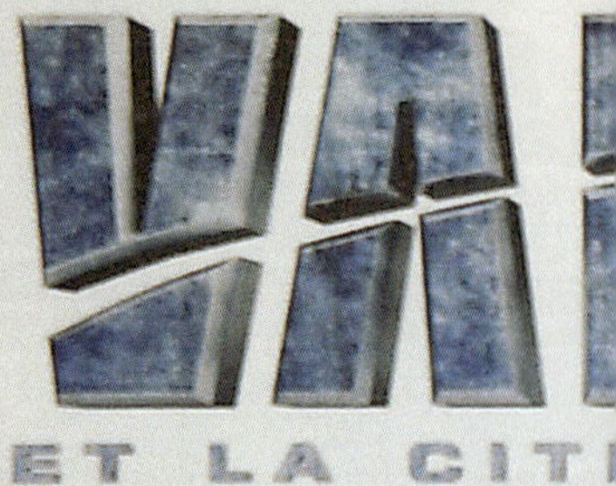

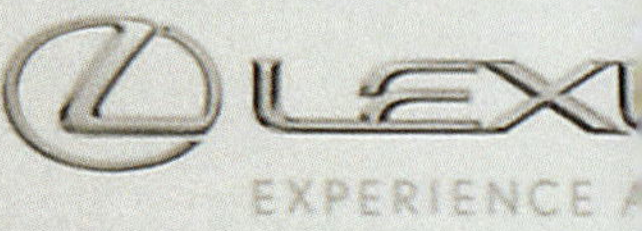

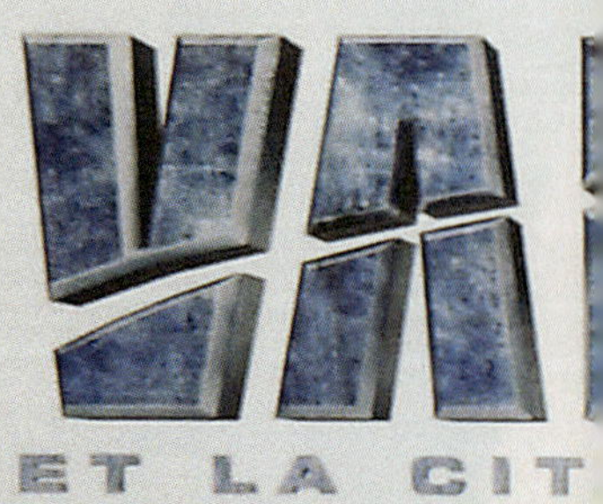

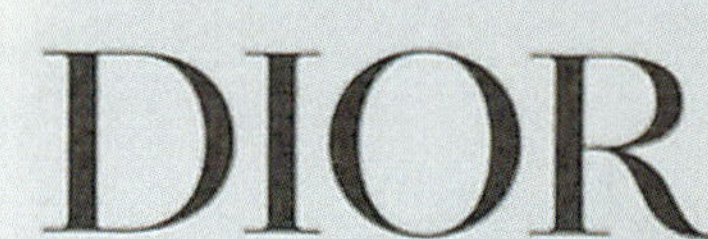
DIOR

VALERIAN
ET DES MILLE PLANÈTES

LE PLANÈTES

OCS
100% cinéma séries

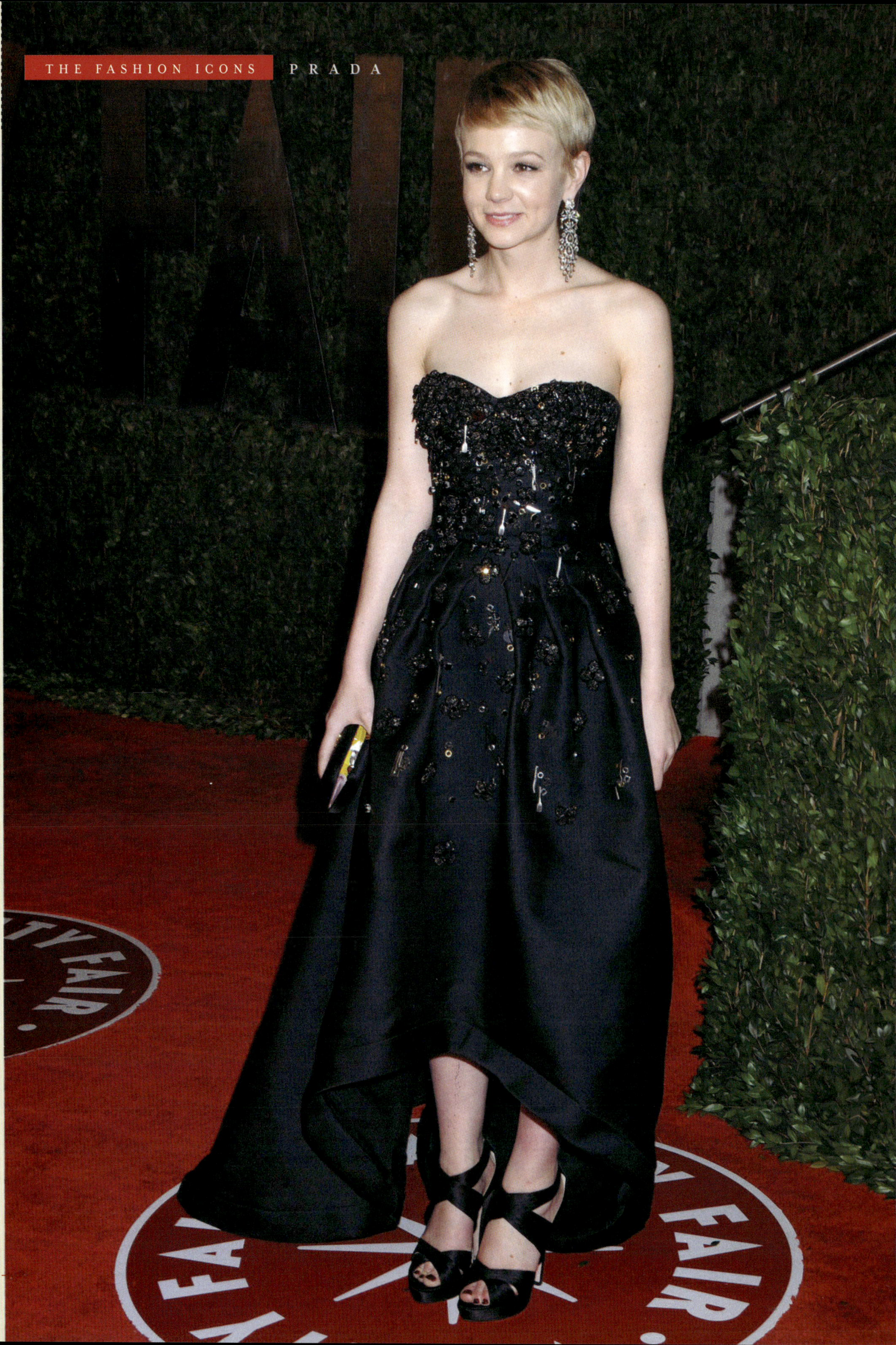

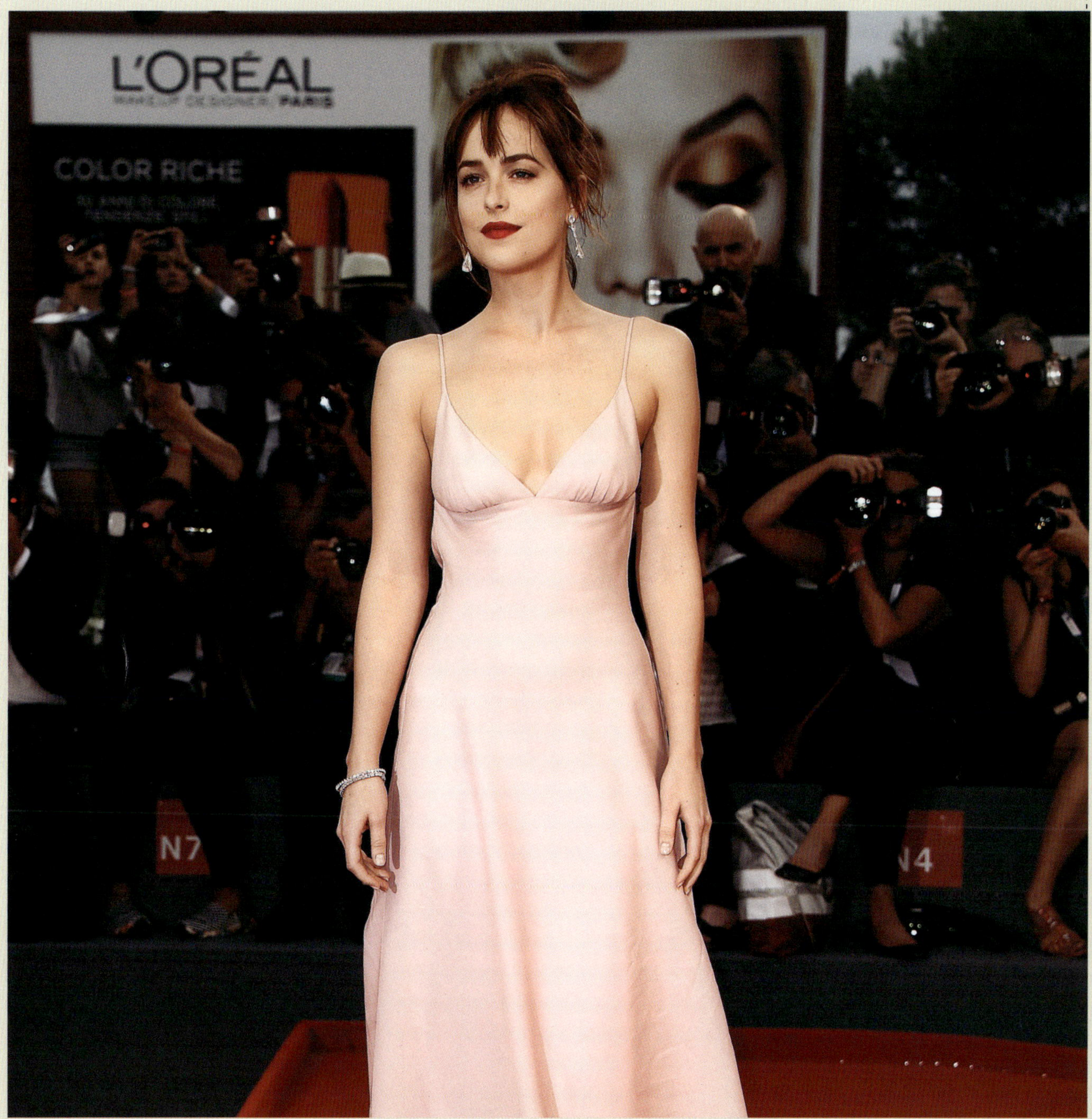

CAREY MULLIGAN

British actress Carey in a strapless black Prada dress with beaded embellishments at the 2010 Oscars.

DAKOTA JOHNSON

Dakota wears a floor-length, blush pink Prada slip dress at the 2015 Venice Film Festival.

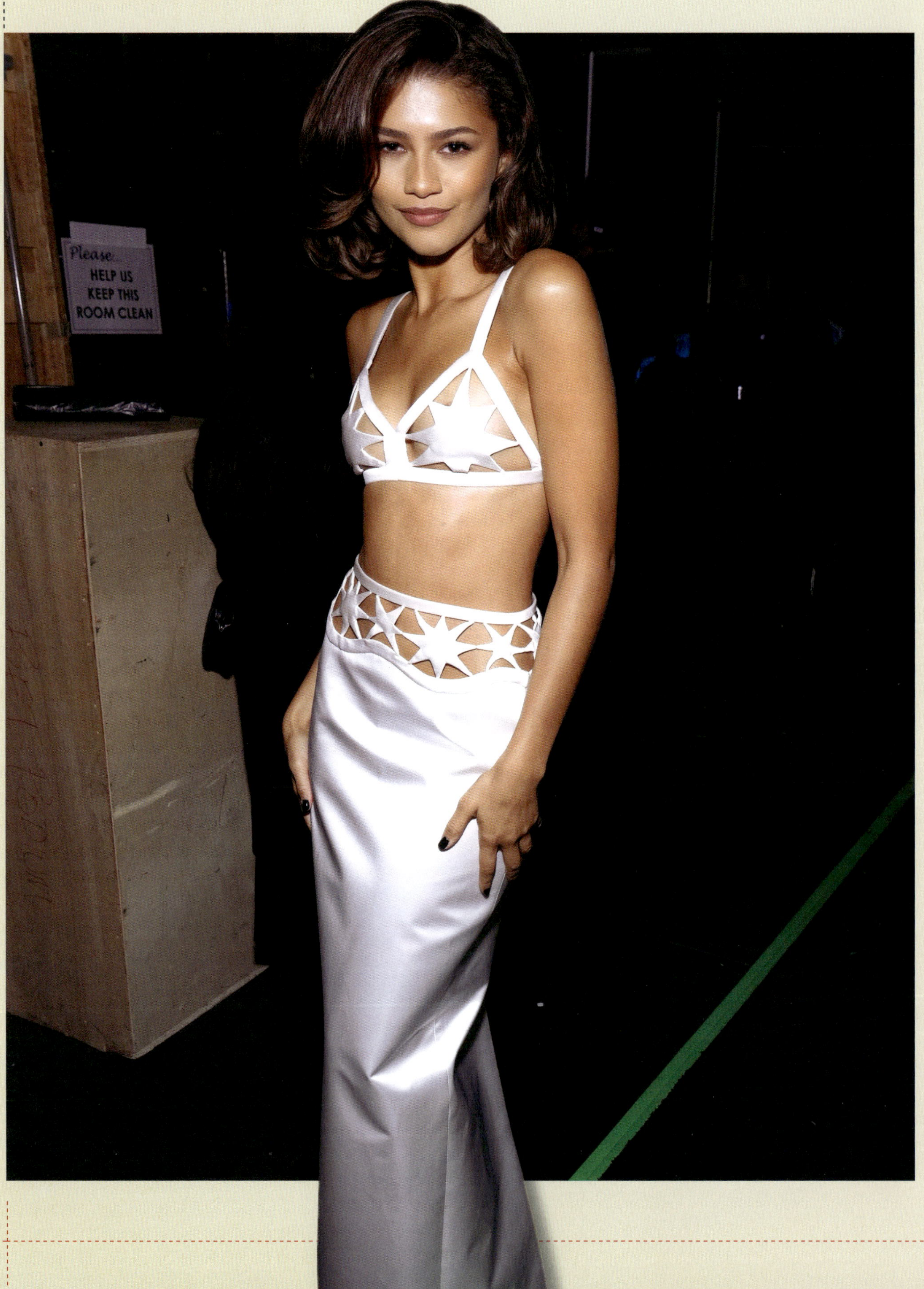
Please...
HELP US
KEEP THIS
ROOM CLEAN

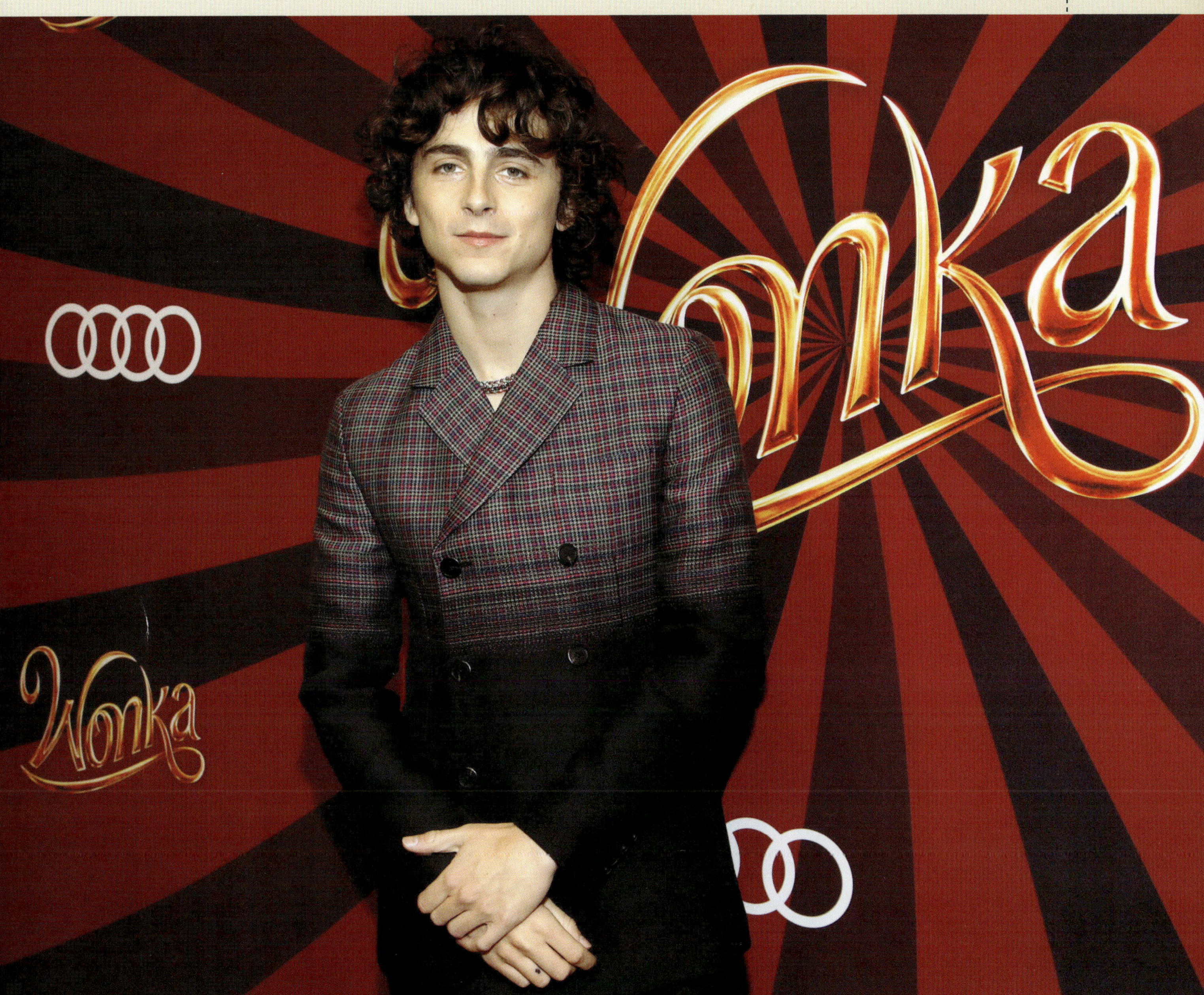

ZENDAYA

Fashion risk-taker Zendaya has worn Prada to several high-profile events. Here she models vintage Prada from the Spring 1993 collection at the NAACP Image Awards in 2023.

TIMOTHÉE CHALAMET

At the 2023 premiere of *Wonka*, Timothée opted for a sleek tailored Prada suit in a bold colour choice.

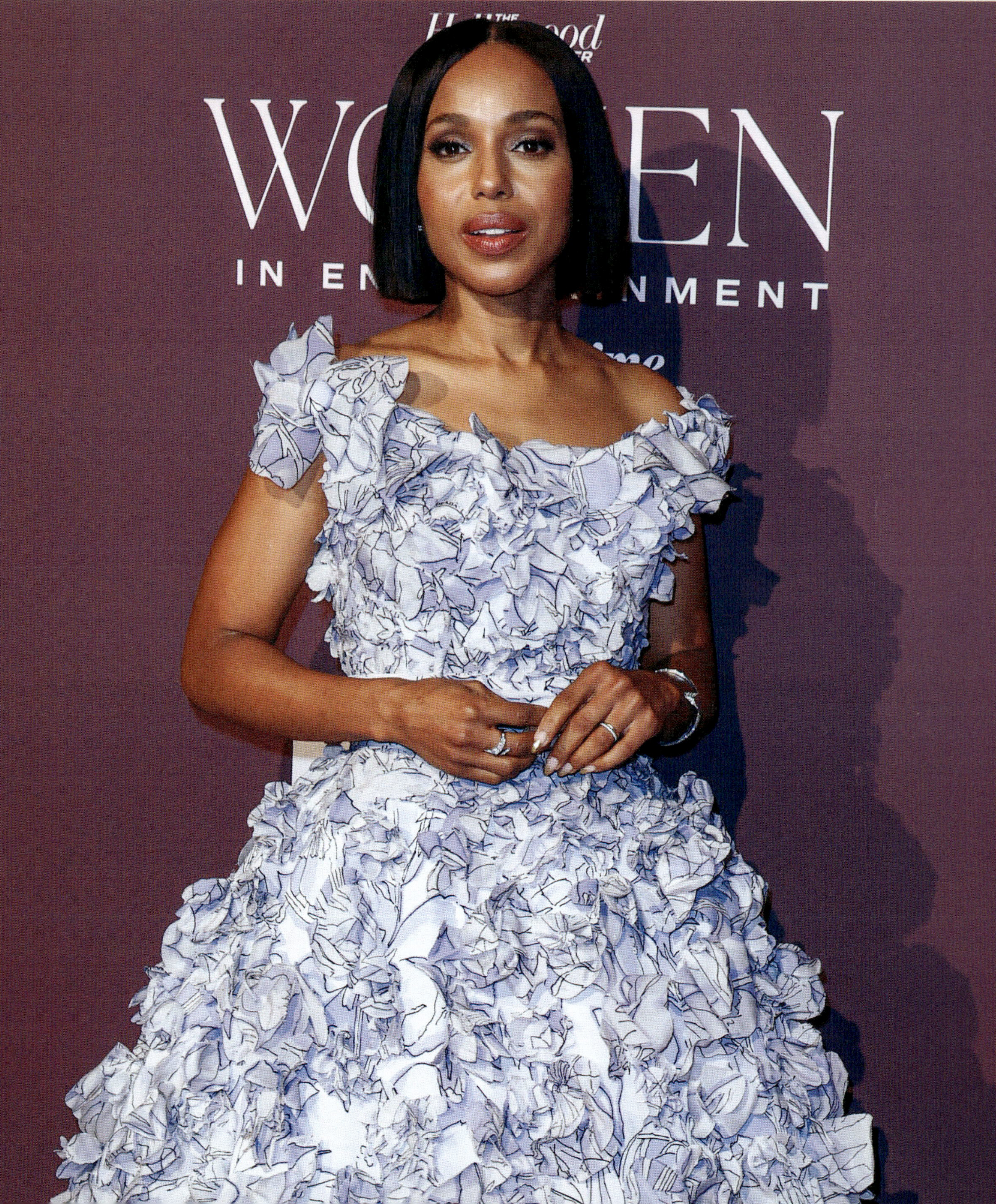

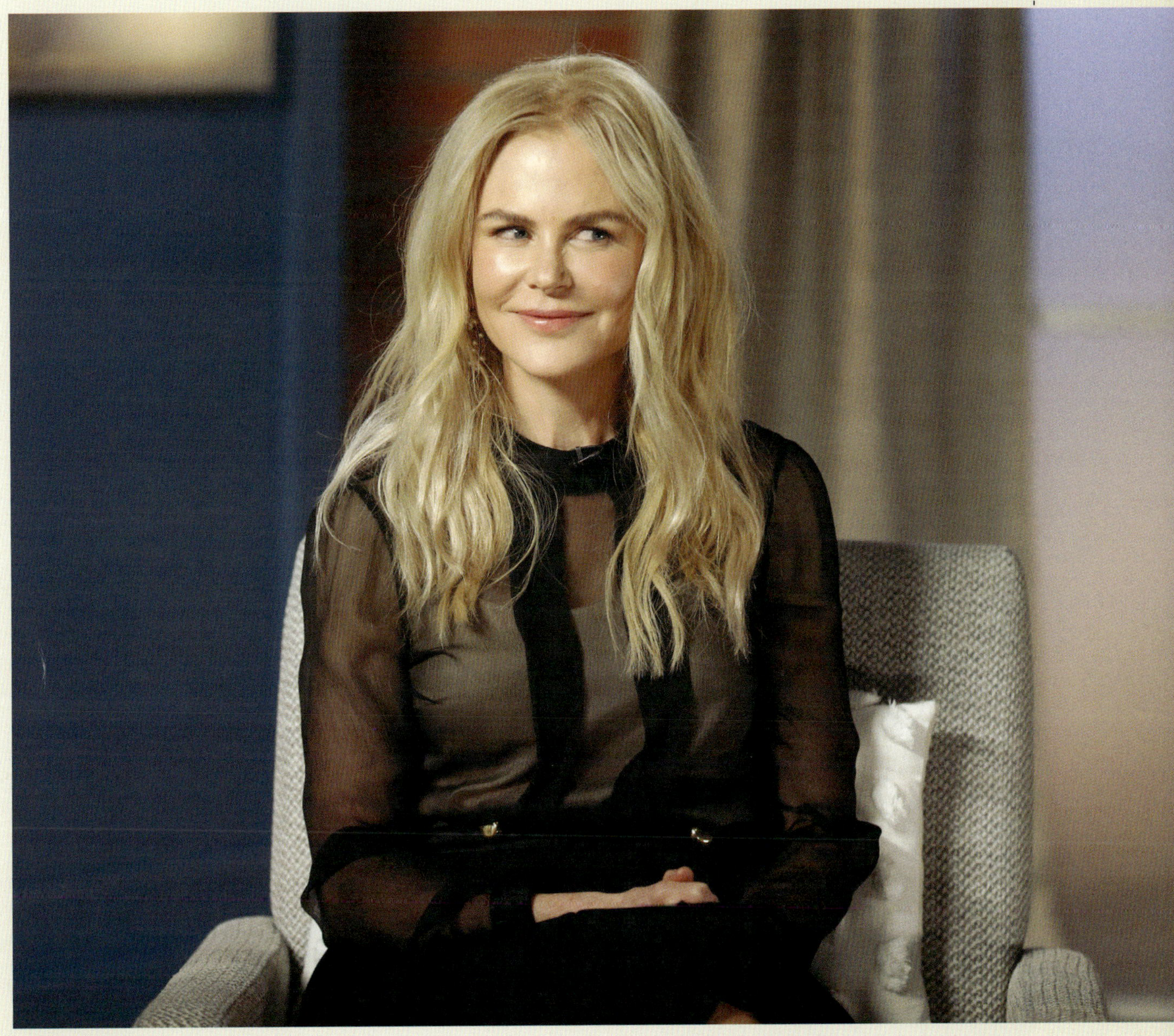

KERRY WASHINGTON

In 2023, Kerry wore this beautiful Prada dress embroidered with crepe marocaine flowers at the Hollywood Reporter's Women in Entertainment event.

NICOLE KIDMAN

Nicole is another Prada lover, equally stunning in a chic gown like the custom-made number worn to the 2011 Golden Globes. Or in the tailored black pleated skirt and chiffon blouse ensemble here from the Prada Spring 2019 collection.

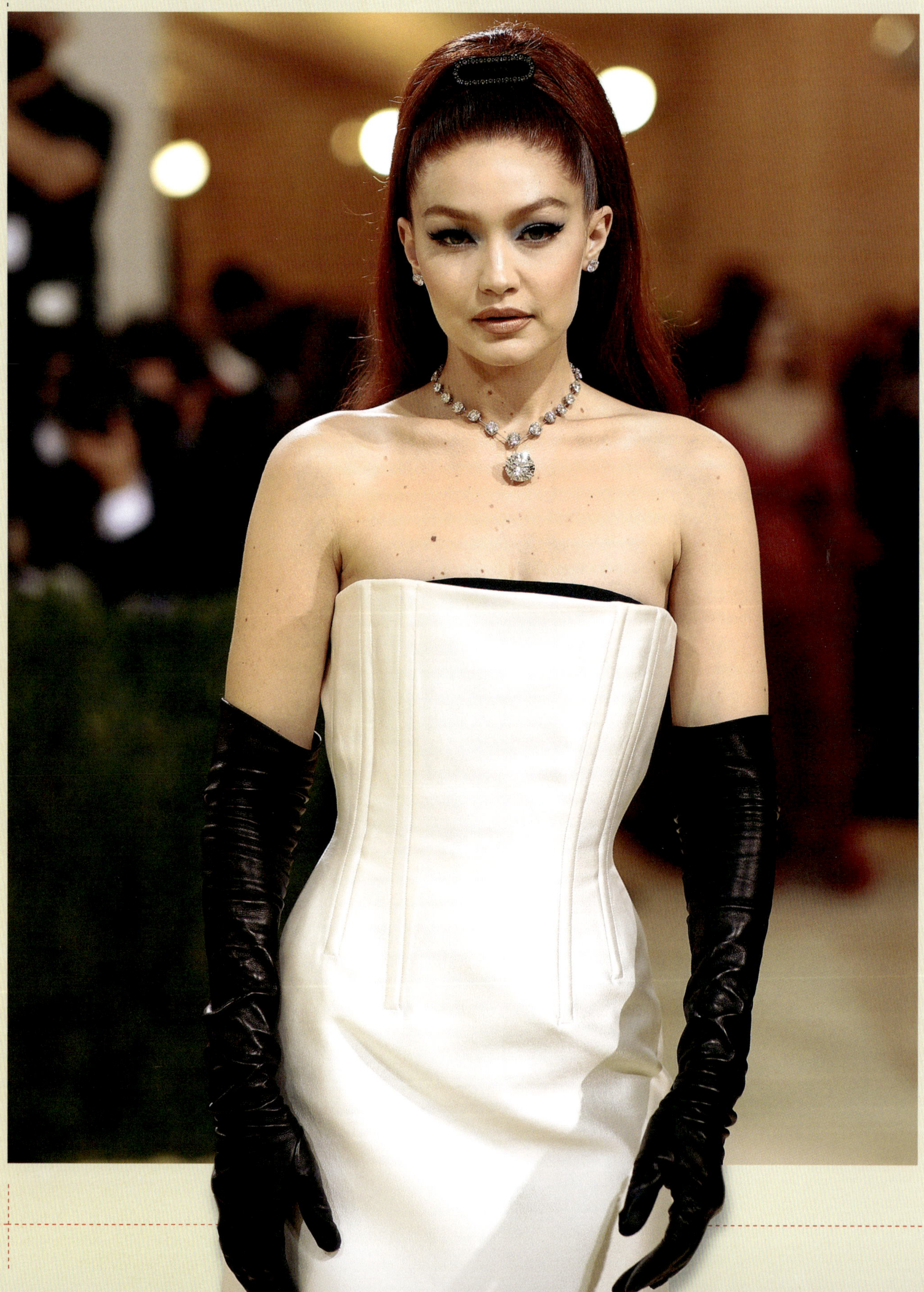

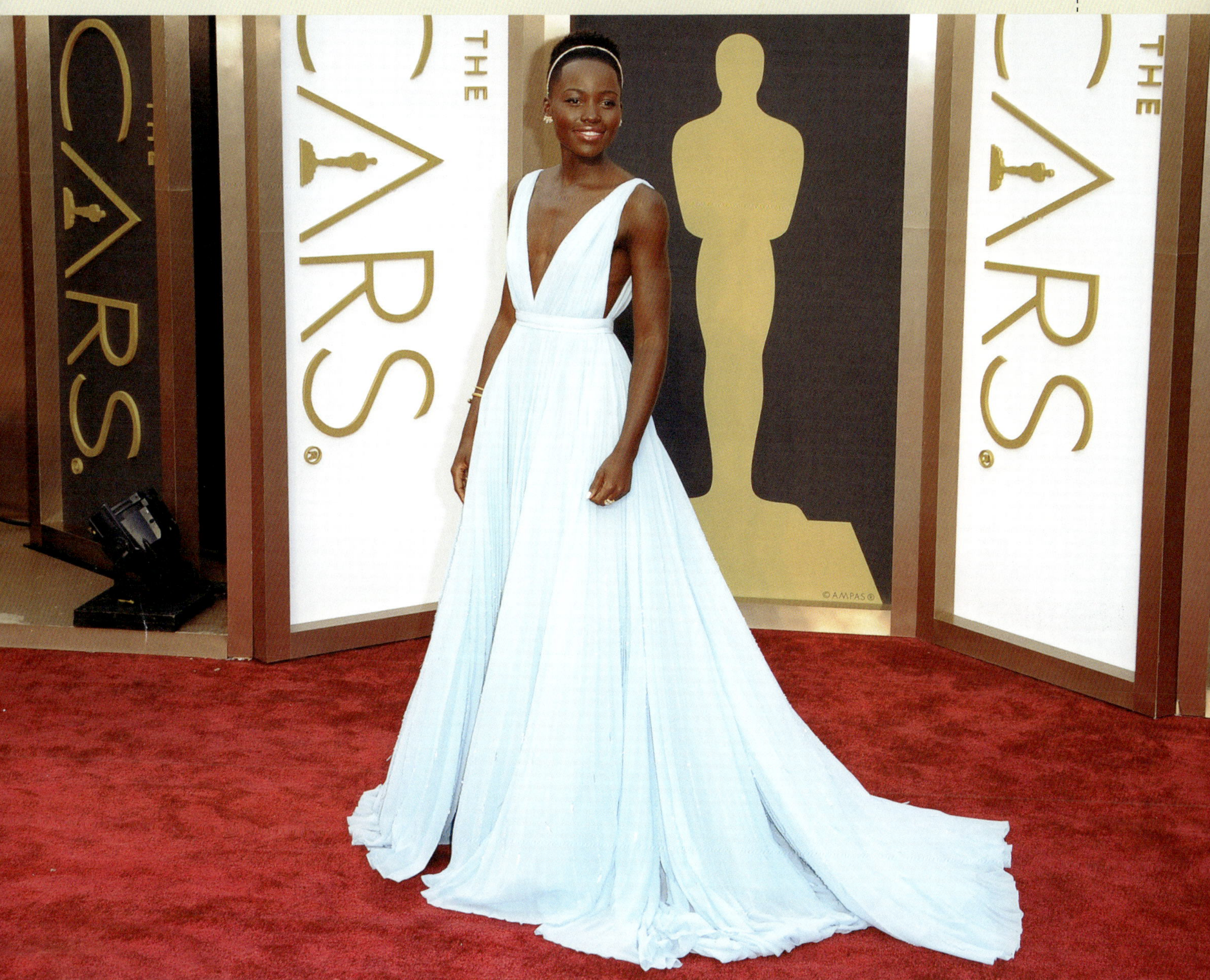

GIGI HADID

Model Gigi regularly wears Prada. At the 2021 Met Gala, she wore a strapless and structured white gown with visible boning details, giving it a sleek, sculptural silhouette. This gown was paired with dramatic, opera-length black leather gloves.

LUPITA NYONG'O

In 2014 Lupita made her Academy Awards debut in a powder blue, custom Prada gown. She took home an Oscar for her role in *12 Years A Slave*, and could not have been better dressed for the occasion.

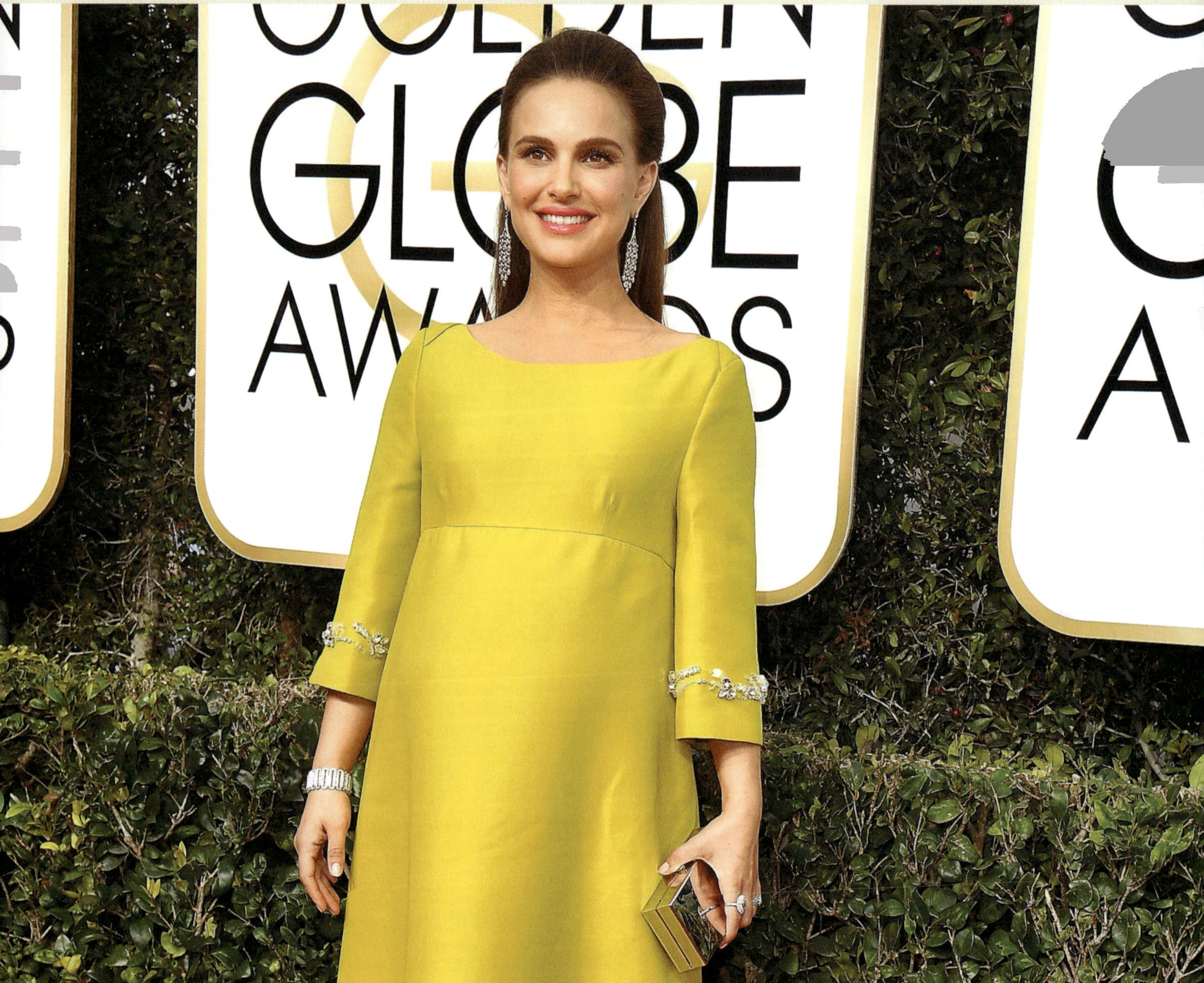

NATALIE PORTMAN

Natalie Portman has worn Prada for various red-carpet events, including the Oscars and film premieres. Here she channels Jackie Kennedy, whom she played in the biopic *Jackie*, at the 2017 Golden Globes.

MARGOT ROBBIE

Prada loves Margot as much as Margot loves Prada. Here she wears a strapless jacquard two-piece set in soft shades of blush and silver, from the 2018 Spring collection, at the 2018 Santa Barbara Film Festival.

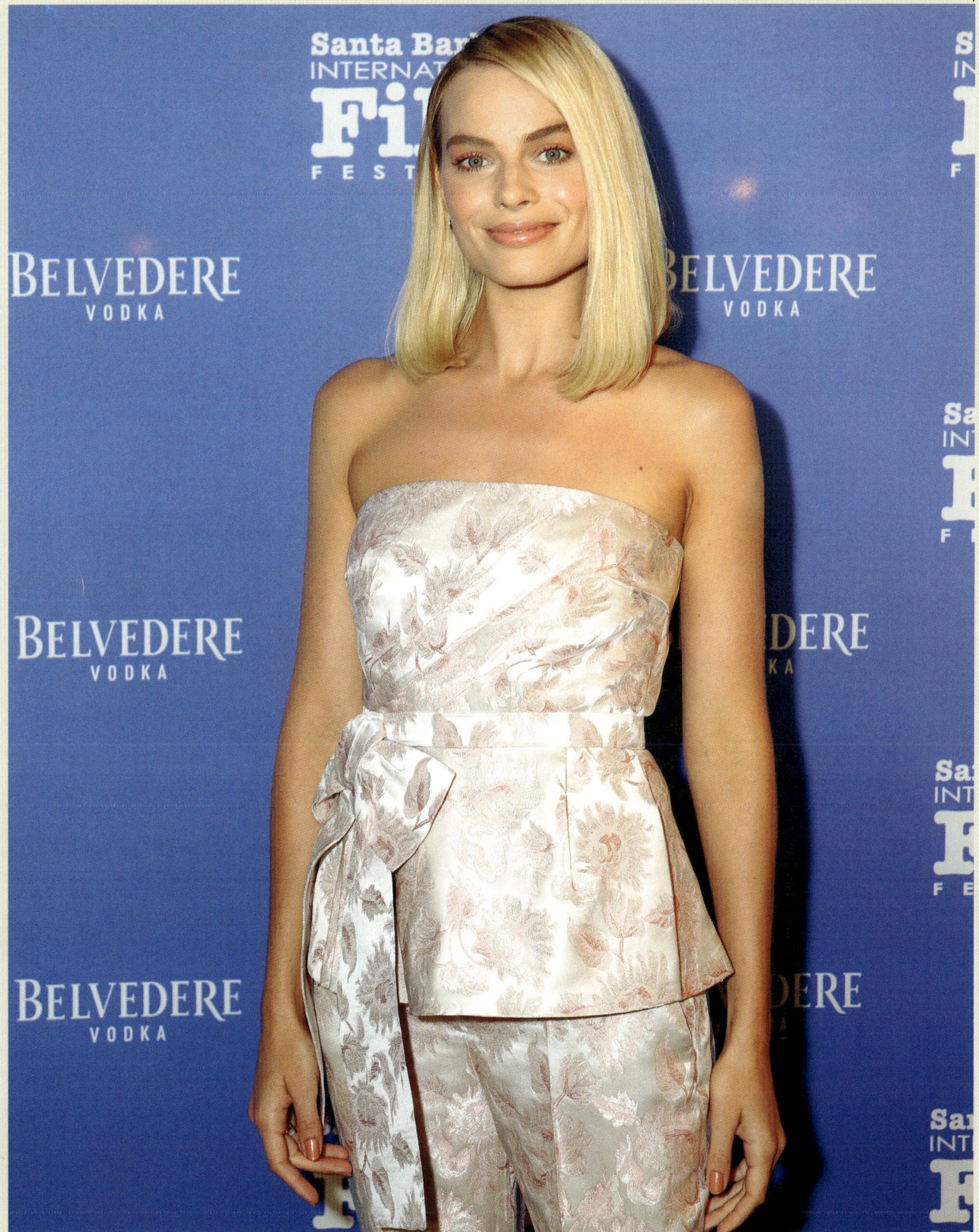
Santa Bar
INTERNAT
Fil
FEST
BELVEDERE
VODKA
BELVEDERE
VODKA
BELVEDERE
VODKA

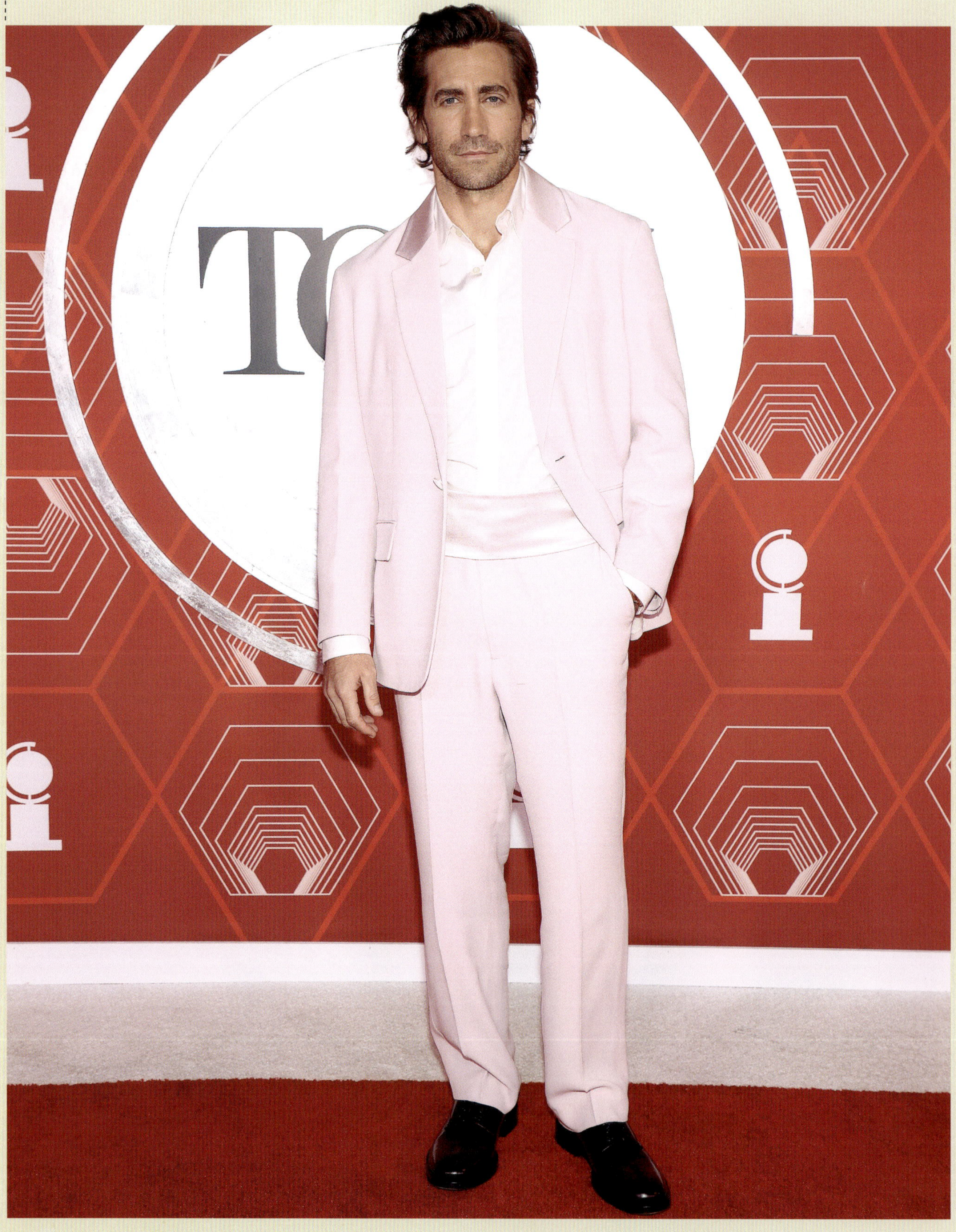

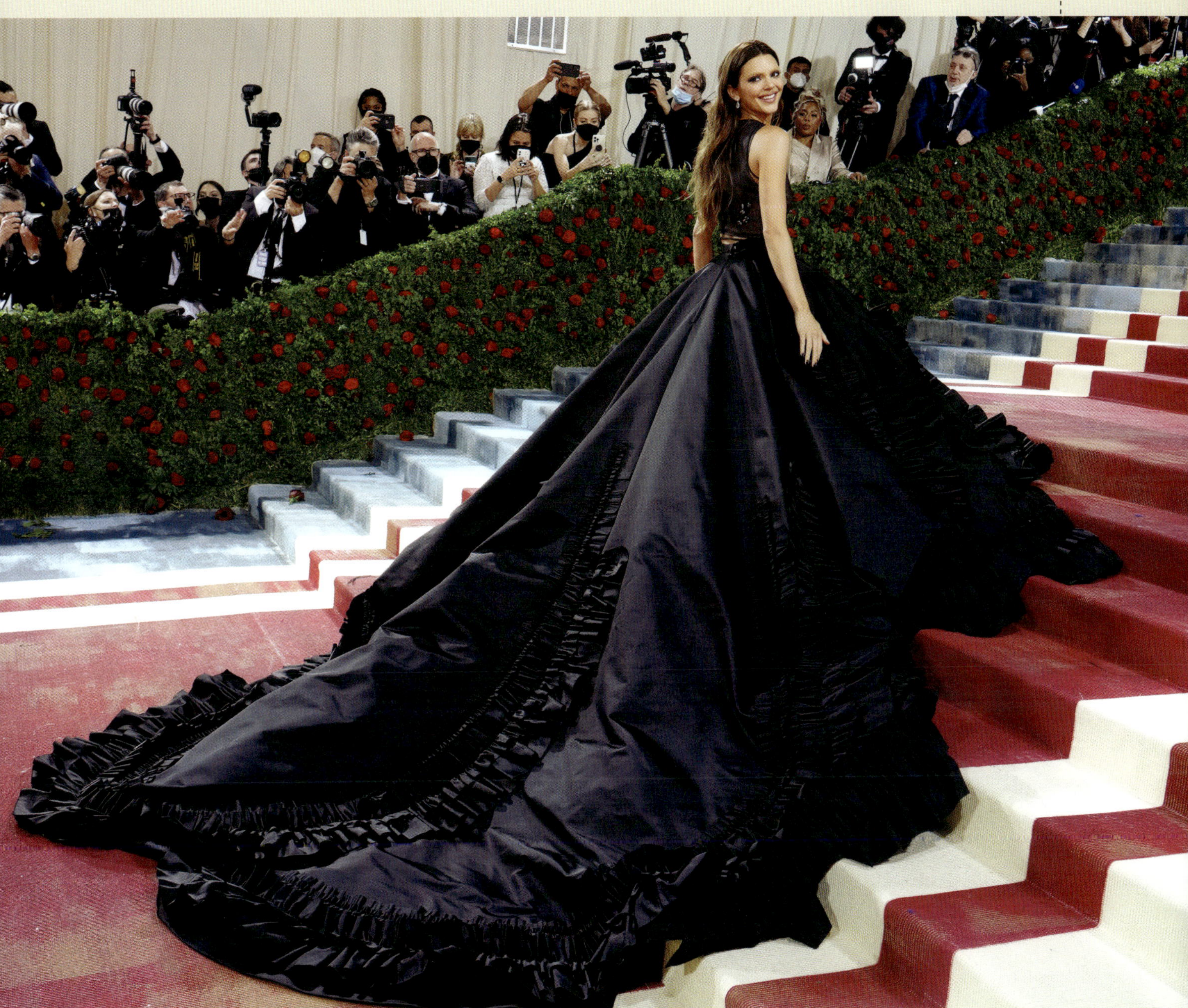

JAKE GYLLENHAAL

Jake in a custom Prada pink tuxedo with a light pink tuxedo shirt and satin cummerbund at the 2021 Tony Awards.

KENDALL JENNER

Kendall Jenner has walked in Prada runway shows and is frequently seen wearing the brand's luxury pieces. For the 2022 Met Gala, she wore a voluminous, custom black taffeta.

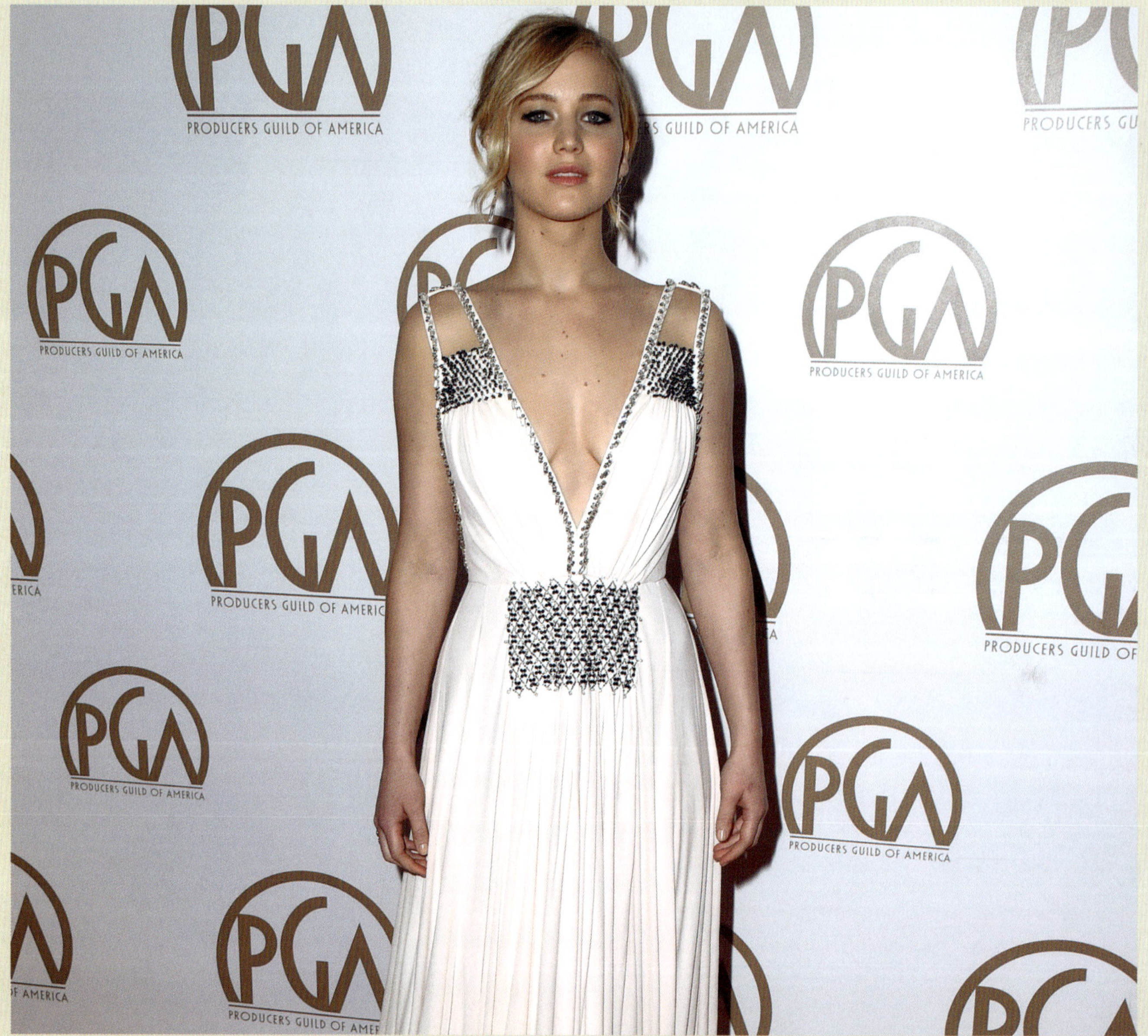

JENNIFER LAWRENCE

Jennifer Lawrence has chosen Prada for numerous award ceremonies and premieres. At the 2015 Producers Guild Awards she wowed in this Prada custom gown in pale pink with silver detailing and Prada crisscross strap platform sandals.

GWYNETH PALTROW

La Paltrow in head-to-toe Prada at the 2011 Venice Film Festival. Silk Prada organza T-back bow detail gown, Prada satin box clutch, Prada platform peep-toe heels.

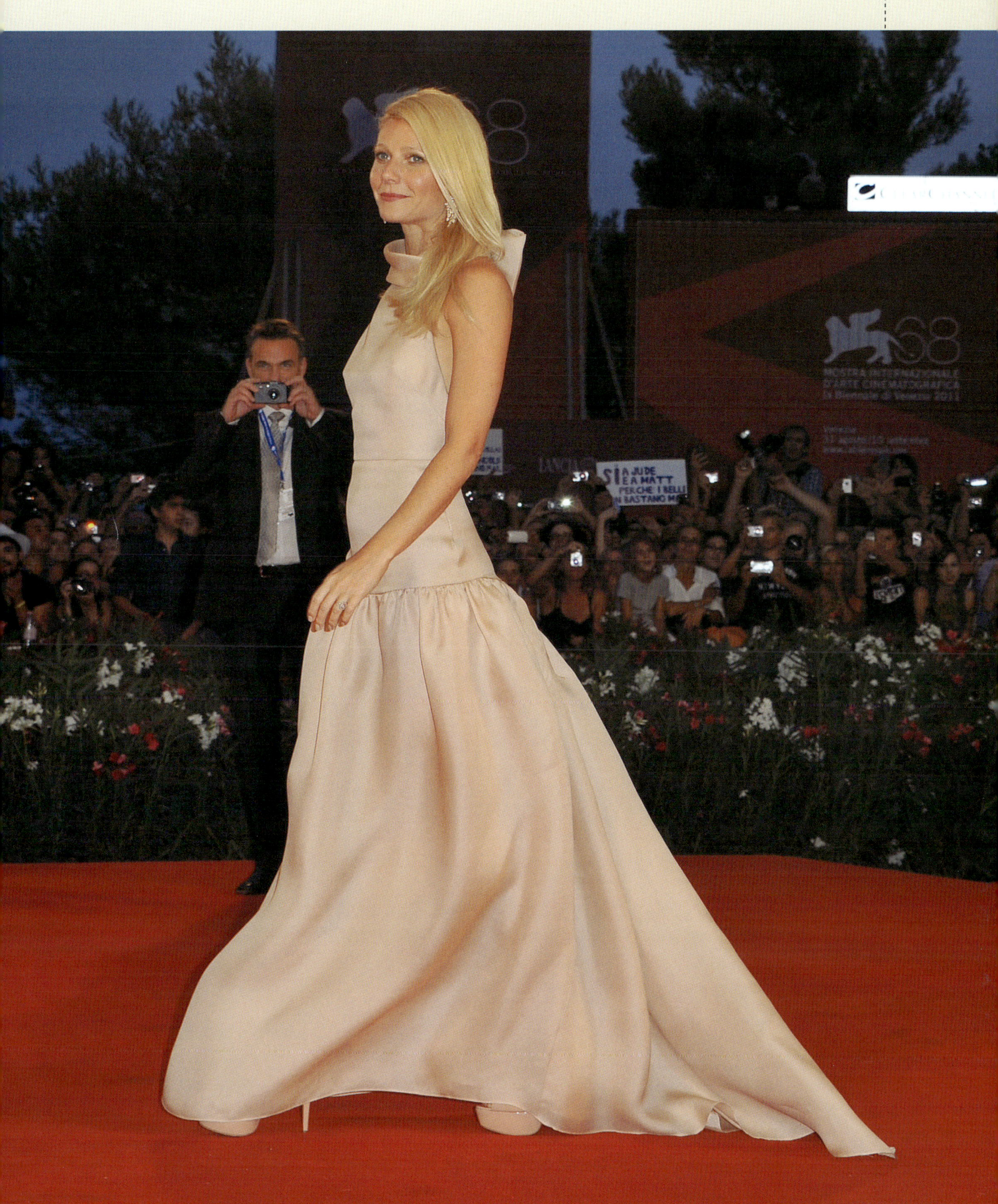

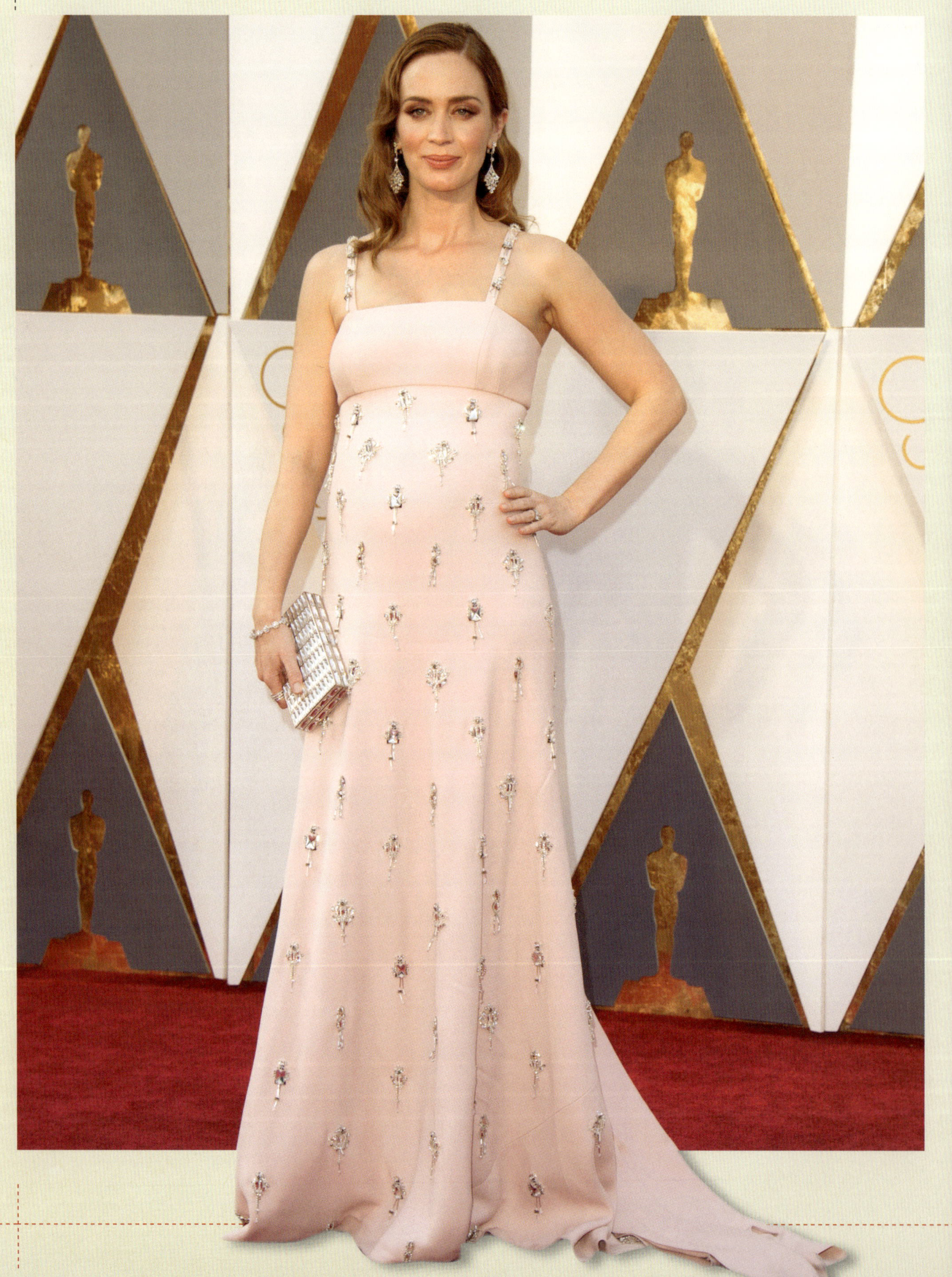

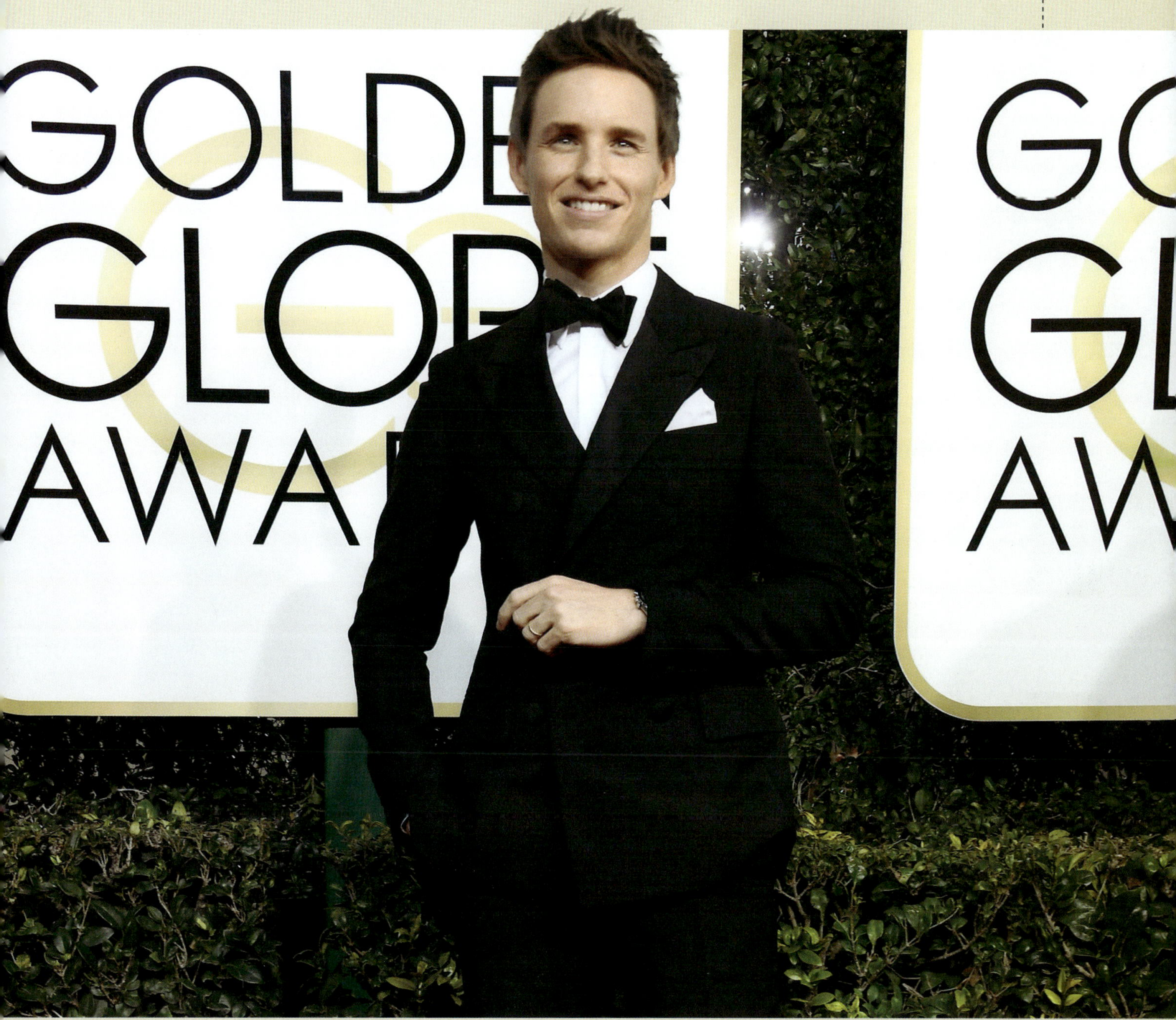

EMILY BLUNT

The Devil Wears Prada actress wears Prada (what else?) on the red carpet – a custom dress in baby pink at the 2016 Academy Awards.

EDDIE REDMAYNE

Oscar winner Eddie in head-to-toe Prada at the 2017 Golden Globes.

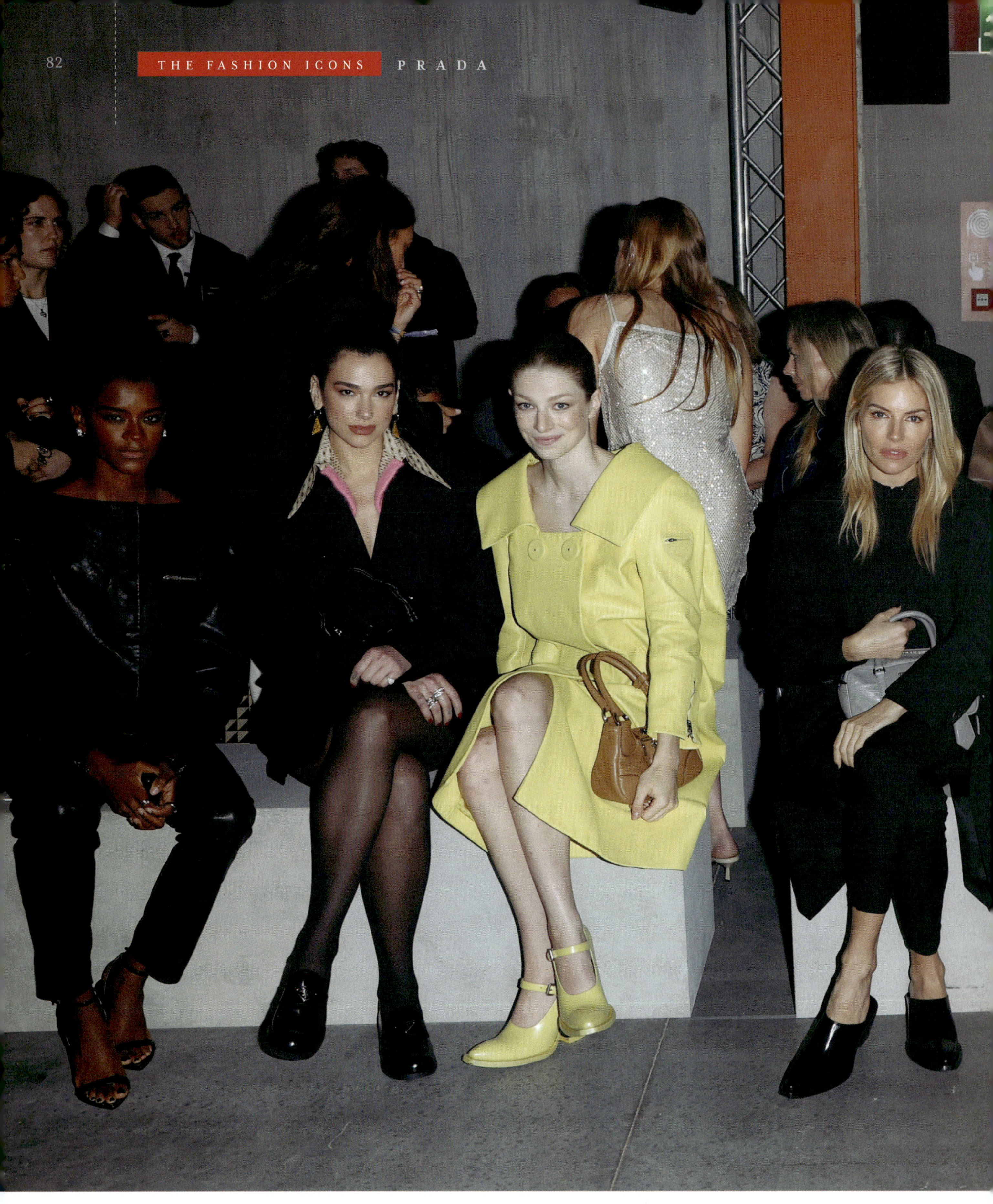

ABOVE: (L-R) Letitia Wright, Dua Lipa, Hunter Schafer, Sienna Miller, Thuso Mbedu, Claire Foy, Ellie Bamber and Naomi Ackie attend Prada Fall/Winter 2023 Womenswear Fashion Show, 23 February, 2023 in Milan, Italy

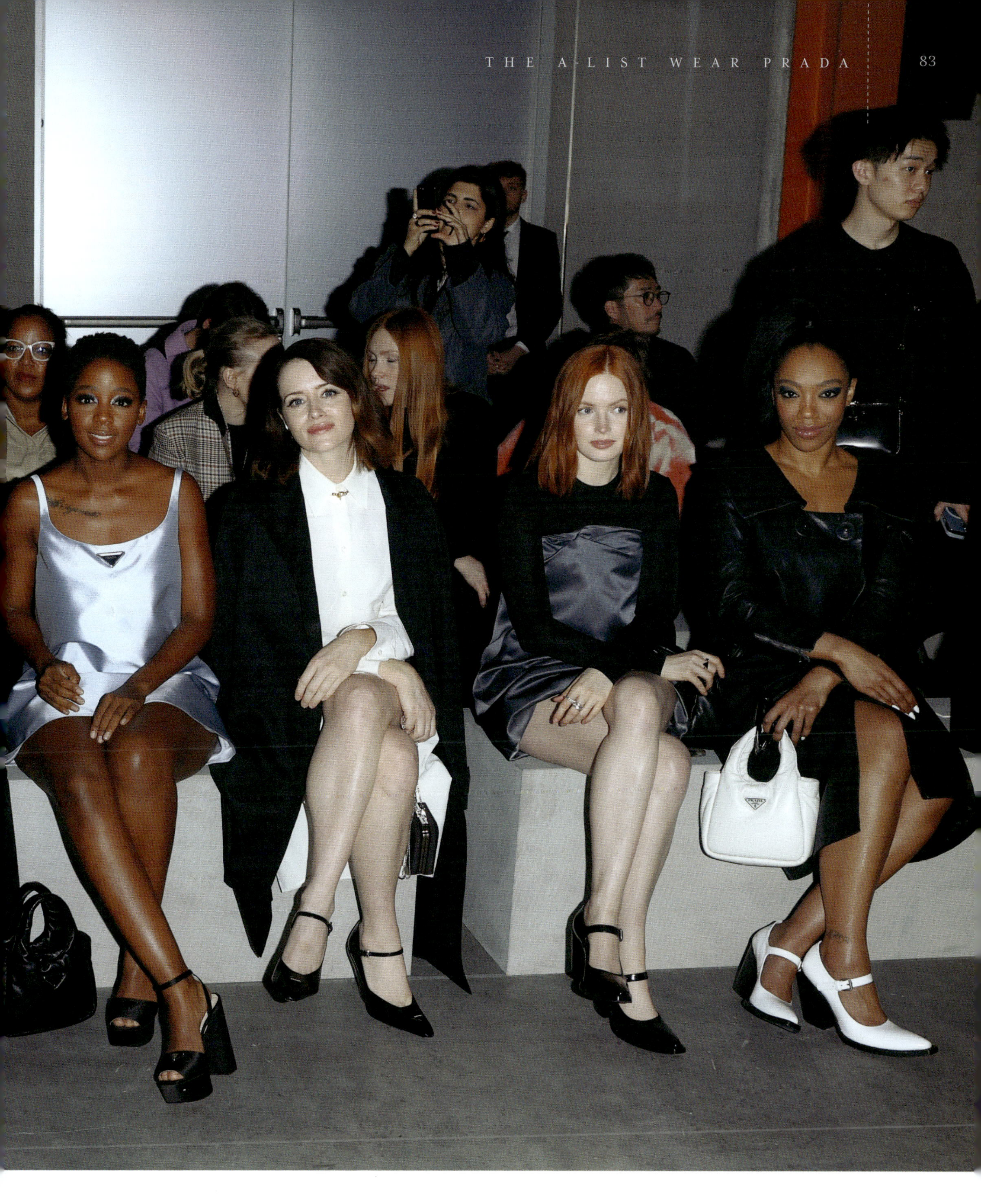

PRADA MEN

"I wanted to try to push some freedom into the men's clothes"
Miuccia Prada

Prada launched its men's ready-to-wear line in 1993 and it quickly became known for its minimalist yet sophisticated style - clean lines, sharp tailoring, and an understated elegance. As with the women's RTW, it blended traditional tailoring with innovative materials and cutting-edge design. Prada Menswear emphasized simplicity and sophistication which stood in contrast to the flashier styles of the era. The designs were praised for pushing boundaries, including experiments with fabrics, cuts, and silhouettes that challenged conventional menswear. Not surprisingly, Prada's growing influence in the menswear market attracted high-profile clients and celebrities. In 2020, Prada announced a ground-breaking collaboration with Raf Simons, well known for his innovative approach to menswear. The Simons-Prada partnership introduced fresh perspectives, combining Raf's avant-garde influence with Miuccia Prada's minimalist approach. Since then, collections have explored themes like fluidity and simplicity, often focusing on the architecture of clothing and exploring freedom of movement in menswear.

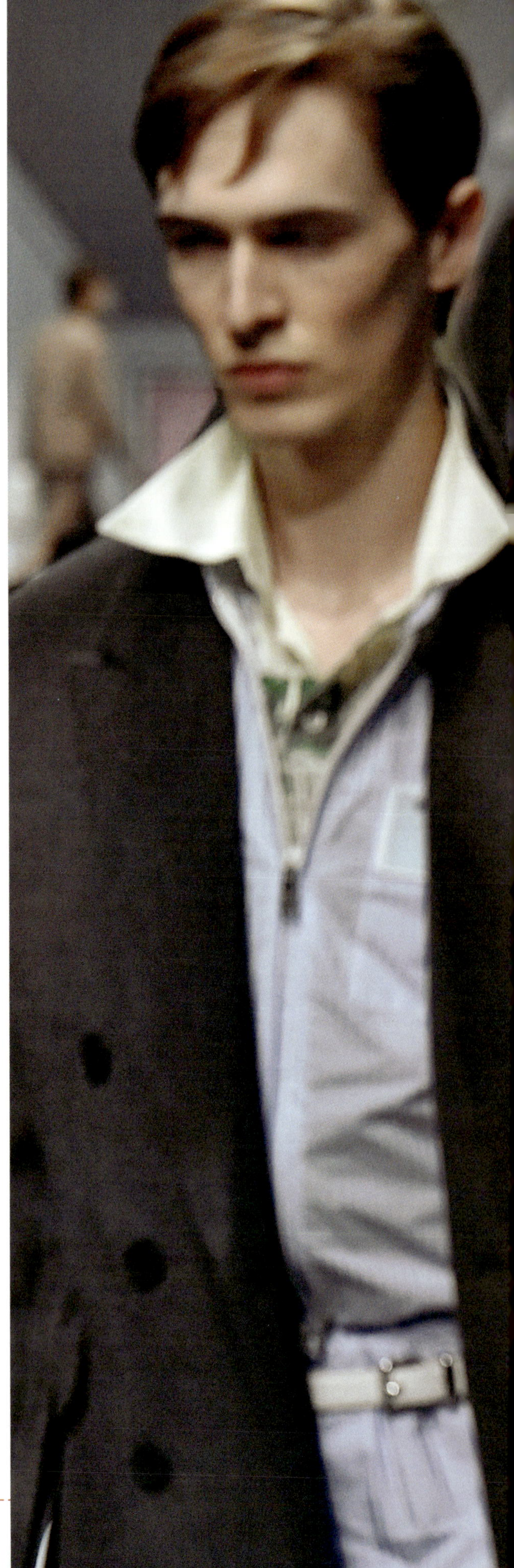

RIGHT: Prada Runway, Milan Men's Fashion Week, Spring/Summer 2018

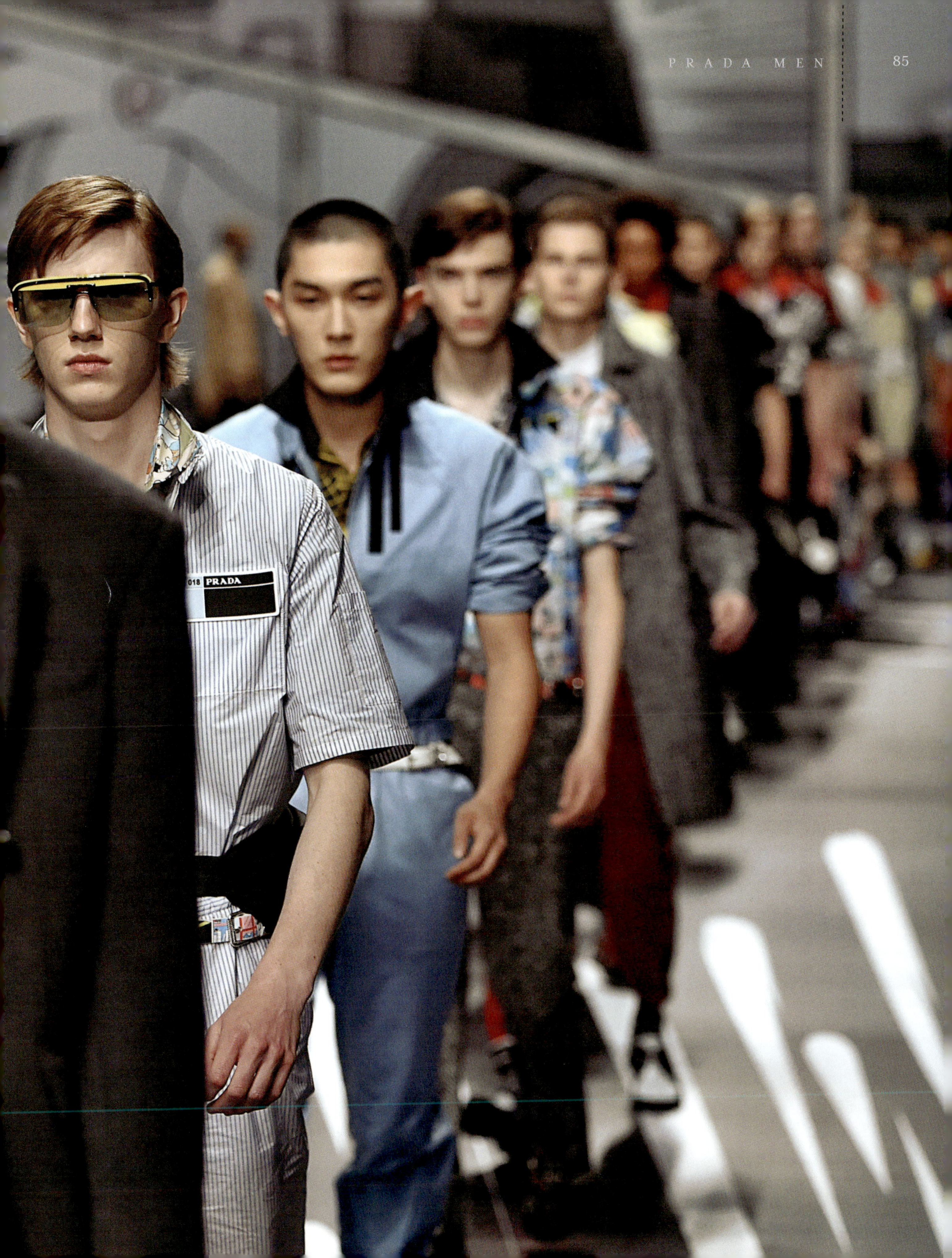

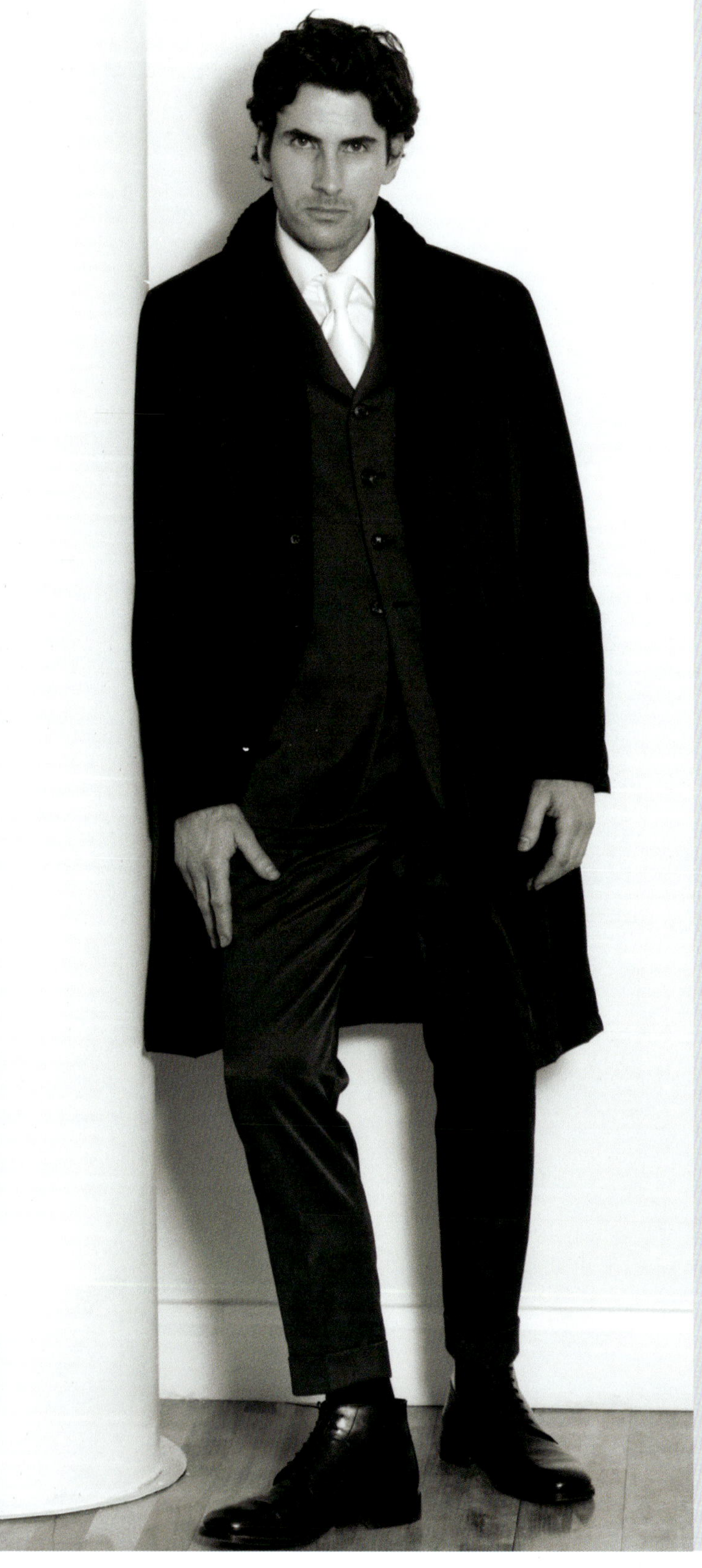

Prada's menswear line continues to seamlessly blend traditional craftsmanship with contemporary design, offering a range of clothing and accessories that cater to the modern man. The collections include tailored suits, jackets, leather goods, printed shirts, cashmere sweaters, wool trousers, coats with clean lines, and accessories that balance classic Italian craftsmanship with subtle experimentation. The brand is known for its sharp silhouettes and innovative use of materials, such as Re-Nylon and stretch fabrics, which juxtapose traditional men's suits with technologically advanced textiles. Prada menswear continues to innovate while honouring its minimalist roots, blending luxury with thoughtful experimentation and reinforcing its role as a defining brand in contemporary men's fashion. Here are some of Prada's most iconic and influential menswear collections over the years.

FALL/WINTER 1995

Prada's Fall/Winter 1995 menswear collection showcased a minimalist aesthetic characterized by clean lines and tailored silhouettes. The collection featured a palette of muted tones, emphasizing classic menswear staples reimagined with modern sensibilities. The advertising campaign for the collection was photographed by Peter Lindbergh and featured actor John Malkovich, highlighting how Prada has always liked to blend fashion with cinematic artistry.

ABOVE & OPP PAGE: Prada Menswear Fall/Winter 1995 Ready-to-Wear Collection

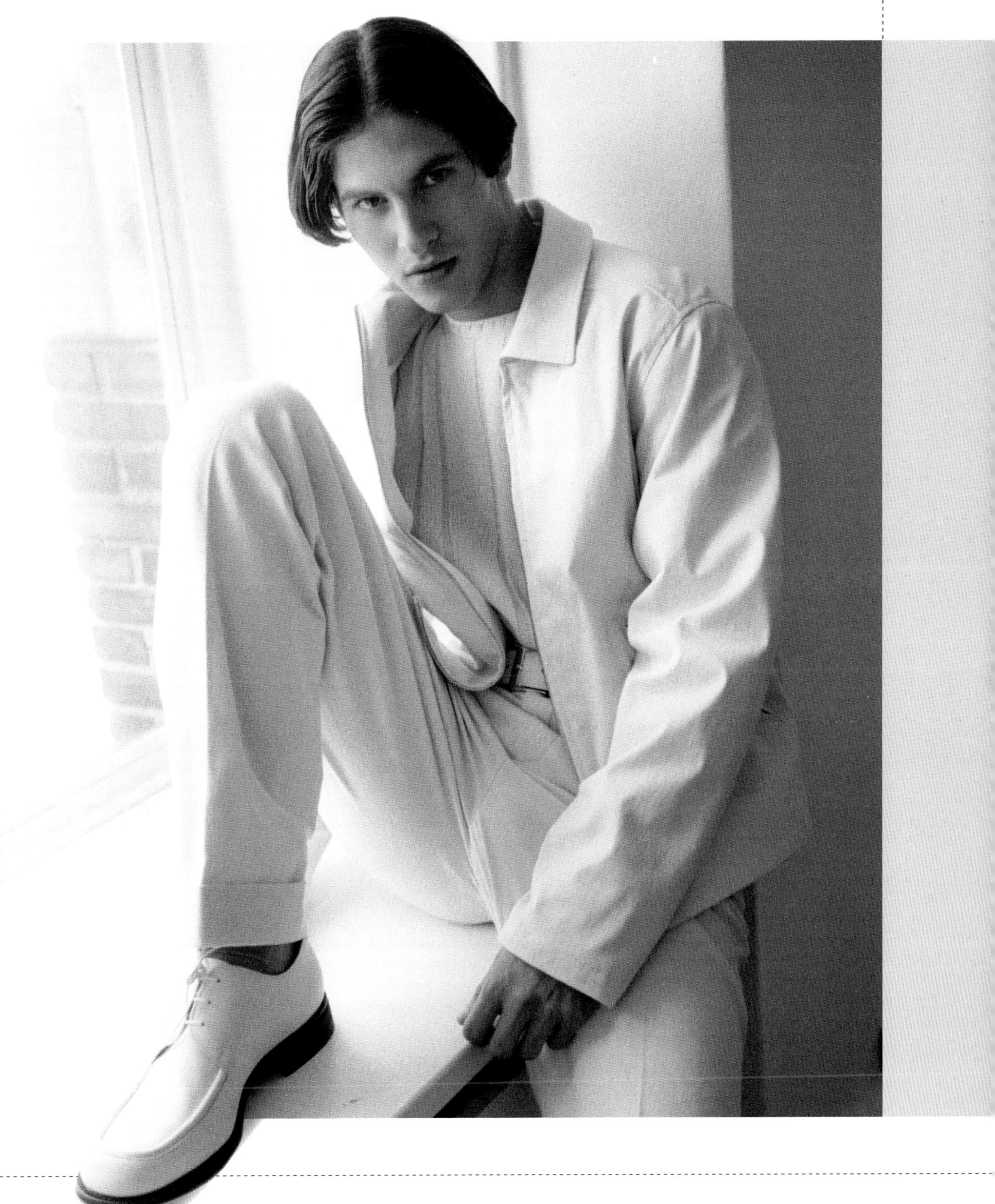

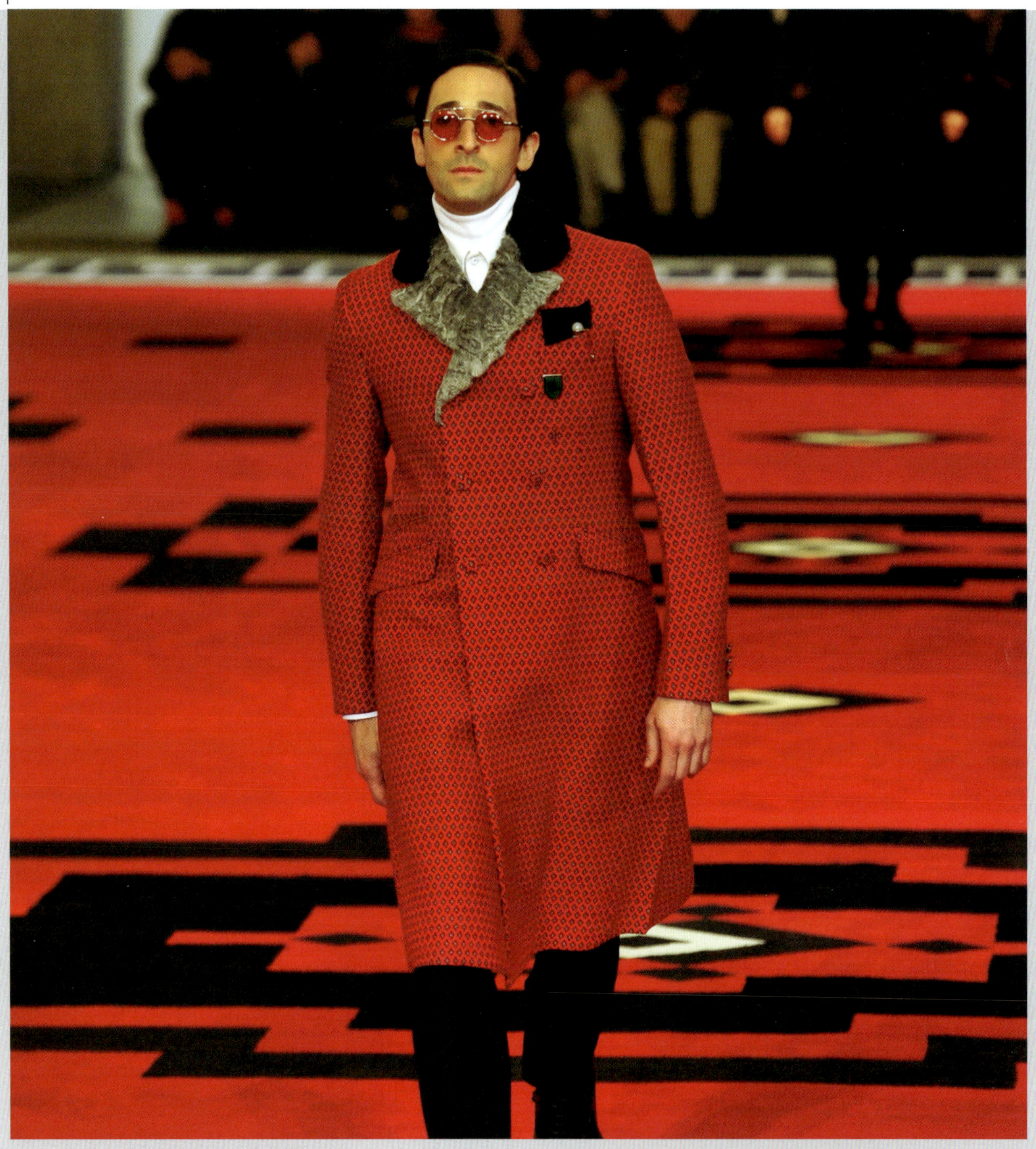

FALL/WINTER 2012

The designs for this collection emphasized sharp tailoring and a retro-futuristic vibe, blending classic menswear elements with avant-garde details. This collection featured a unique twist by incorporating renowned actors such as Gary Oldman, Adrien Brody, and Willem Dafoe as models.

ABOVE: Adrien Brody displays a creation as part of Prada Fall/Winter 2012 Menswear collection
OPP PAGE: A model walks the runway at the Prada show during Milan Men's Fashion Week, Fall/Winter 2016

FALL/WINTER 2016

Prada introduced a nautical theme with a modern twist, featuring sailor collars, striped patterns, and maritime-inspired accessories. The collection balanced traditional seafaring motifs with contemporary silhouettes and materials.

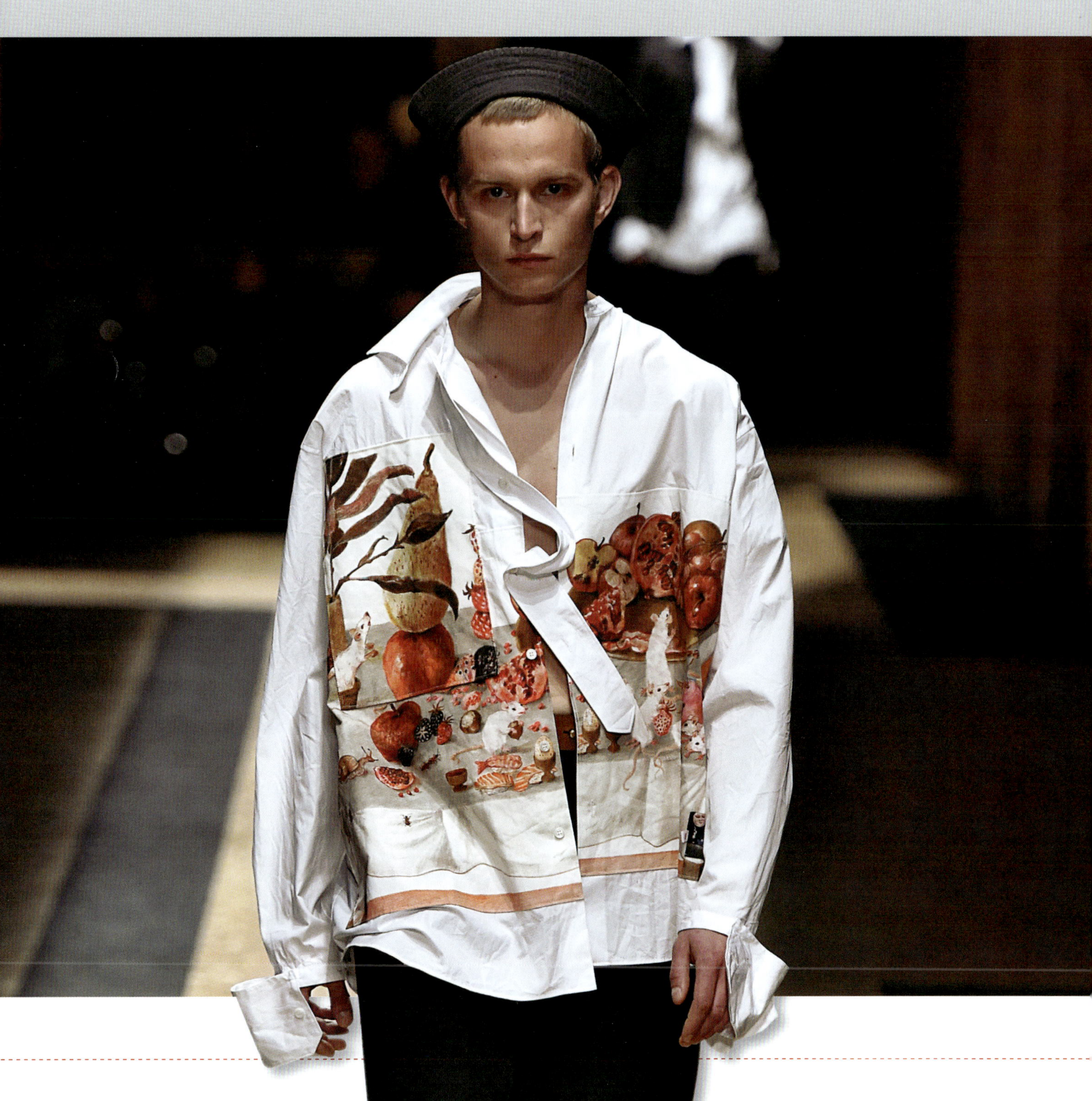

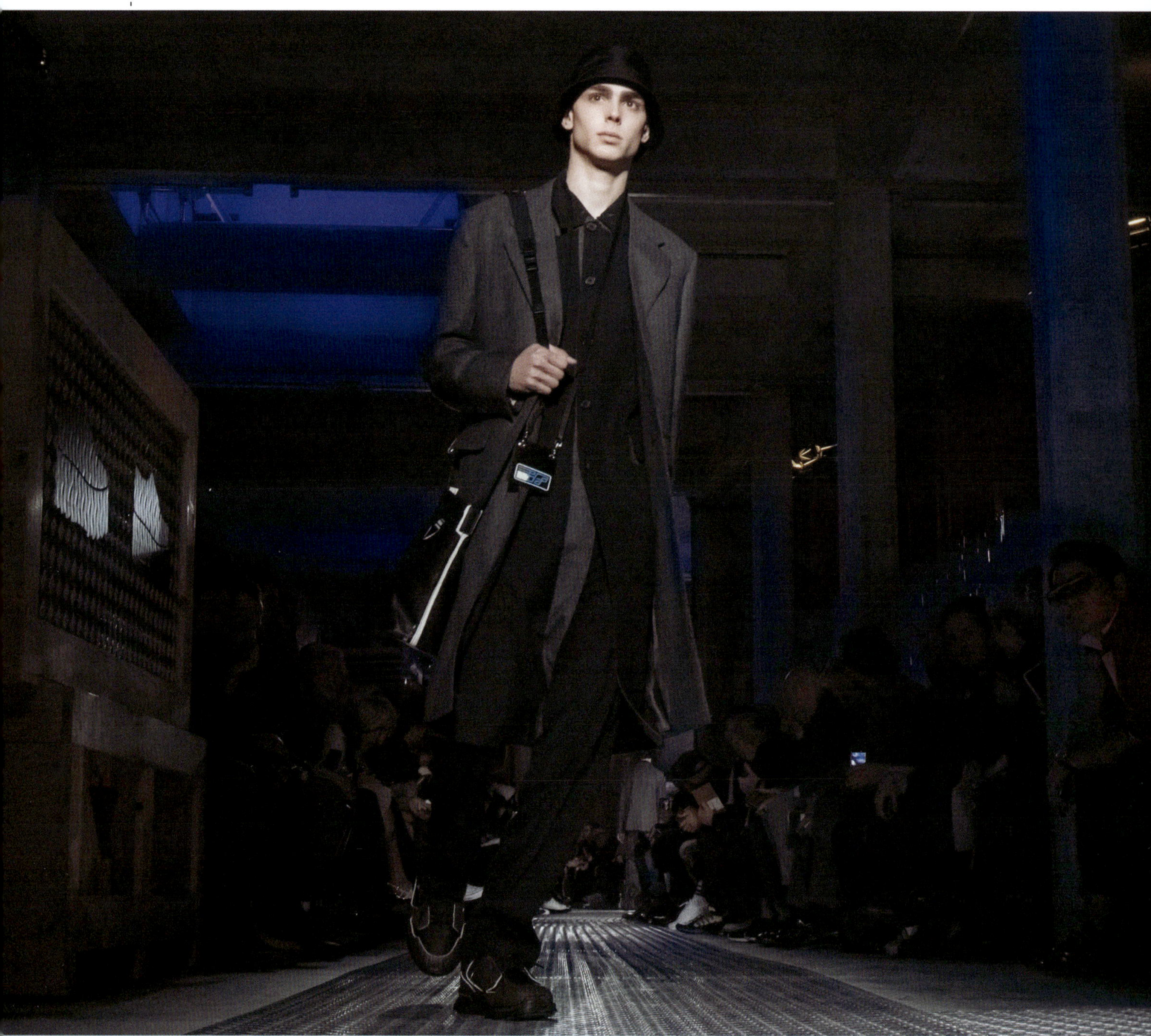

FALL/WINTER 2018

This season marked a return to Prada's roots with a focus on nylon, the material that brought the brand significant acclaim in the 1990s. The collection combined utilitarian designs with luxury, featuring nylon suits, coats, and accessories, highlighting the brand's ability to elevate everyday materials.

ABOVE: Milan Men's Fashion Week Fall/Winter 2018
OPP PAGE: Prada window display in Hamburg, Germany, 27 May, 2022

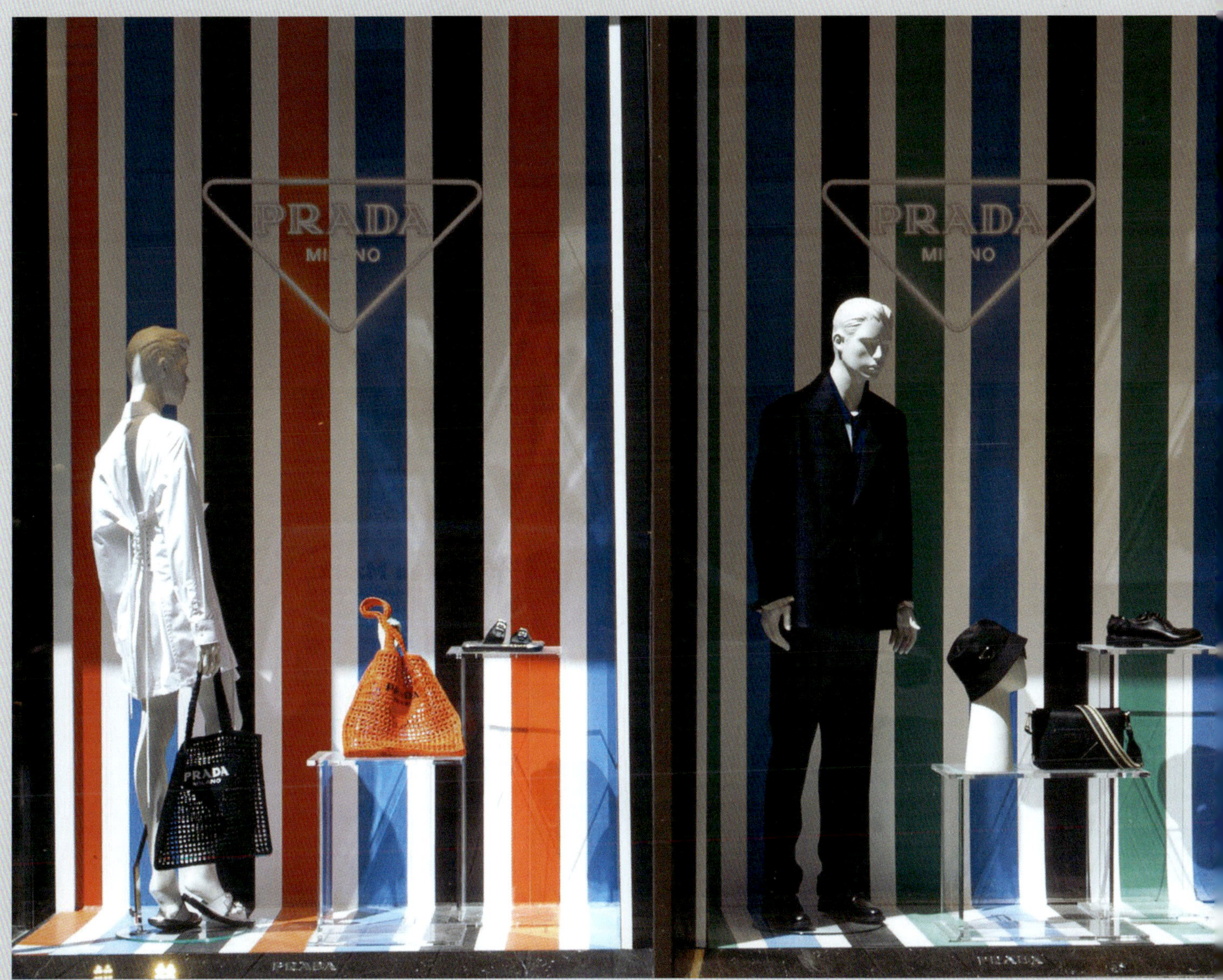

SPRING/SUMMER 2022

The collection, titled 'Possible Feelings' was a collaboration between Miuccia Prada and her recently appointed Co-Creative Director, Raf Simons. It explored themes of freedom and sensuality, featuring bold colours, oversized silhouettes, and innovative fabric combinations. The designs emphasized the human body's freedom and the pleasure of tactility - resulting in a sensuous coming together of surface, texture, and textile.

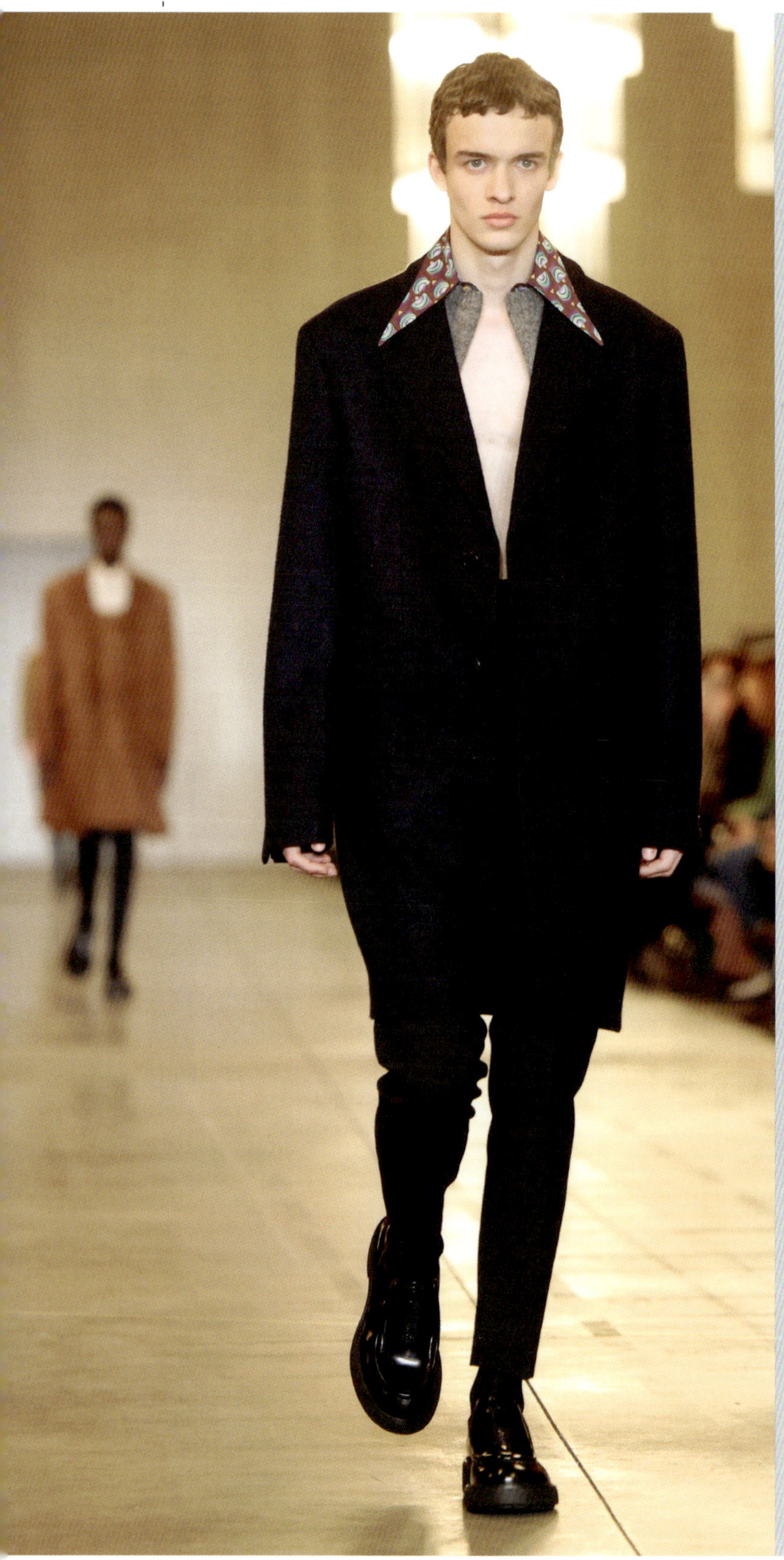

FALL/WINTER 2023

This collection focused on the fundamentals of fashion, emphasizing reduction and simplicity combined with comfort and exaggeration. It featured reductionist tailoring and graphic prints coupled with bold changes in shape and form, thus using the structure and design of the clothes themselves to create dramatic contrasts in volume and style – resulting in unique, avant-garde silhouettes.

SPRING/SUMMER 2024

The collection explored the concept of fashion as fluid architecture around the human body. It emphasized absolute freedom of movement expressed through the foundational garments that clothe the body. For instance, actor Jake Gyllenhaal was noted for wearing a standout Prada shirt featuring a Cuban collar and a flowy silk finish at the Tribeca Festival premiere of his Apple TV courtroom thriller, *Presumed Innocent*.

ABOVE: A model is walking the runway at the Prada fashion show during the Milan Menswear Fall/Winter 2023
OPP PAGE: Prada Runway, Milan Fashion Week, Menswear Spring/Summer 2024

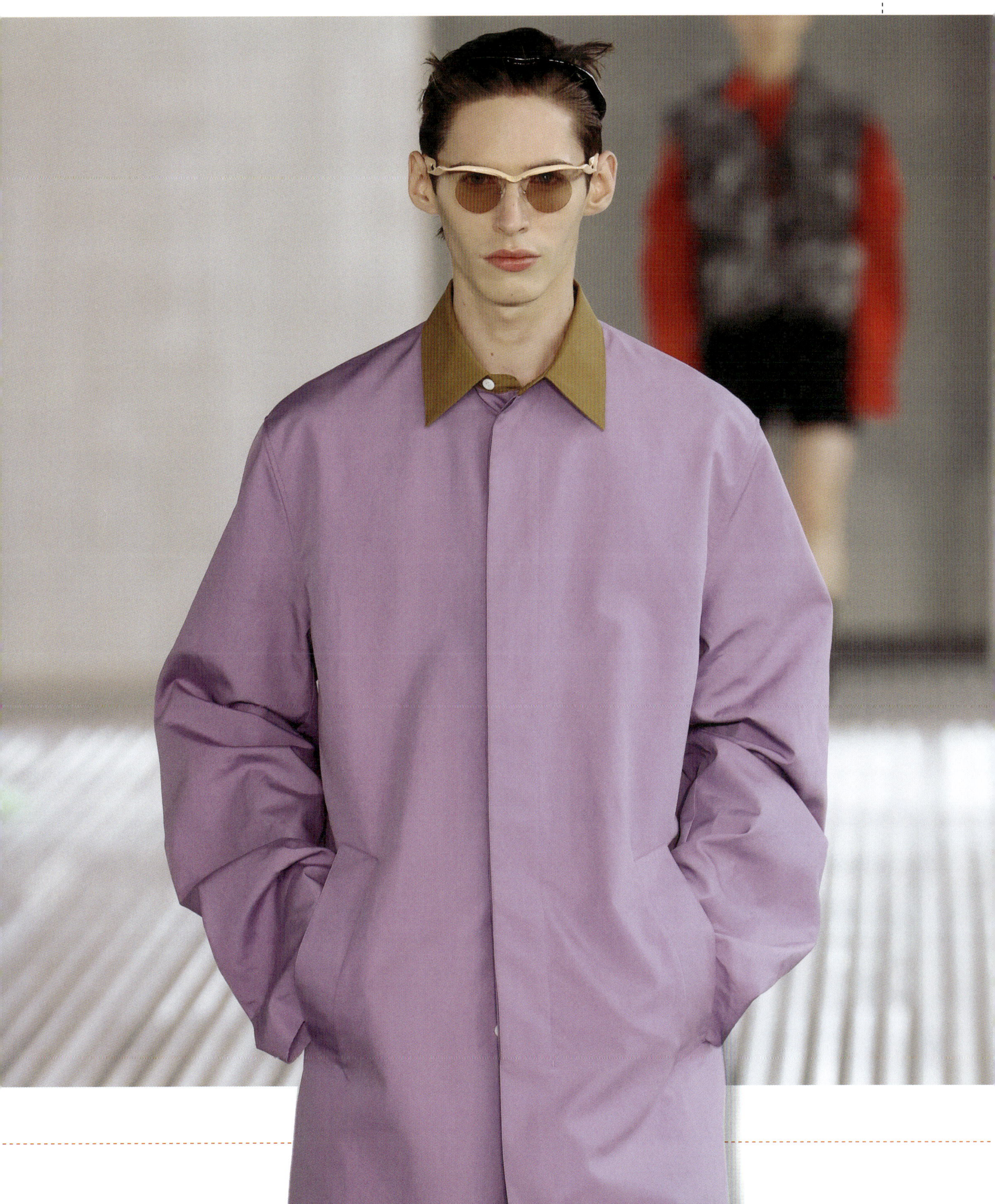

PRADA SUNGLASSES

"Sunglasses are like eyeshadow - they make everything look younger and prettier"
Miuccia Prada

Prada launched its first collection of sunglasses in the late 1990s. This move was part of a broader strategy to expand its brand beyond its established fashion and leather goods lines and into luxury accessories and eyewear. Prada shades quickly gained popularity for their combination of contemporary, elegant, and bold design - crafted with quality materials and incorporating both functionality and style. From classic to avant-garde, they have become iconic - recognized for their innovative designs, distinct branding and influence on luxury eyewear trends.

RIGHT: Close up side view of Prada sunglasses with classic lines and logo detail

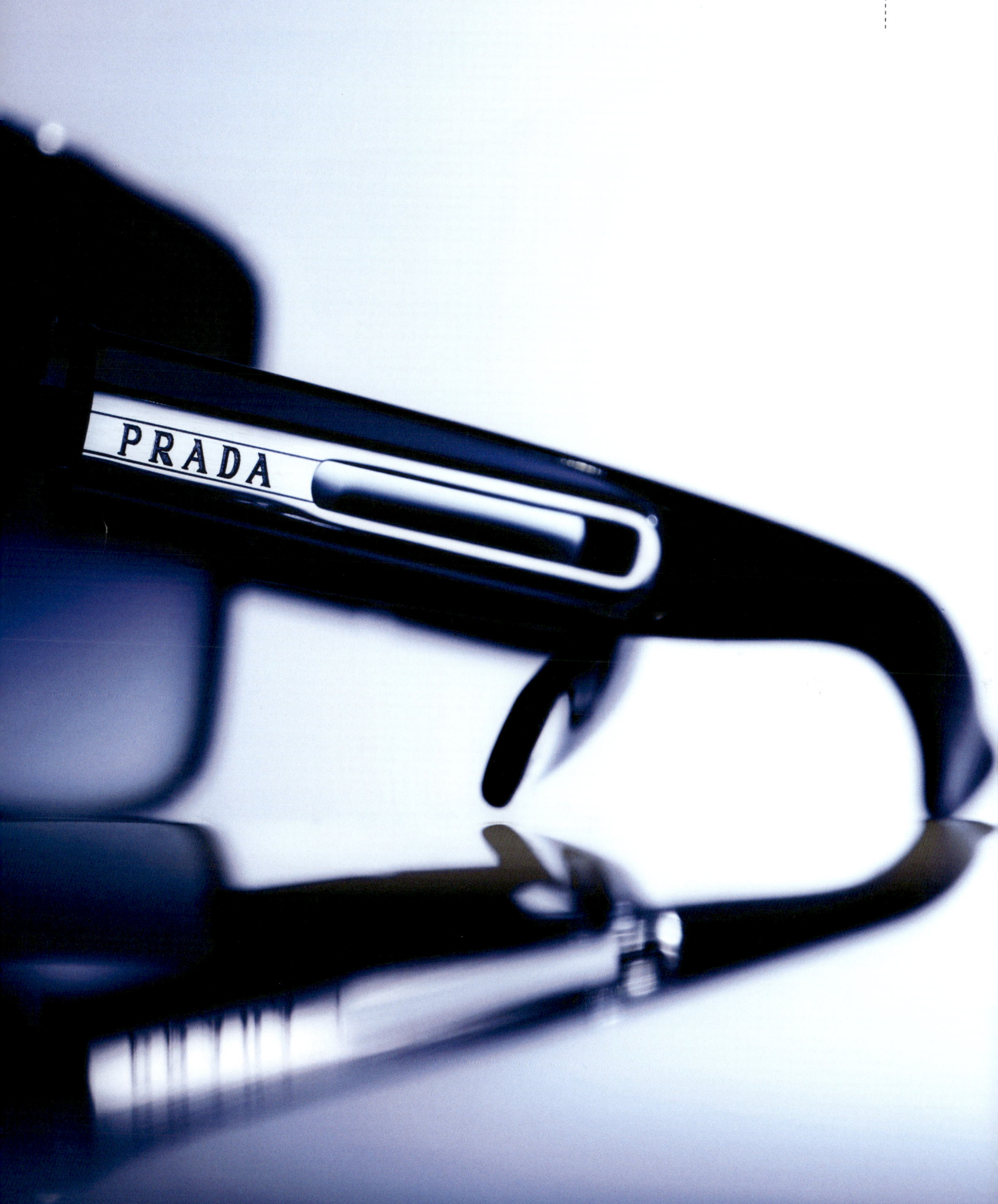
PRADA

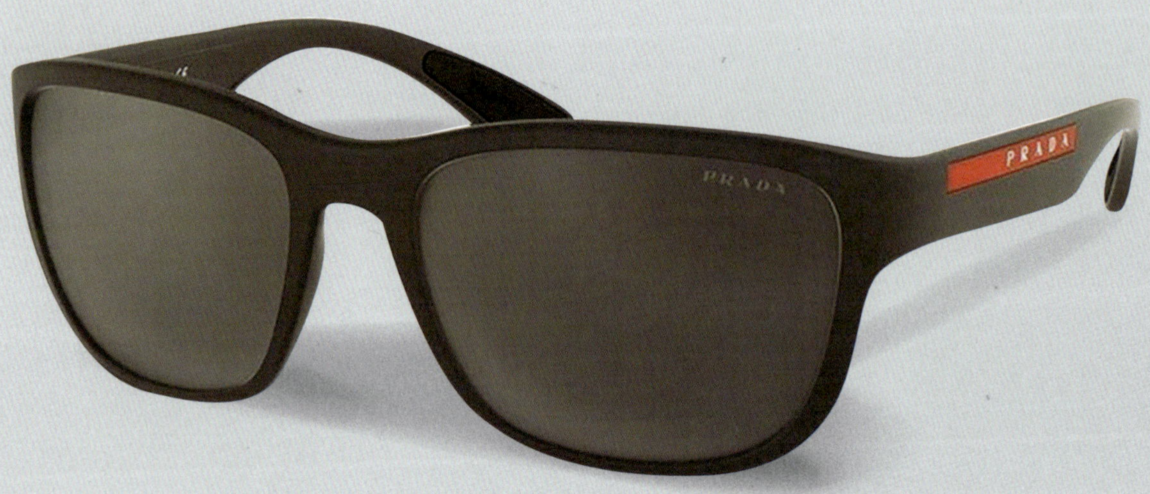

PRADA LINEA ROSA

Known as Prada Sport and launched in 1997, the Linea Rosa line of Prada sunglasses feature sleek designs, bold lines and subtle branding with a focus on functionality and athletic use - blending Prada's luxury appeal with a performance-oriented edge. The Linea Rossa collection is popular for outdoor and activewear, and include designs with polarized lenses and wraparound frames.

SQUARE AND ROUND FRAMES

Prada has produced square and round sunglasses since the early days of its eyewear line. The brand embraced bold, structured square frames early on as part of its approach to create eyewear that

emphasized elegance with an edgy vibe. Prada's round frames emerged as part of a vintage revival trend circa the mid noughties, often featuring thin metal rims for a more retro, classic look, and thus highlighting the label's reputation for merging timeless style with contemporary fashion cues. Prada frequently revisits its classic square and round frames, giving them modern updates through colour variations, lens choices and usage of innovative materials.

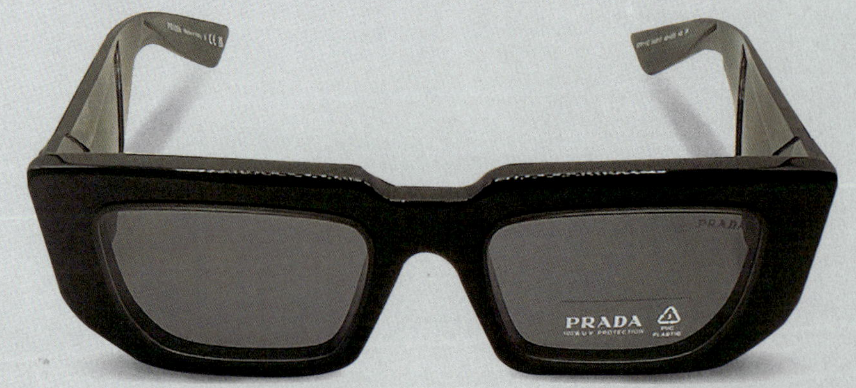

OPP PAGE: 2014 Prada Eyewear advertisment featuring James McAvoy

CLASSIC AVIATORS AND CAT-EYE STYLES

Prada's sunglasses collection includes updated releases of the classic Aviator and Cat-Eye styles, blending timeless elegance with modern detailing. The classic Aviators feature metal frames, echoing the vintage yet minimalist appeal with touches including gradient lenses and slim silhouettes. The Cat-Eye styles offer a glamorous, dramatic, sexy vibe. Prada's specific design accentuates the pointed, upward sweep typical of Cat-Eye frames but also incorporate contemporary twists, such as thicker acetate frames and intricate colourways like tortoiseshell and classic black.

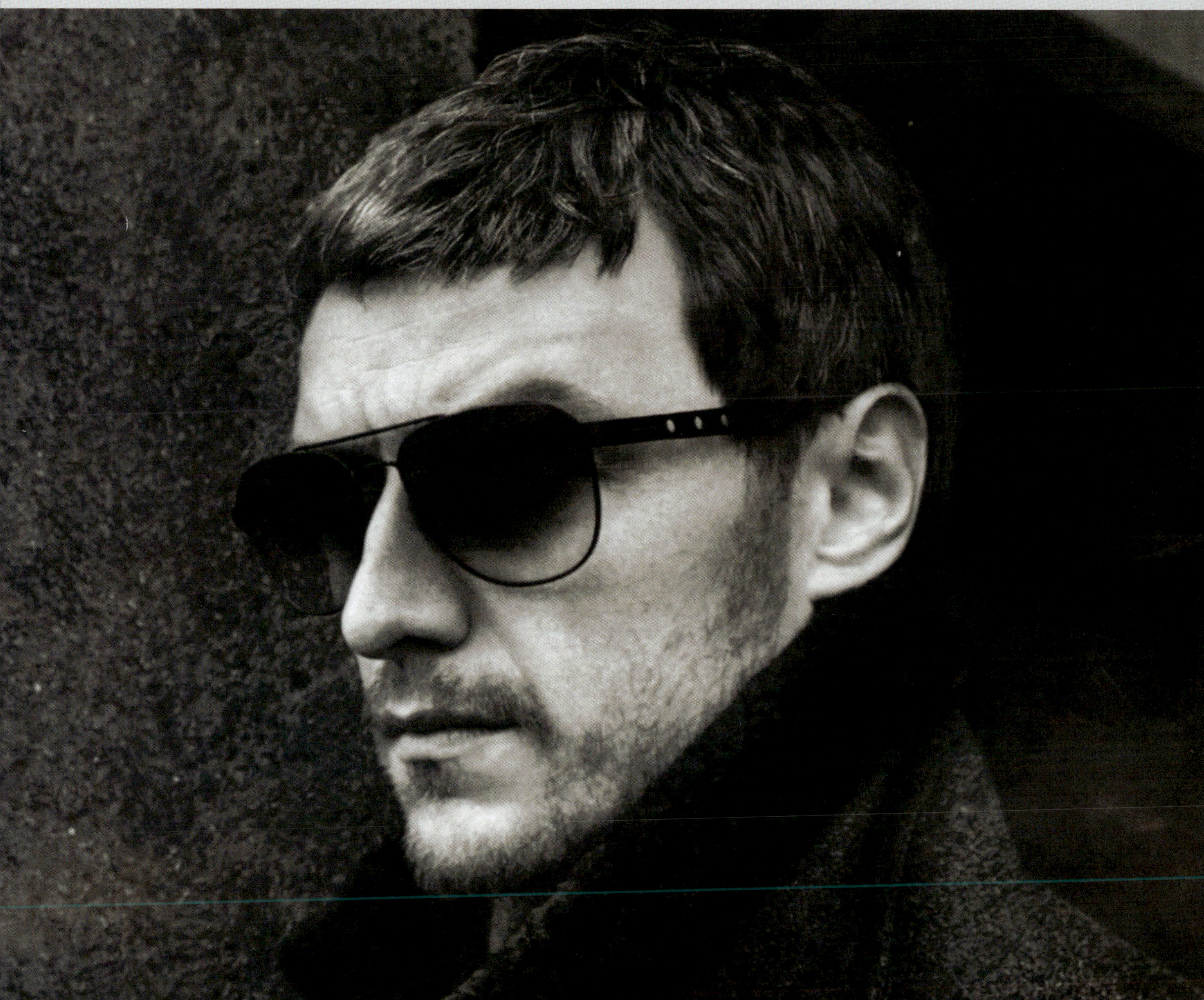

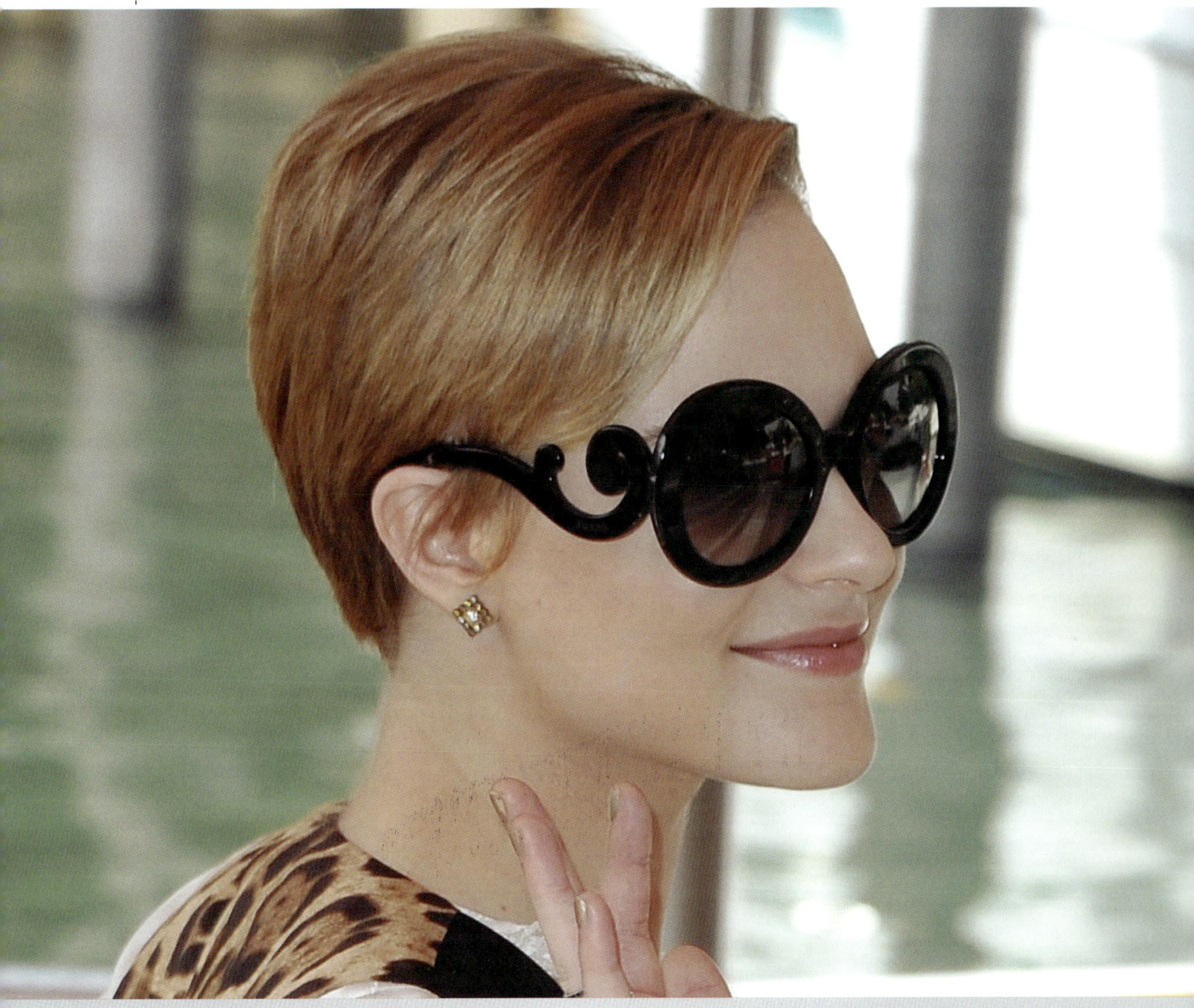

PRADA MINIMAL BAROQUE

The Prada Minimal Baroque collection, first launched in 2011, is famous for its distinctively ornamental and exaggerated styles, inspired by Baroque art. These bold and intricately designed sunglasses feature swirling, sculptural frames and curvy arms that blend high fashion with artistic expression. The PMB line occupies a unique place in Prada's history by merging luxury eyewear with a distinctive aesthetic that's simultaneously playful and sophisticated. Only at Prada.

ABOVE: Actress Evan Rachel Wood arrives at the 68th Venice Film Festival wearing Prada Baroque sunglasses in 2011

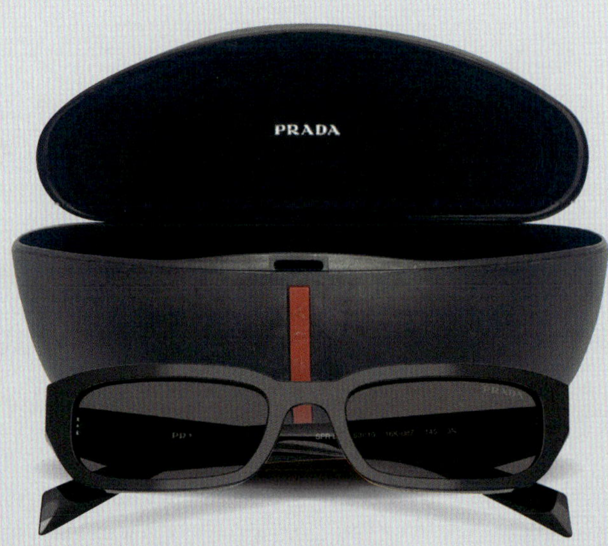

PRADA RE-NYLON SUNGLASSES

Since 2020 Prada has incorporated its Re-Nylon material in various products, including sunglasses. These eco-friendly frames are made from recycled materials like plastic waste, ocean debris and textile remnants – reflecting the brand's commitment to sustainability.

PRADA SYMBOLE COLLECTION

The Prada Symbole Sunglasses Collection, part of Prada's 2024 releases, embodies a bold design that reinforces the brand's iconic triangular motif, linking back to Prada's heritage and style identity. Available in a variety of colours and finishes, including bold acetate frames and gradient lenses, the collection includes options for those seeking both classic and modern styles. The Prada Symbole shades represent the brand's ongoing skills in merging luxury and modernism. Iconic design with a contemporary twist.

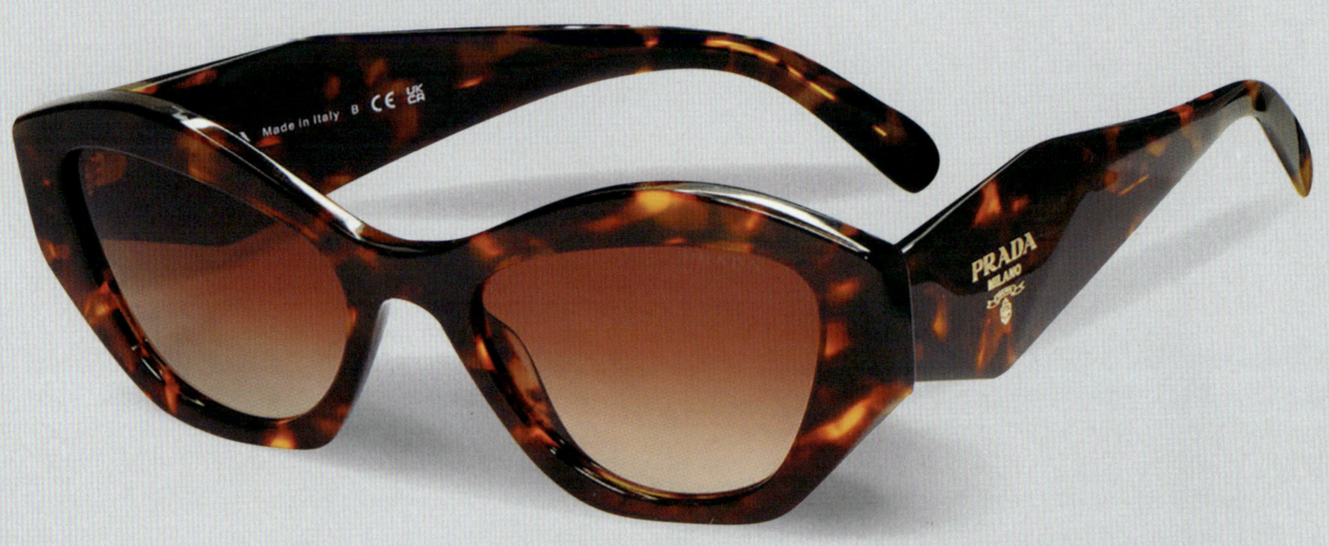

ICONIC PRADA

Prada boasts several truly iconic pieces and styles that are considered 'classics' in the fashion world. These items have stood the test of time and are emblematic of Prada's minimalist yet innovative aesthetic. Each of the following items has become synonymous with Prada's dedication to quality, innovation, and a timeless approach to luxury fashion. Yet the brand continually reinterprets its classics, keeping them fresh and modern while honouring the original designs.

PRADA NYLON BAGS

Nylon Backpack (Vela): Originally released in 1984, Prada's nylon backpack was ground-breaking for its use of industrial nylon material in luxury fashion. Its minimalist design and utilitarian aesthetic make it an enduring classic. The backpack was re-issued in 2000 and 2005 respectively.

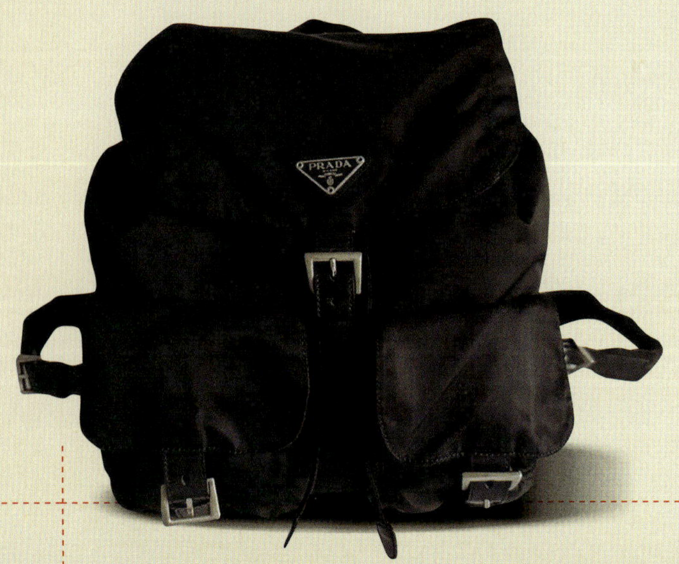

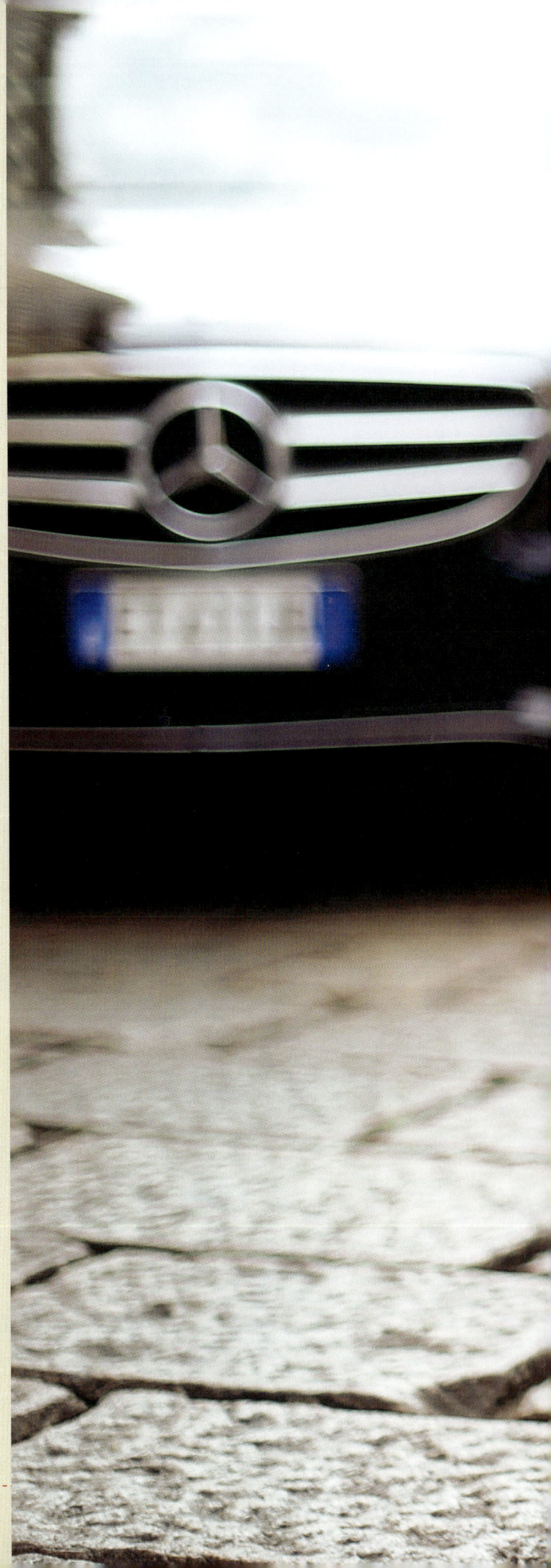

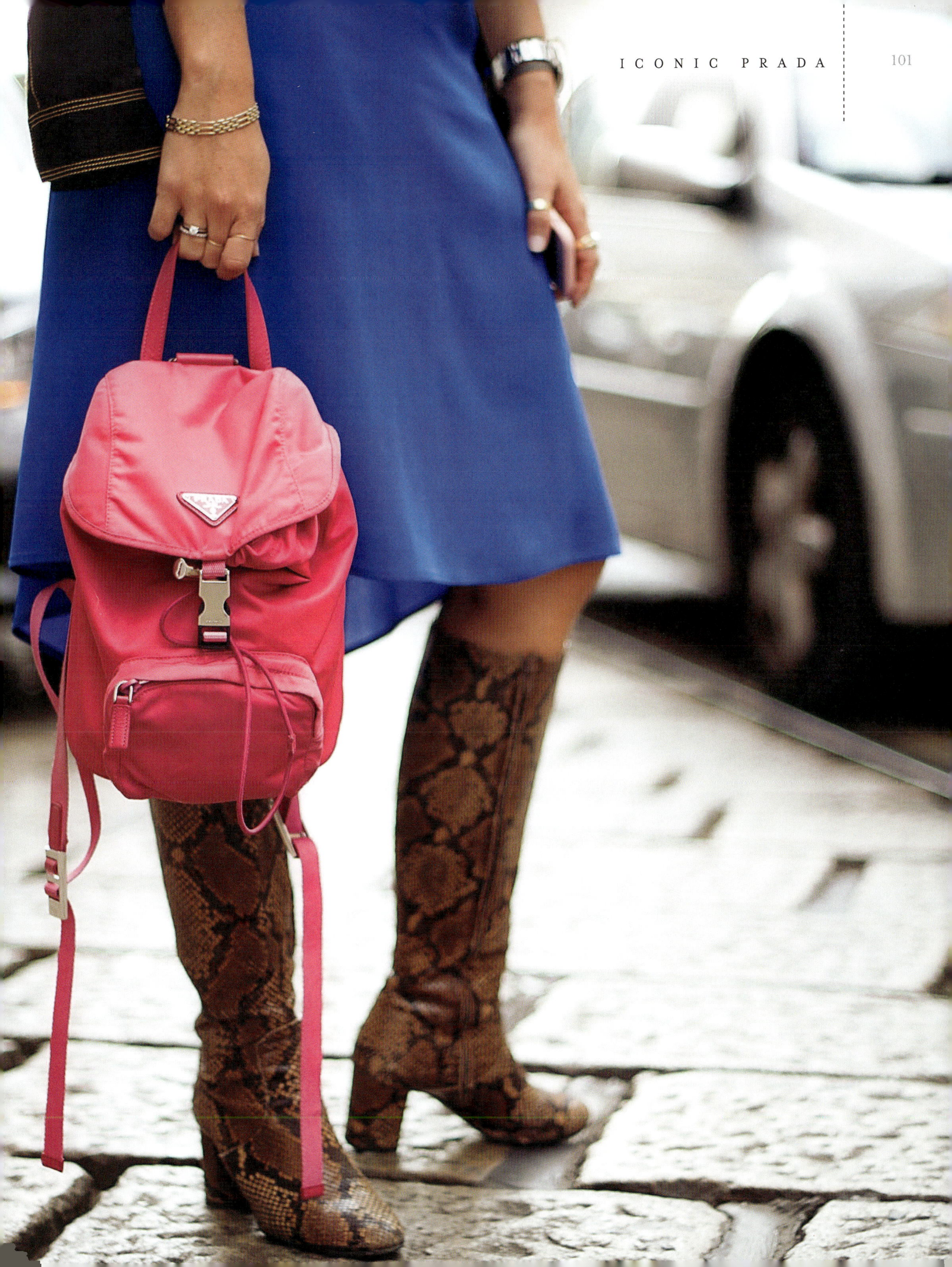

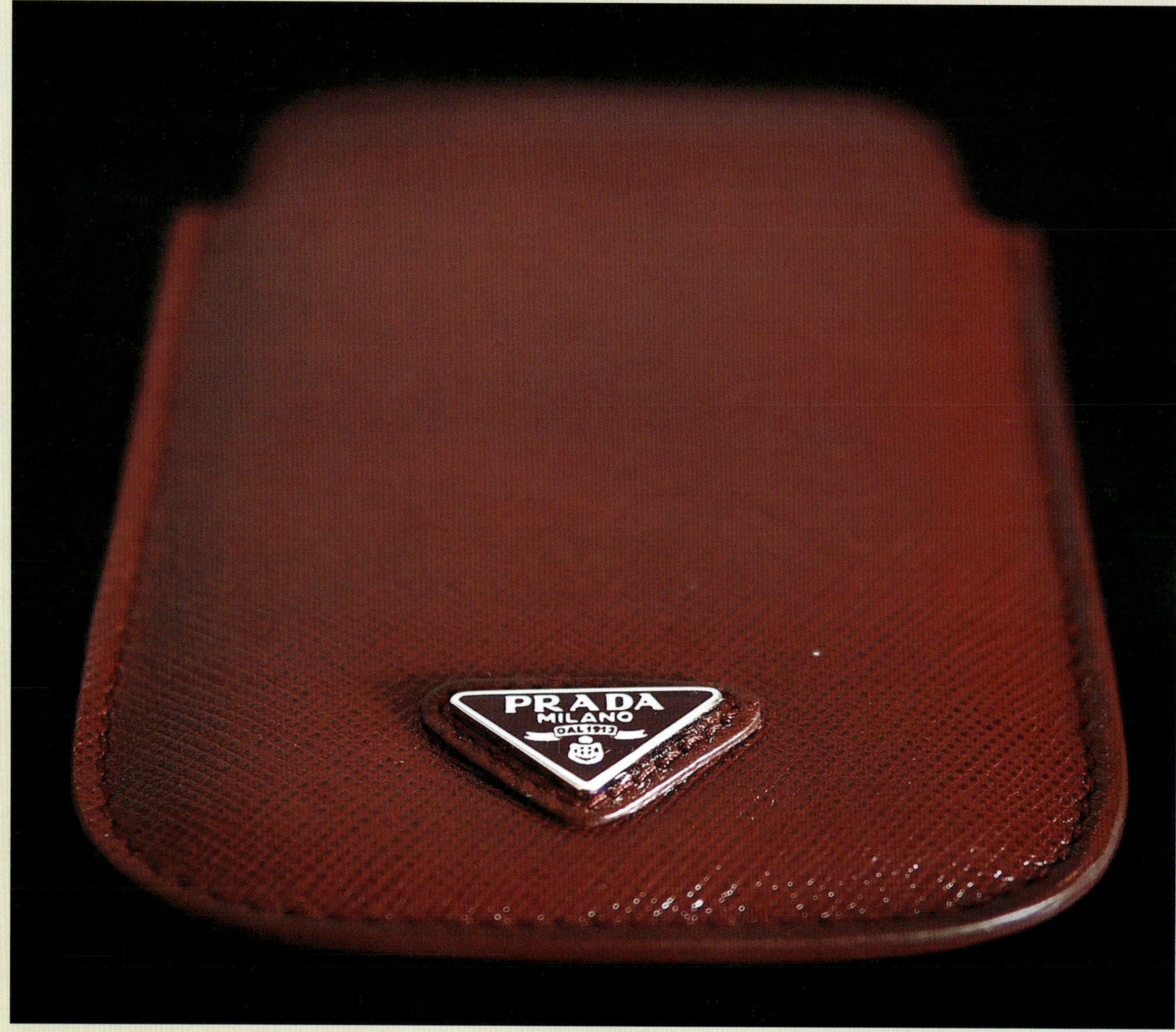

PRADA LOGO TRIANGLE

Metal logo triangle: Often displayed prominently on bags, shoes, and accessories, this logo has become a Prada signature. It subtly reinforces the brand's identity and is recognized instantly as a mark of Prada's quality.

THE PRADA SAFFIANO LEATHER TOTE (GALLERIA BAG)

The Saffiano Leather Totes: Made from Saffiano leather, developed by Mario Prada to be both durable and luxurious, these leather totes are highly sought after. The Galleria tote, a structured bag in Saffiano leather, is a classic piece for both daily and formal use.

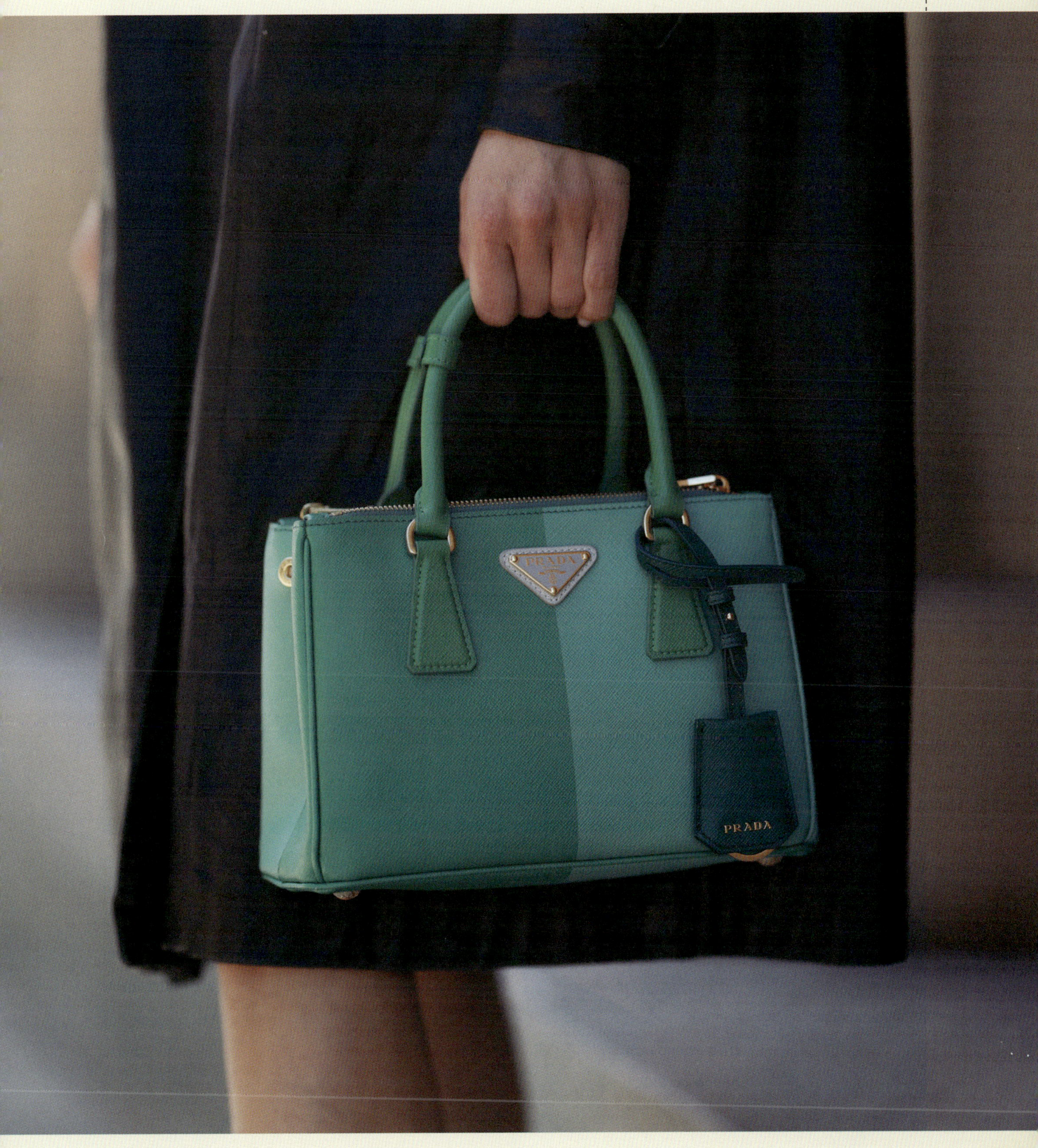

PRADA'S MINIMALIST SHOES

Loafers: The chunky Prada loafers, especially the Monolith version, have a classic shape with a modern edge, making them a go-to in fashion.

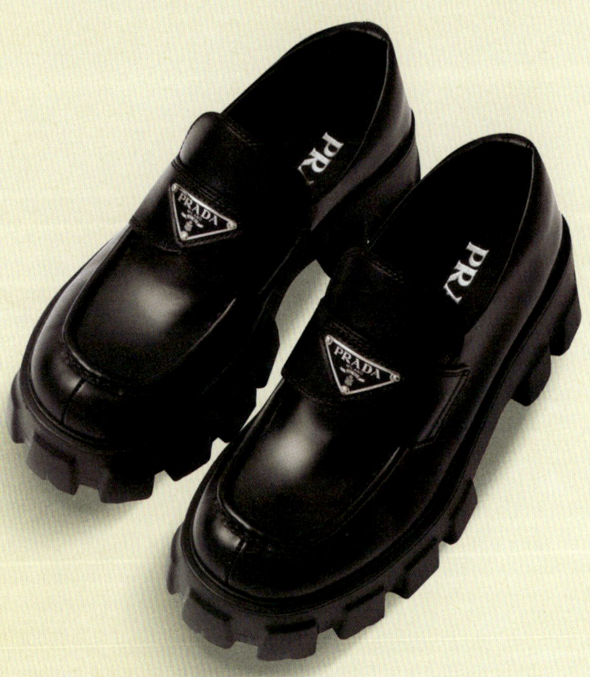

Prada Mary Janes, classic pumps and ballet flats: Known for their clean lines, Prada's sleek Mary Jane heels, classic pumps and ballet flats have also become timeless items, often seen on and off the runway.

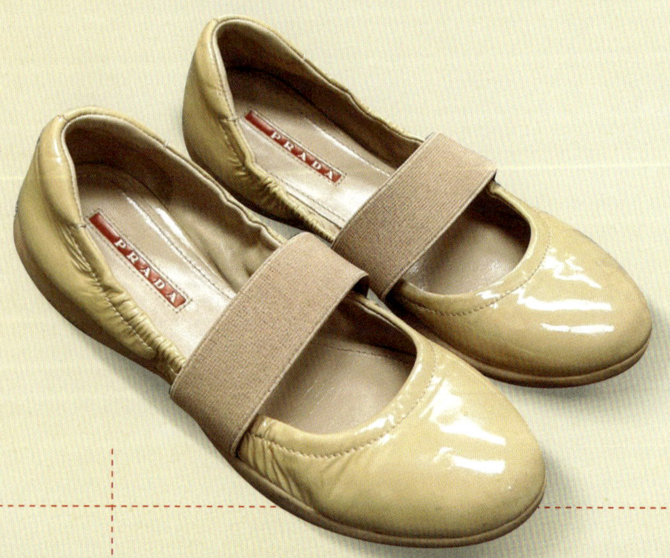

PRADA OUTERWEAR

Double-Breasted Coats: Prada's double-breasted wool coats are known for their precision tailoring and minimalist design. They are a favourite among those looking for timeless elegance in outerwear.

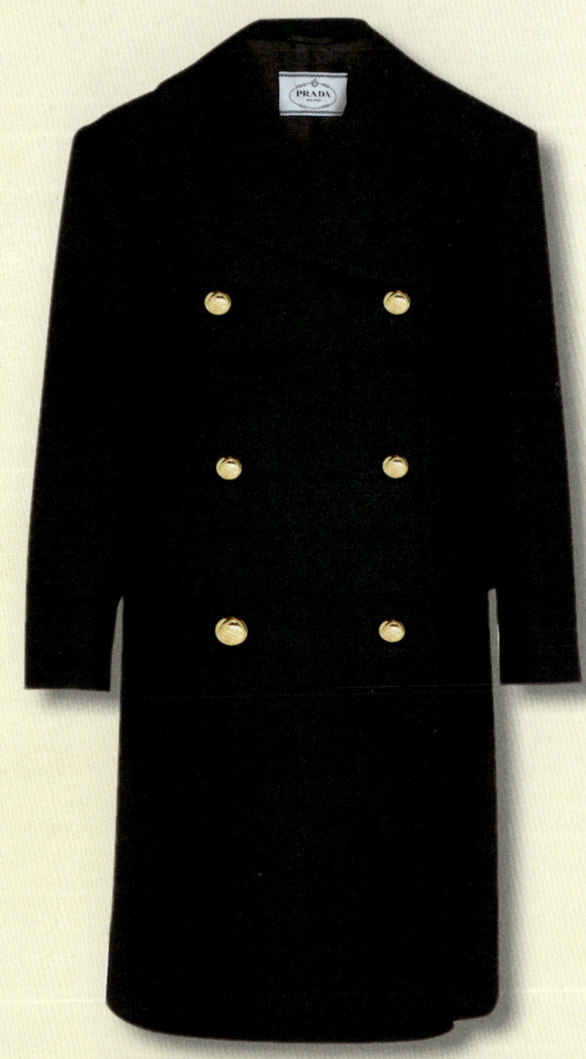

Puffer Jackets: Prada also pioneered high-fashion puffer jackets in nylon, combining practicality with high fashion.

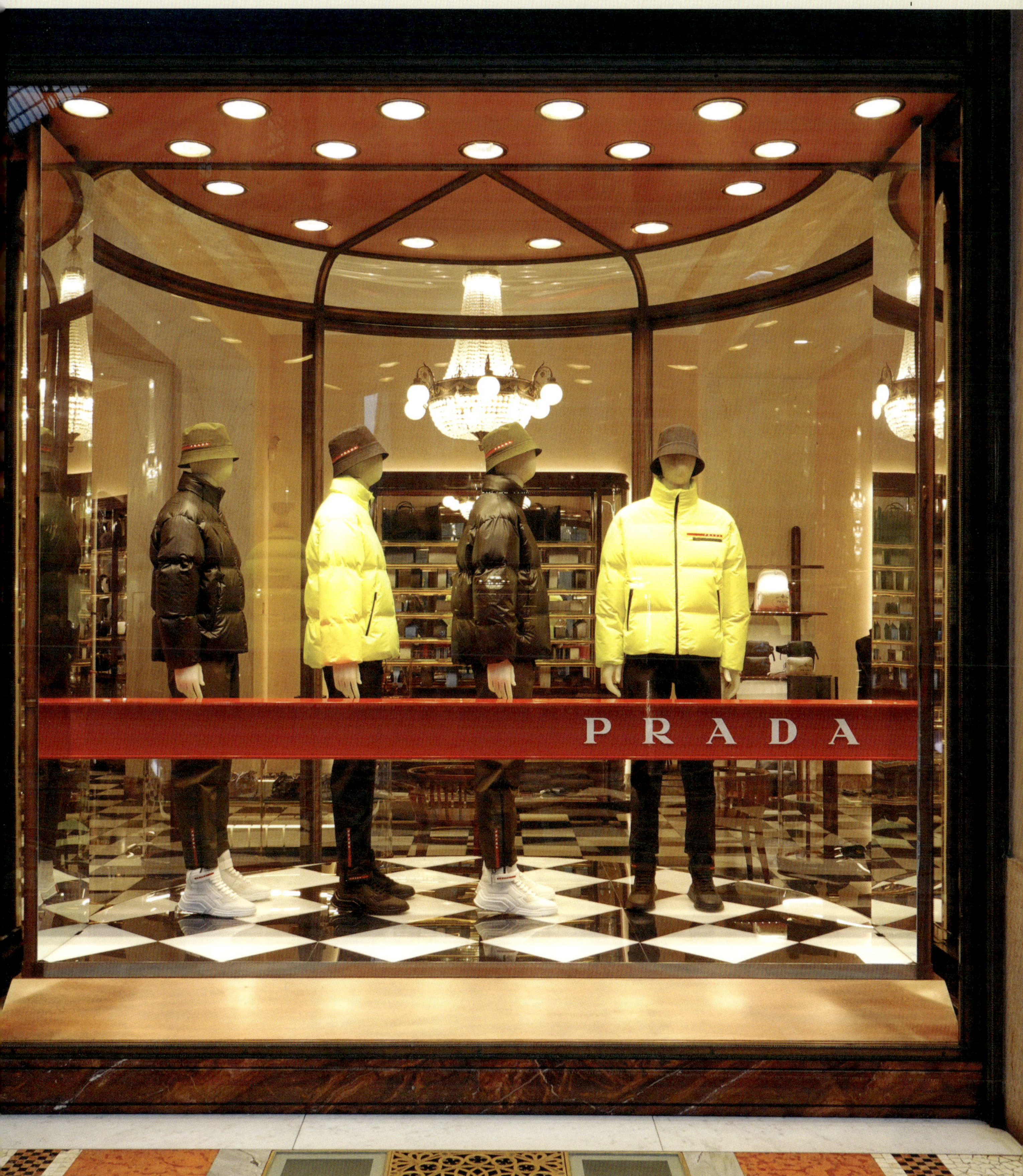
PRADA

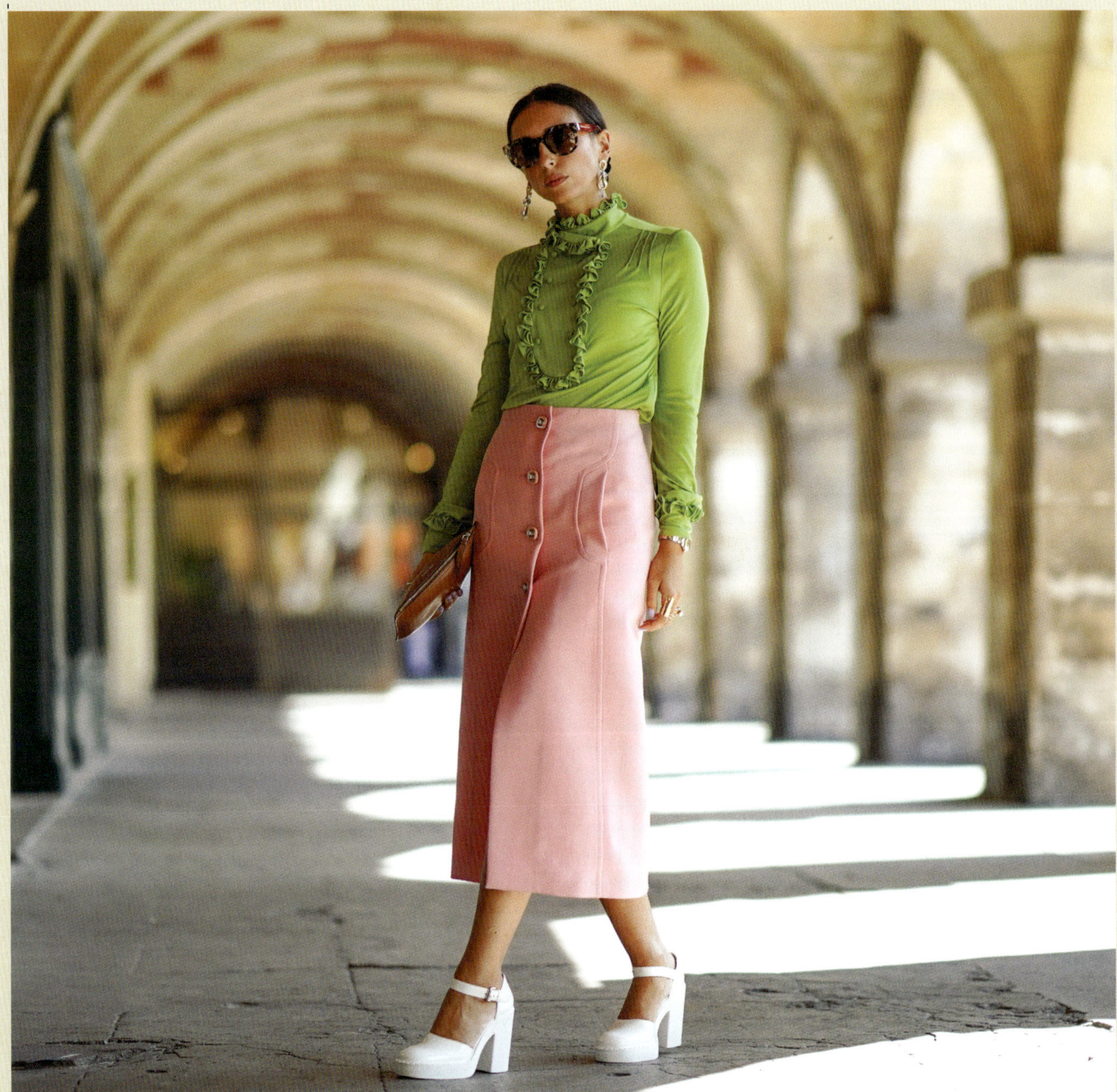

PRADA READY-TO-WEAR BASICS

Pencil Skirts: Prada's pencil skirts are tailored and sleek, often in luxe fabrics that give a sophisticated edge to a simple silhouette.

Slim Knit Sweaters and Cardigans: Prada's sweaters and cardigans, often in monochromatic colours with fine tailoring, are must-have basics in many a wardrobe.

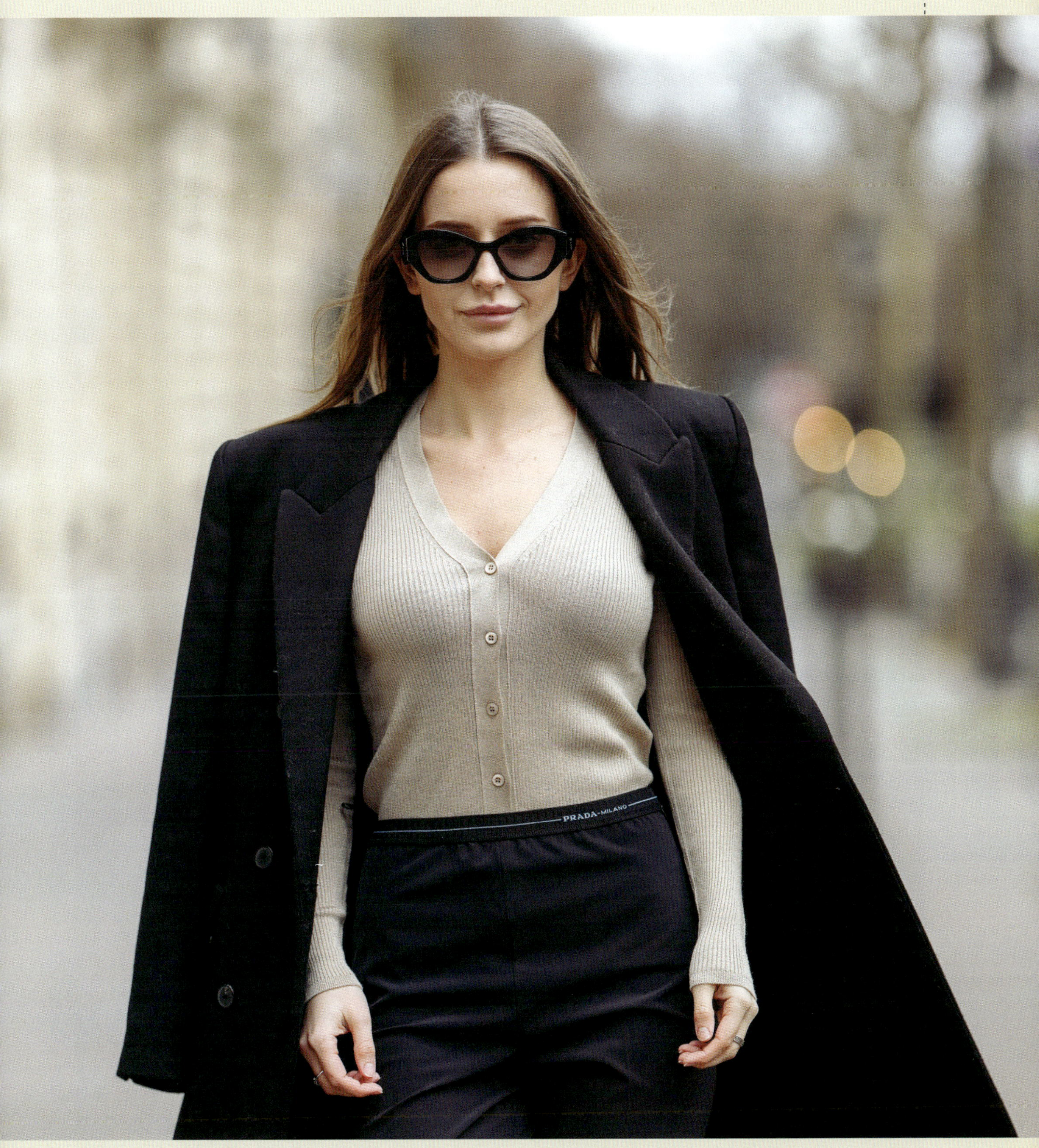

PRADA LINEA ROSSA COLLECTION

Linea Rossa: This line focuses on technical, performance-based apparel, often with a distinctive red stripe logo.

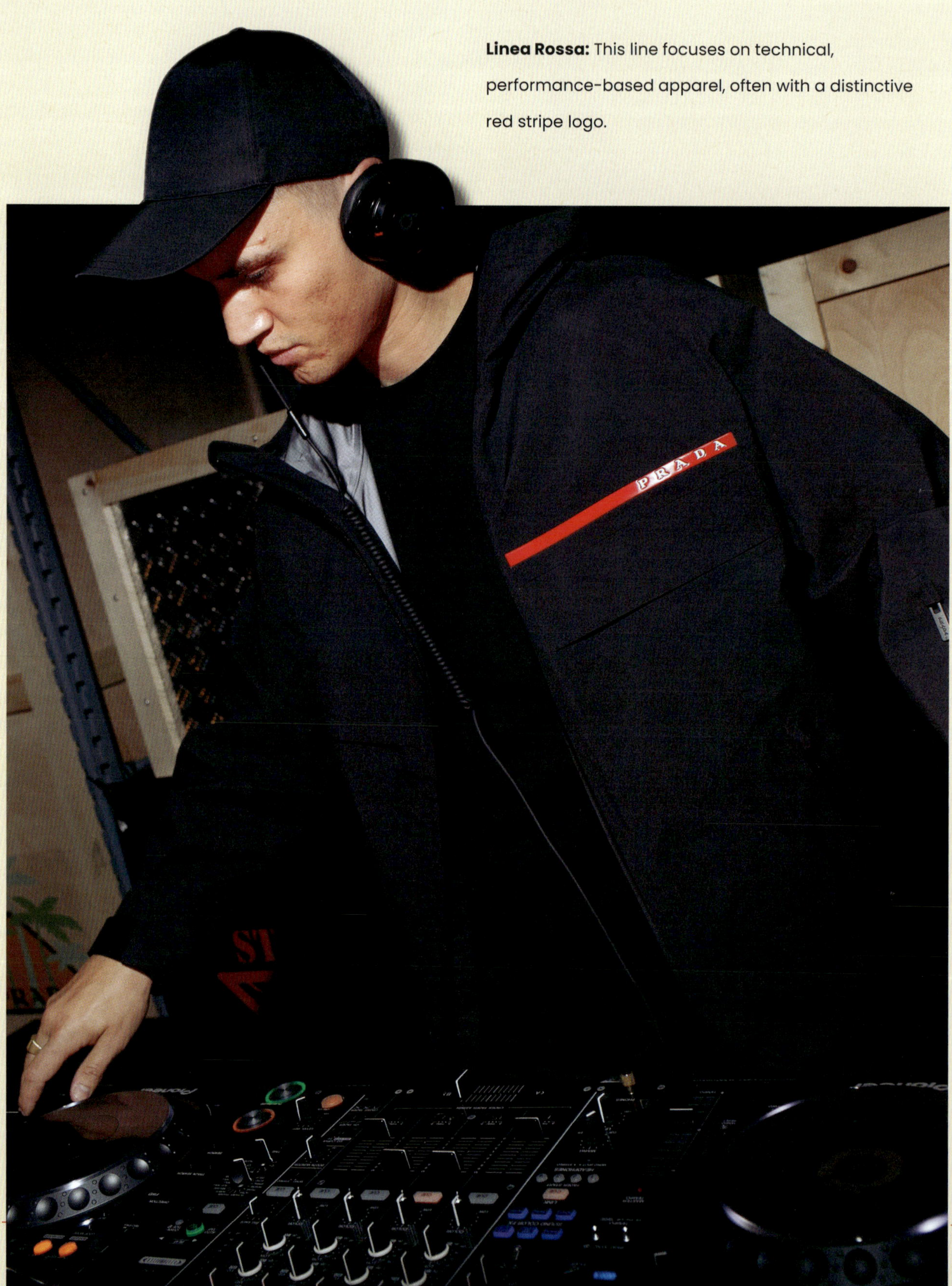

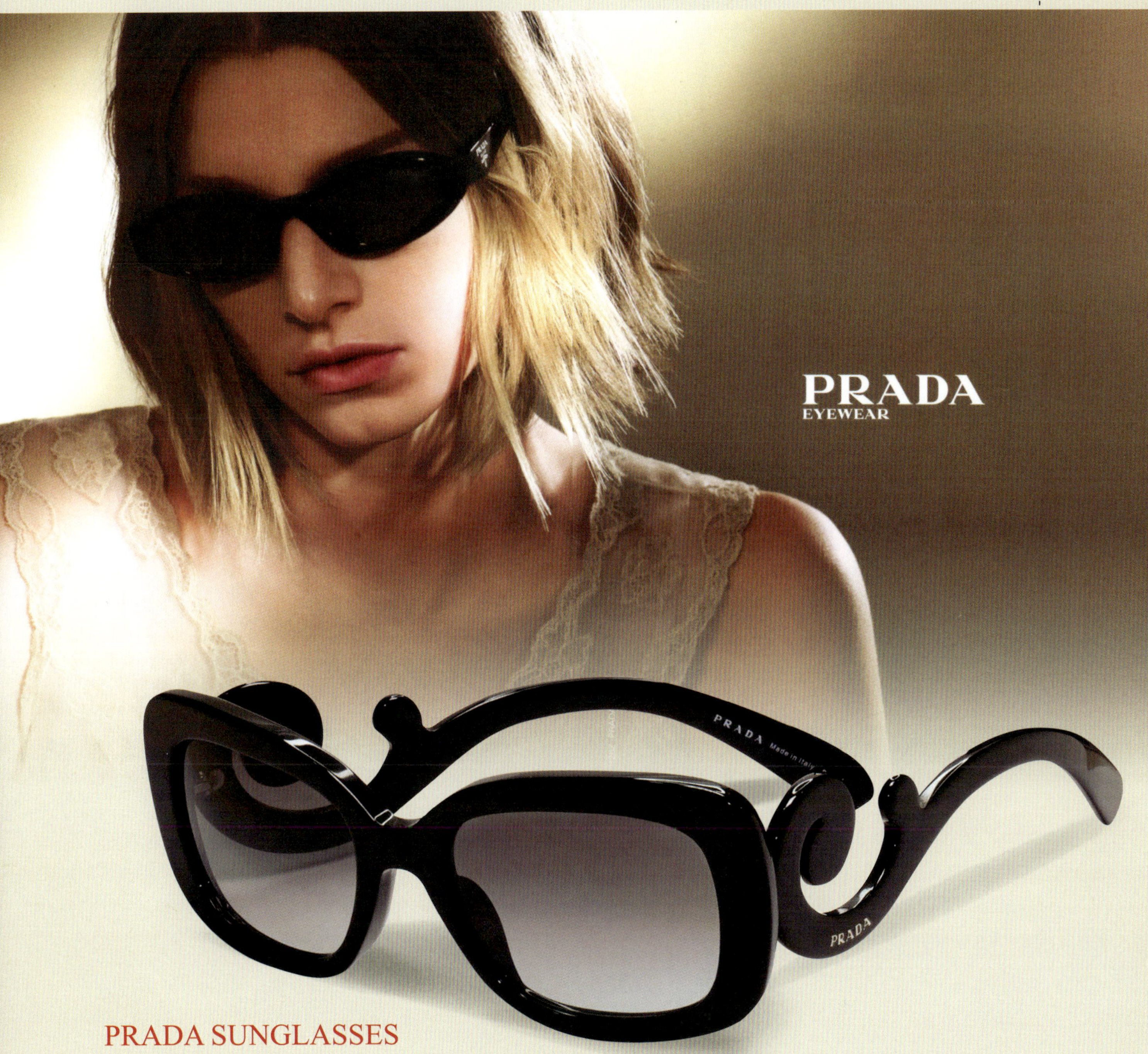

PRADA SUNGLASSES

Baroque Sunglasses: The Baroque style, with its dramatic swirls and ornate design, became an instant classic and remains one of Prada's most distinctive eyewear designs.

Minimalist Frames: Prada also produces minimalist frames that focus on form and function, appealing to fans of understated elegance.

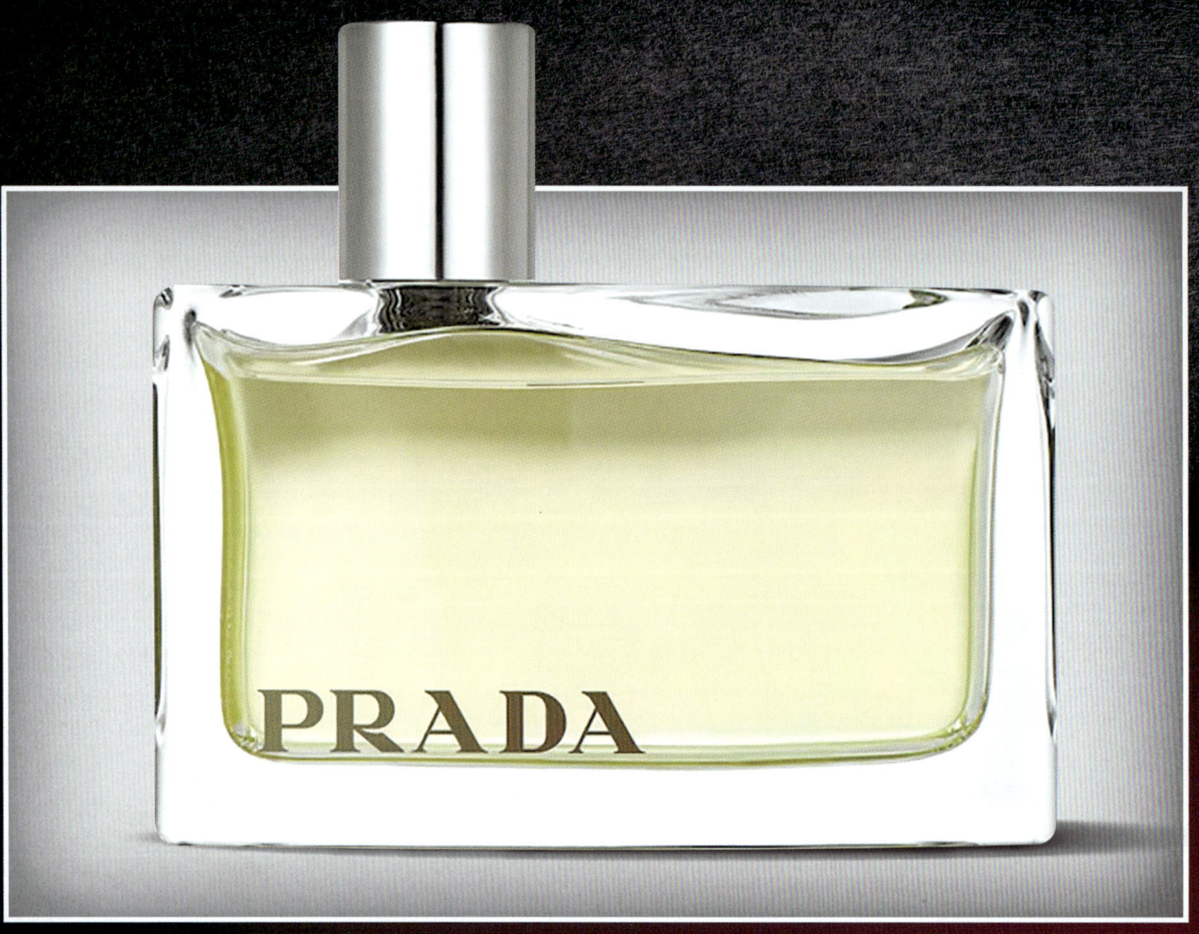

PRADA FRAGRANCES

Prada Amber: The original scent from Prada, 'Amber', was launched in 2004 and has become a classic fragrance for those who love warm, luxurious scents with notes of patchouli and vanilla. In all, Prada has launched 96 fragrances over the last 20 years.

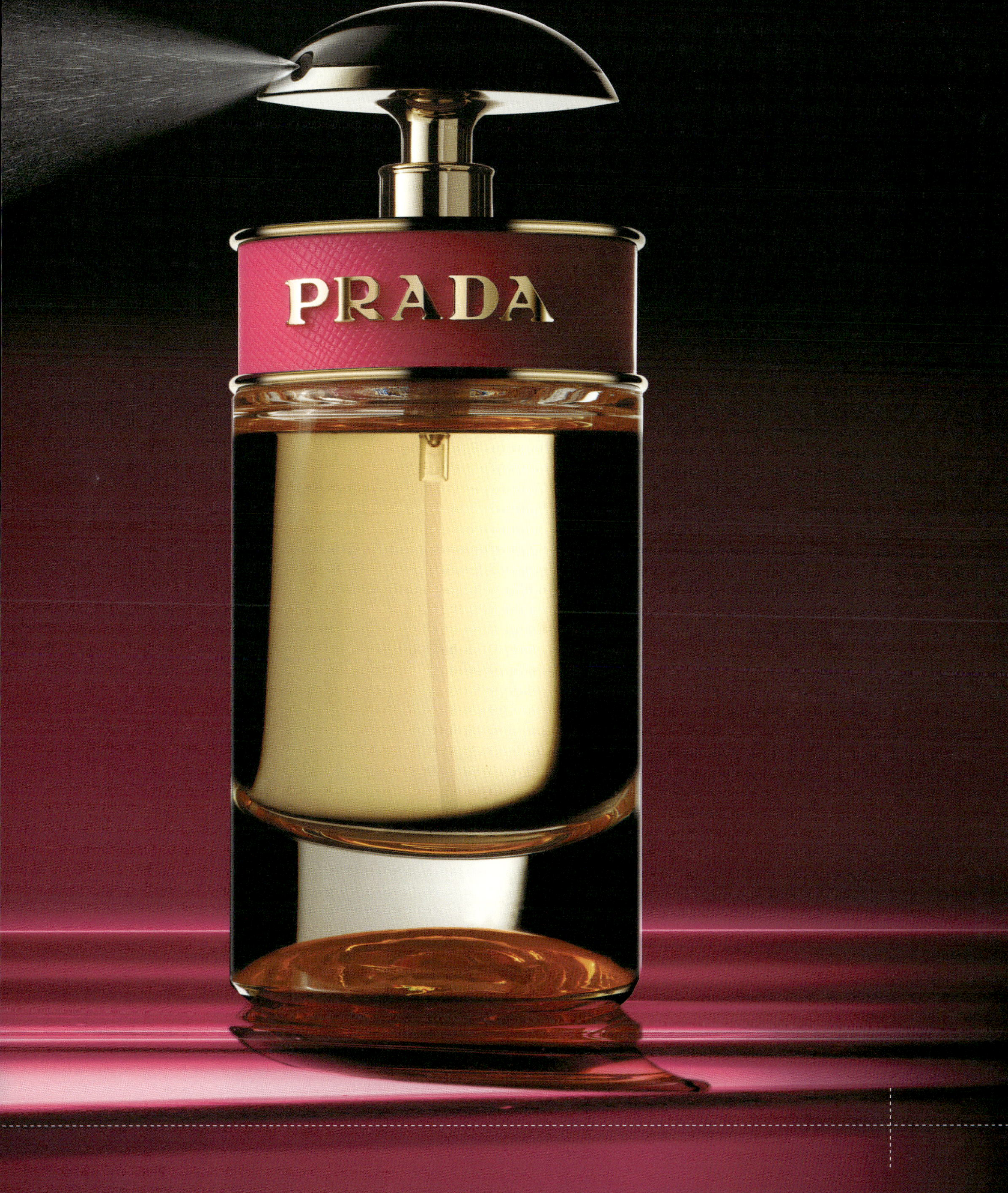
PRADA

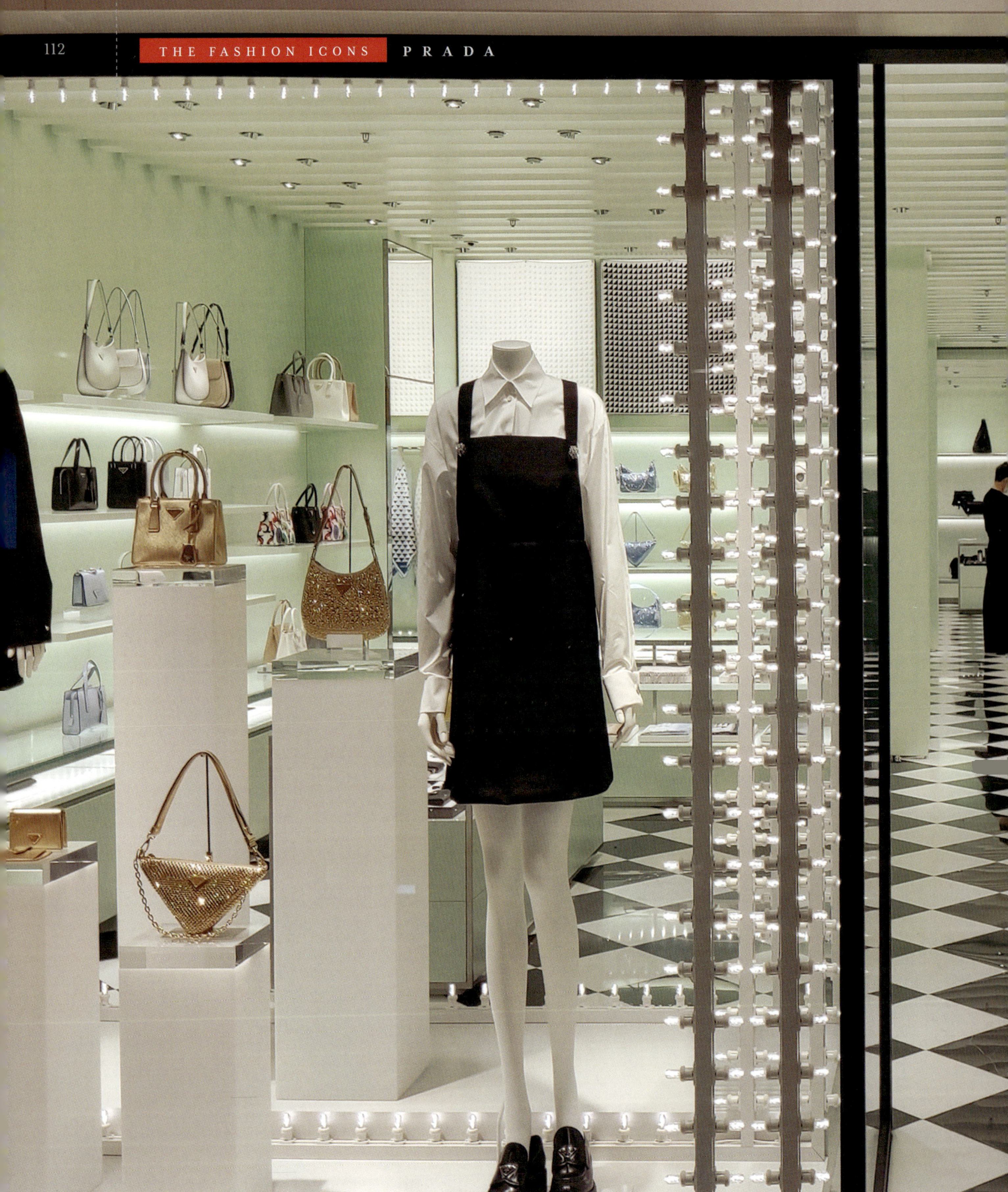

ABOVE: A modern interior is blended with the iconic Prada chequered floor at this Prada store, Pacific Place, Hong Kong, China

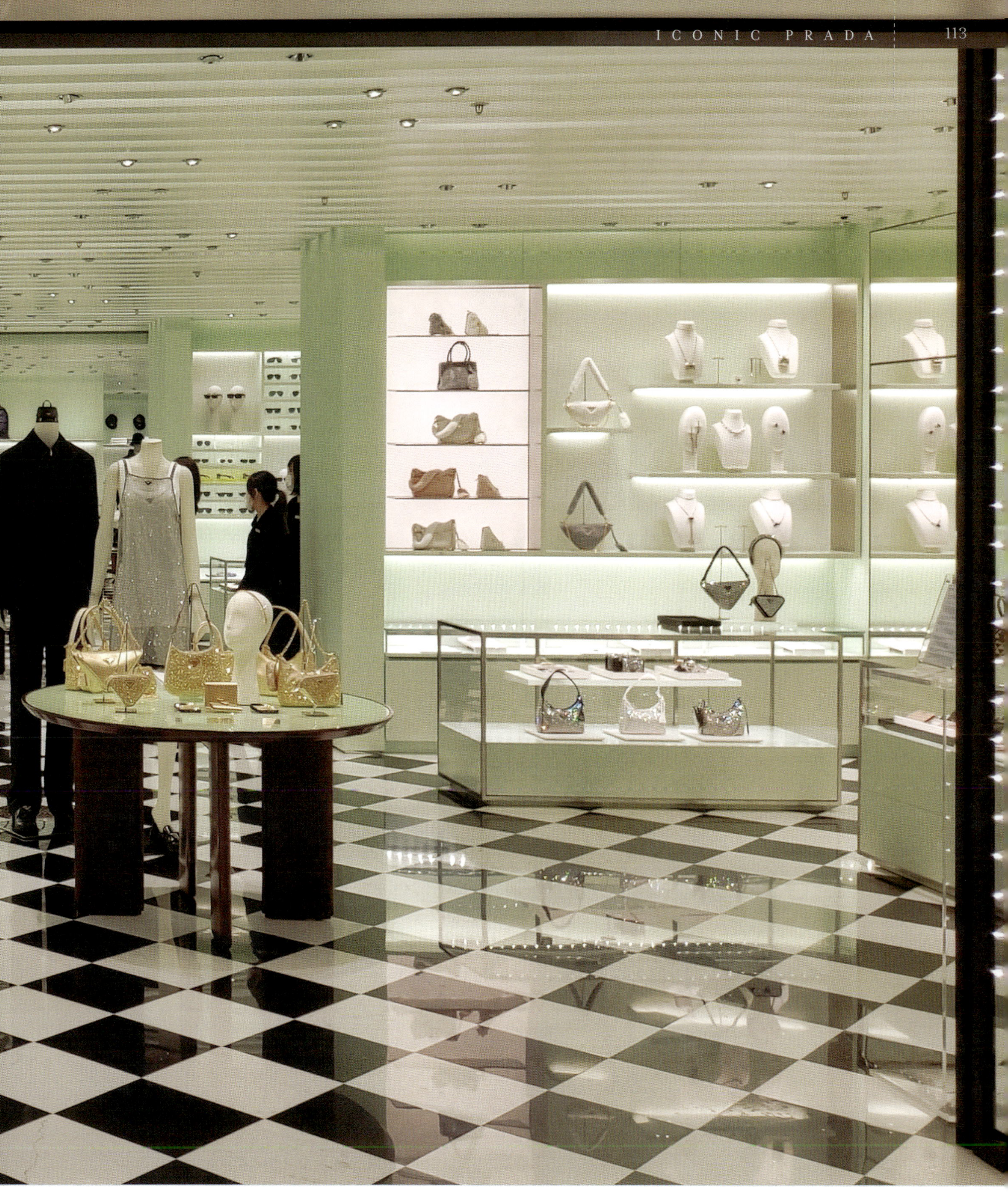

MIU MIU

"Miu Miu is a way of having fun. It's young, it's more spontaneous. It's playful and whimsical. It is the little sister who isn't burdened by the same kind of expectations as Prada"
Miuccia Prada

Miu Miu was created by Miuccia Prada in 1993 as a response to a desire for a more youthful, experimental, and fun line that contrasted with the more established and sophisticated aesthetic of Prada. The brand allowed Miuccia to explore her creative freedom and less serious side. It was her own, highly personal innovation with the brand's name of 'Miu Miu' being Miuccia's own childhood nickname.

'Miu Miu is a space where we can take risks, embrace youth, and bring out that playfulness which isn't always possible with Prada,' she announced at the launch of the brand.

While Prada focused on understated luxury and timeless pieces, Miu Miu offered an opportunity to push boundaries and play with bold colours, prints, and unconventional styles. Miuccia created Miu Mia as Prada's unconventional, edgier, more exciting little sister. This contrast allowed Miu Miu to develop its own distinct identity, appealing to different consumer tastes while still being part of the Prada fashion house. A brand which would appeal to those still wanting luxury but with a more youthful, rebellious spirit. From a business perspective, Miu Miu helped Prada diversify its portfolio by appealing to a different demographic and segment of the luxury market. The launch of Miu Miu allowed the Prada Group to capture new customers without diluting the Prada brand's core identity.

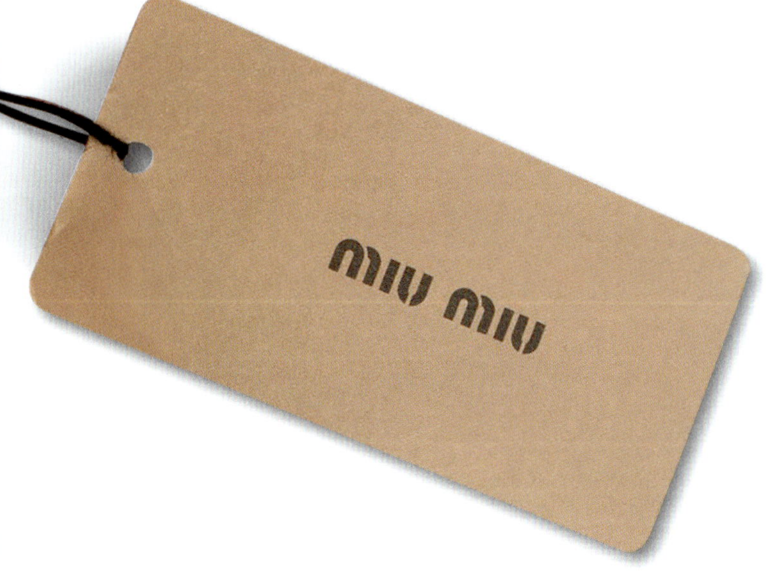

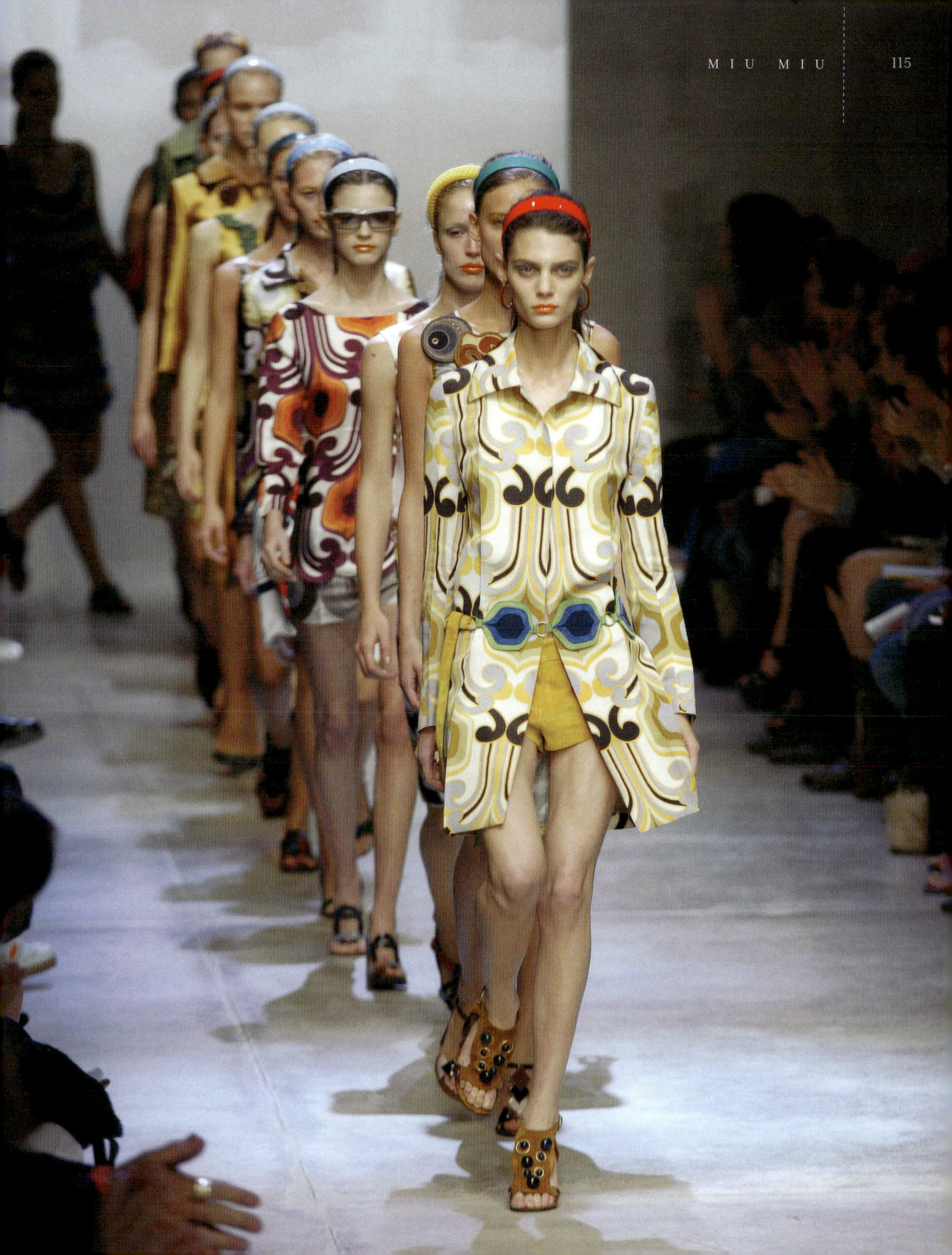

Some of Miu Miu's most iconic designs include…

THE MATELASSÉ HANDBAGS

Coming in various sizes and colours, Miu Miu's Matelassé handbags are among the brand's most recognizable accessories. These bags feature a unique quilted texture that gives them a distinctive, luxurious appearance. The Matelassé technique creates a pleated, padded effect, adding depth and dimension to the leather. A true Miu Miu signature piece.

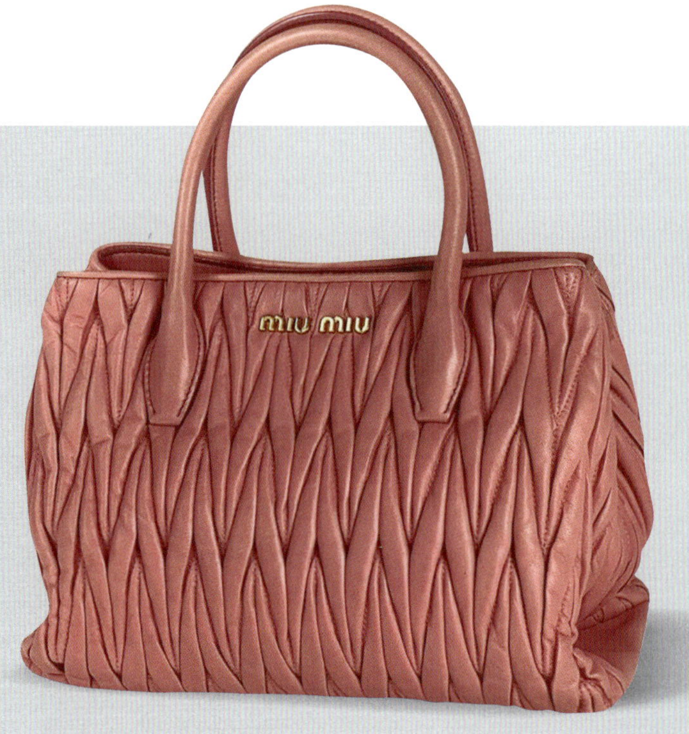

CRYSTAL-EMBELLISHED SANDALS

The range of crystal-embellished sandals have become a Miu Miu staple with the brand frequently incorporating sparkling details such as bold crystals on the heels or straps. Blends glamour with a playful twist.

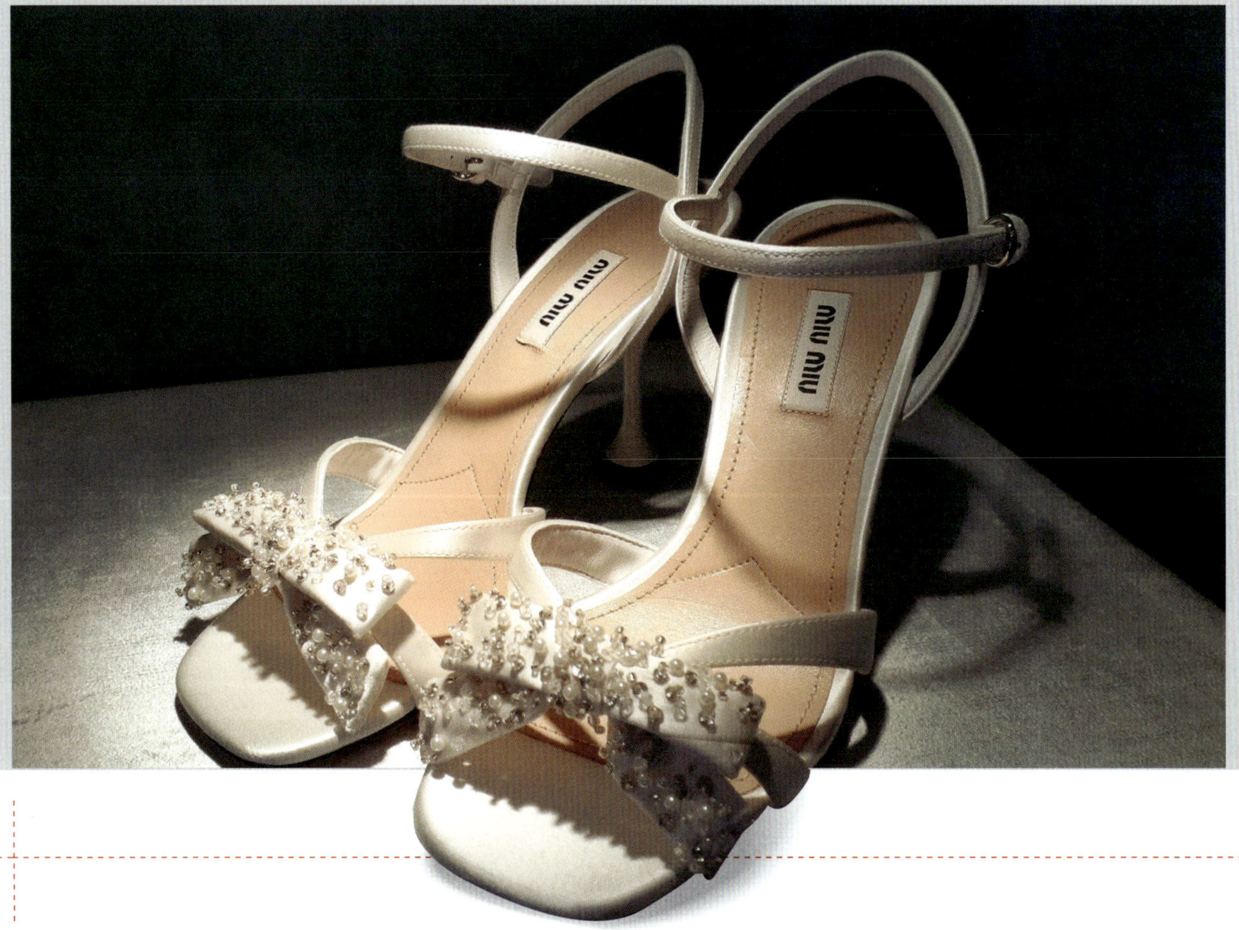

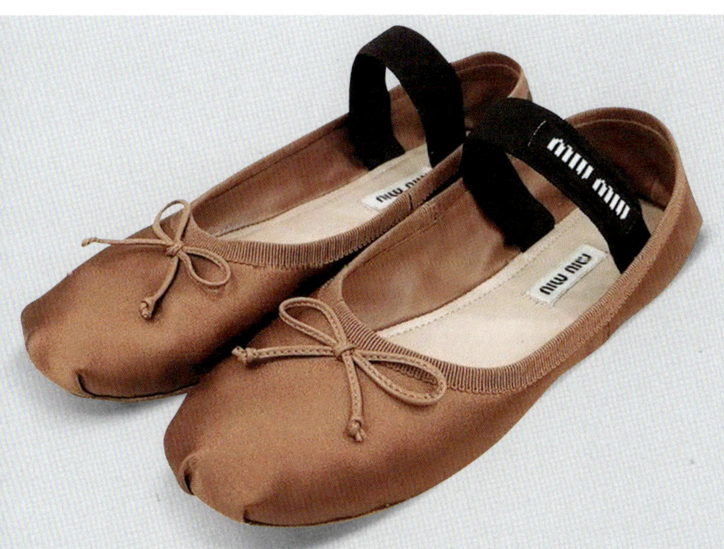

MIU MIU BALLET FLATS

Miu Miu's ballet flats, particularly those decorated with crystals, ribbons, and metallic details have become classics. These flats, often with a punk edge or dainty feminine feel, are a favourite among fashion enthusiasts for their mix of elegance and playful charm. The lace-up ballet flats with ribbon ties from the Fall/Winter 2016 collection were particularly influential and widely copied.

THE MICRO MINI SKIRT

Miu Miu made headlines with their ultra-low-rise micro mini-skirts in the Spring/Summer 2022 collection. Often paired with cropped tops or oversized blazers, the skirts became a global sensation - seen on runways, magazine covers and social media. The skirt's retro 2000s feel, with visible underwear bands and a provocative, edgy design, was hailed as a fashion moment of the year.

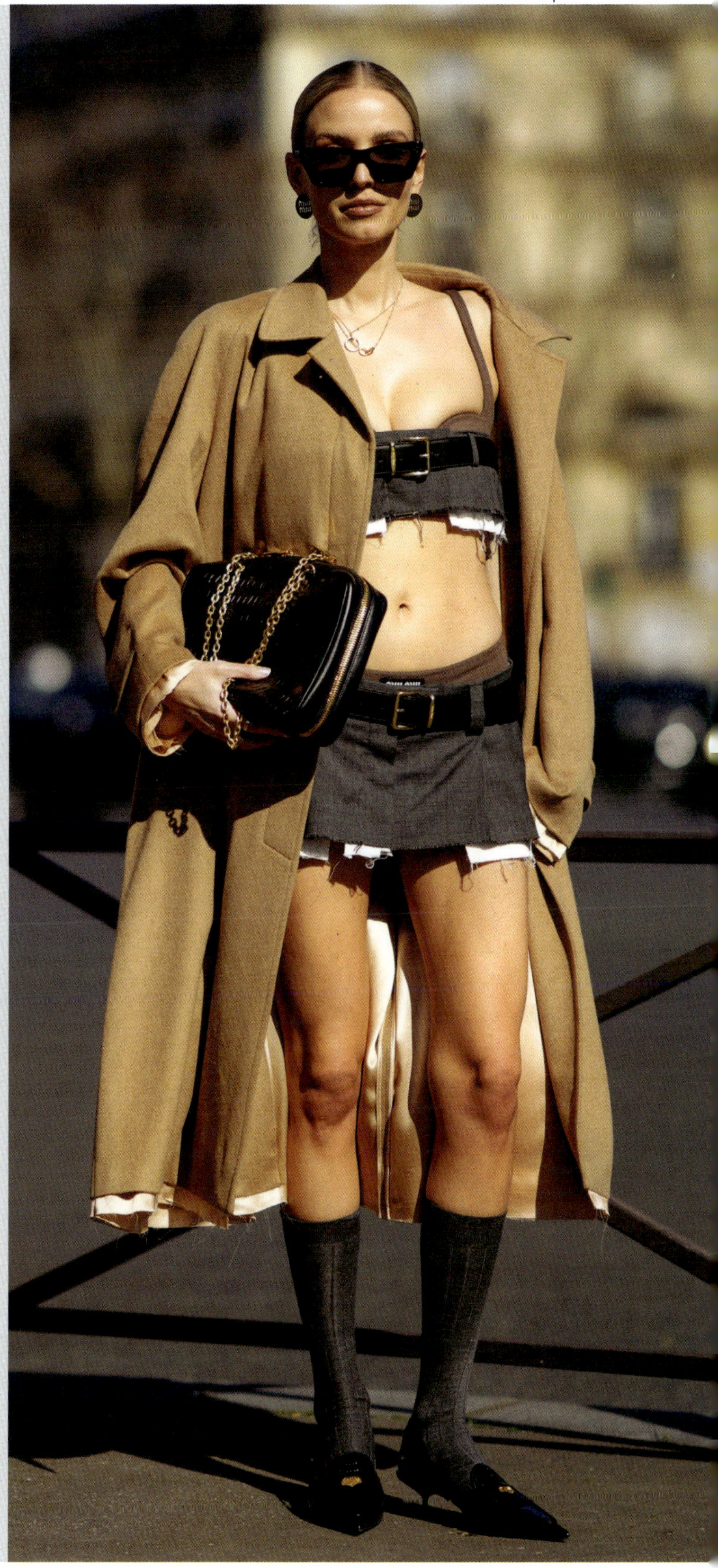

ABOVE: Leonie Hanne wears a belted micro mini skirt with matching cropped top and beige long coat, all from Miu Miu during Paris Fashion Week, 2022

NOSTALGIC KNITWEAR

Miu Miu often reinvents retro-inspired knitwear, from oversized sweaters to cropped cardigans, with girly embellishments. Knitwear featuring quirky designs like argyle patterns, bows, and glittery details is classic Miu Miu. Think 'school-girl' and 'cosy' chic.

DAISY PRINT DRESSES

Miu Miu's daisy print dresses, often made with silk or lightweight fabrics, have become one of the brand's most beloved designs – romantic and retro-inspired yet simultaneously modern.

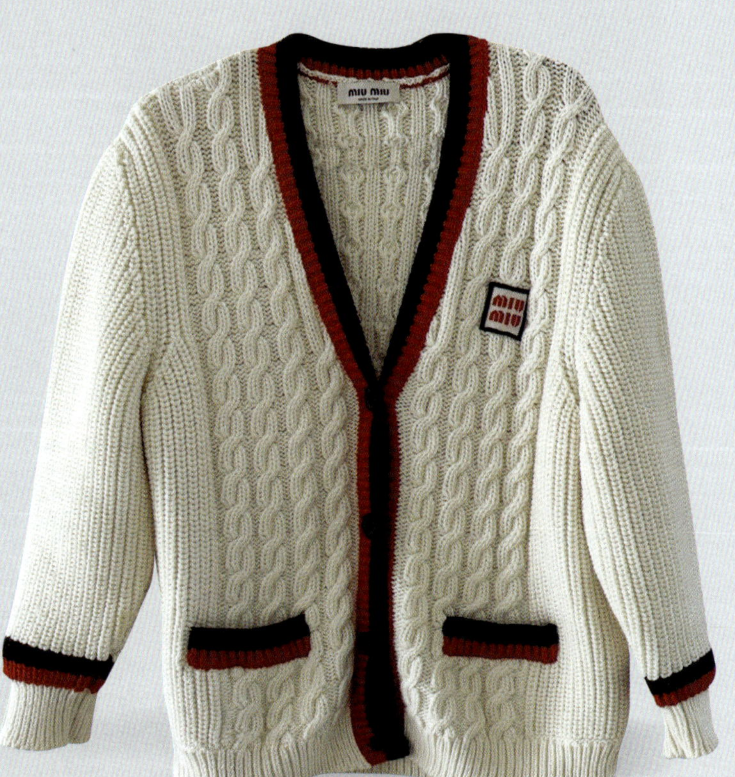

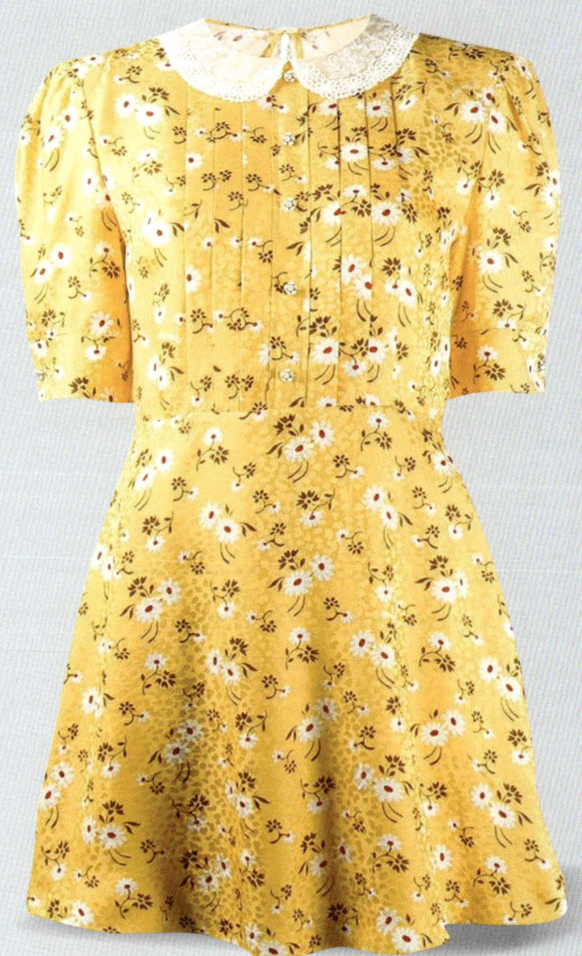

CHUNKY PLATFORMS

Miu Miu's platforms have gained iconic status. Whether in the form of platform sneakers or boots, these shoes are characterized by their bold design, exaggerated height, and mix of feminine and rebellious elements.

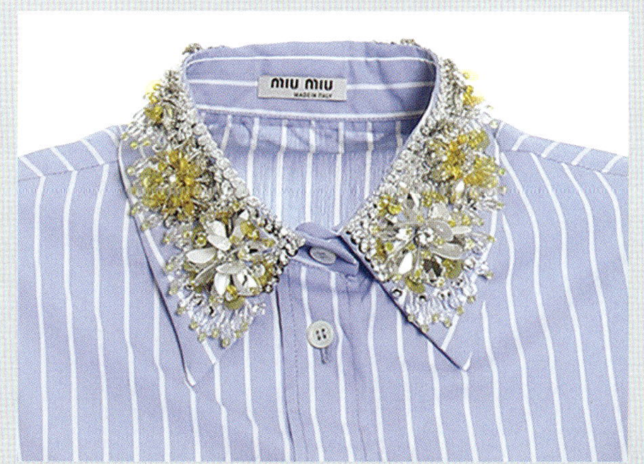

EMBELLISHED COLLARS

One of Miu Miu's signature design details is the embellished collar. Often detachable, these collars feature intricate beadwork, crystals, or lace, transforming simple dresses or tops into statement pieces.

SUNGLASSES

The brand's cat's-eye shades with bold frames are a favourite among fashion influencers. Often oversized with playful shapes, glittery details, or striking patterns, Miu Miu eyewear is once seen, never forgotten.

COATS AND OUTERWEAR

From faux fur coats with bold prints to military-inspired jackets with luxe detailing, Miu Miu outerwear is designed to make a statement while blending classic and avant-garde styles.

In the words of Miu Miu herself...*'Miu Miu is about trying to find an elegance that is not bourgeois. It's for the girl who wants to express her own identity, be independent, and show her personal style'.*

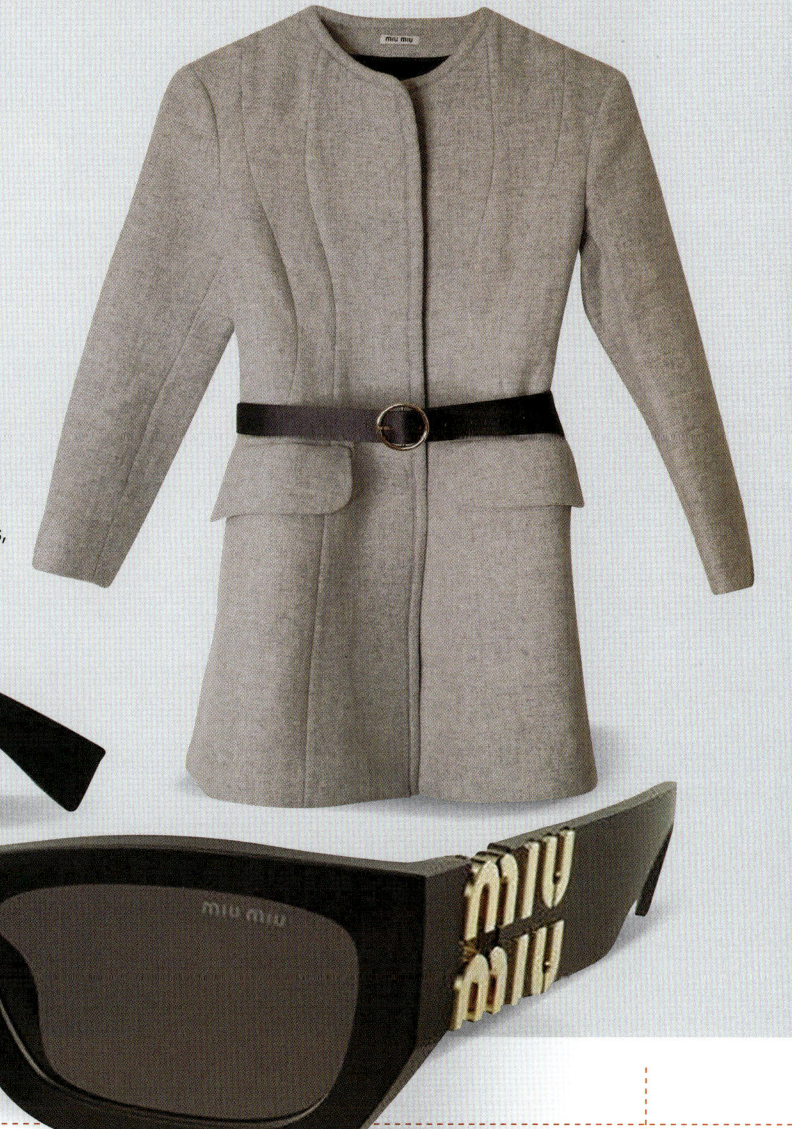

MIU MIU MUSES

Miu Miu is loved by many a celebrity – and Miu Miu loves them right back...

CATHERINE, PRINCESS OF WALES

The Princess favours Miu Miu - especially during the holiday season. A festive favourite is a red, cashmere-jacquard Miu Miu cardigan, adorned with rose designs and pearl bobble buttons which she wore at the 2021 'Royal Carols: Together at Christmas' service, and then again at a Christmas tea party two years later. On Christmas Day 2017, she wore a Miu Miu red and green tartan coat to church.

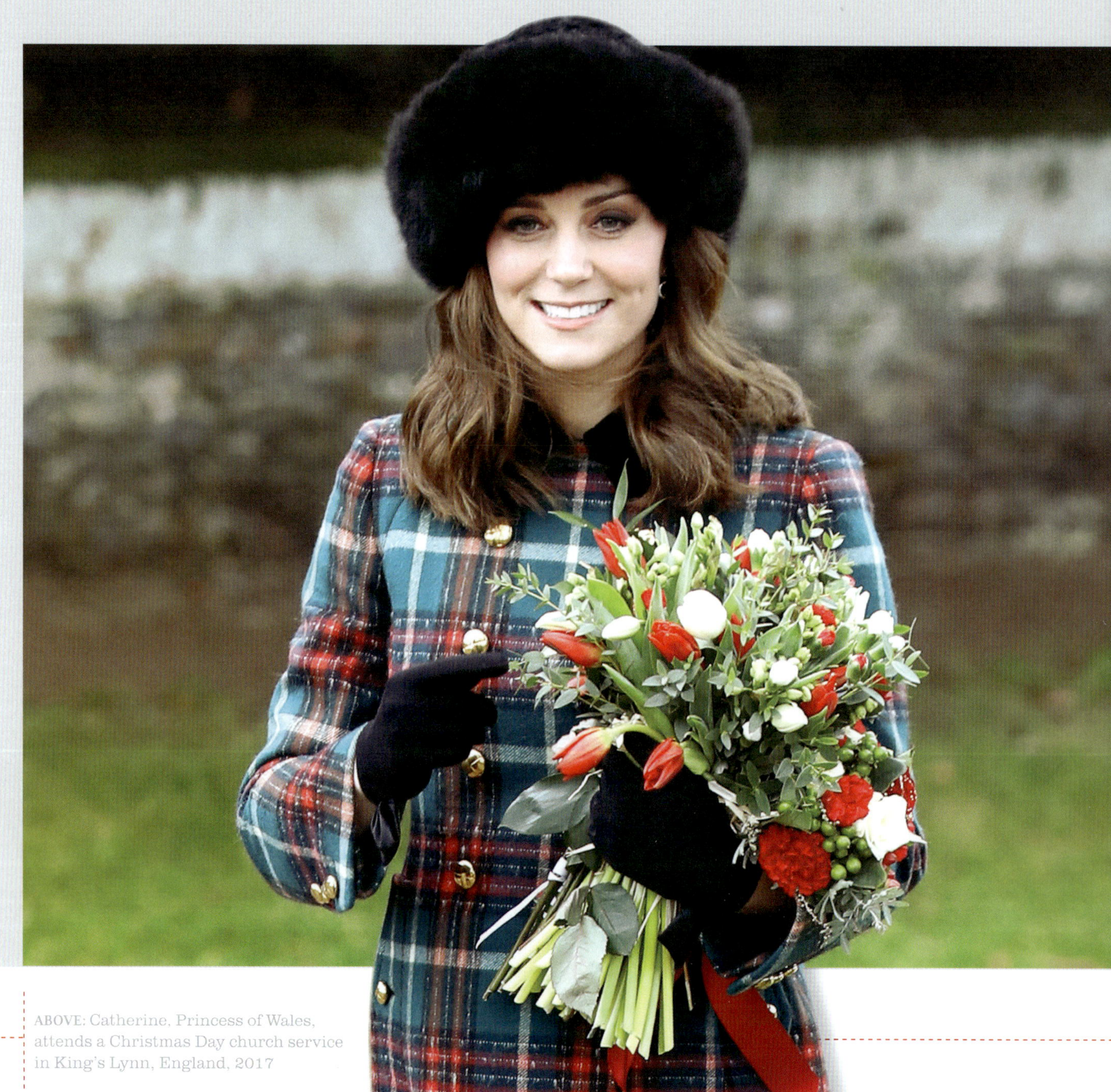

ABOVE: Catherine, Princess of Wales, attends a Christmas Day church service in King's Lynn, England, 2017

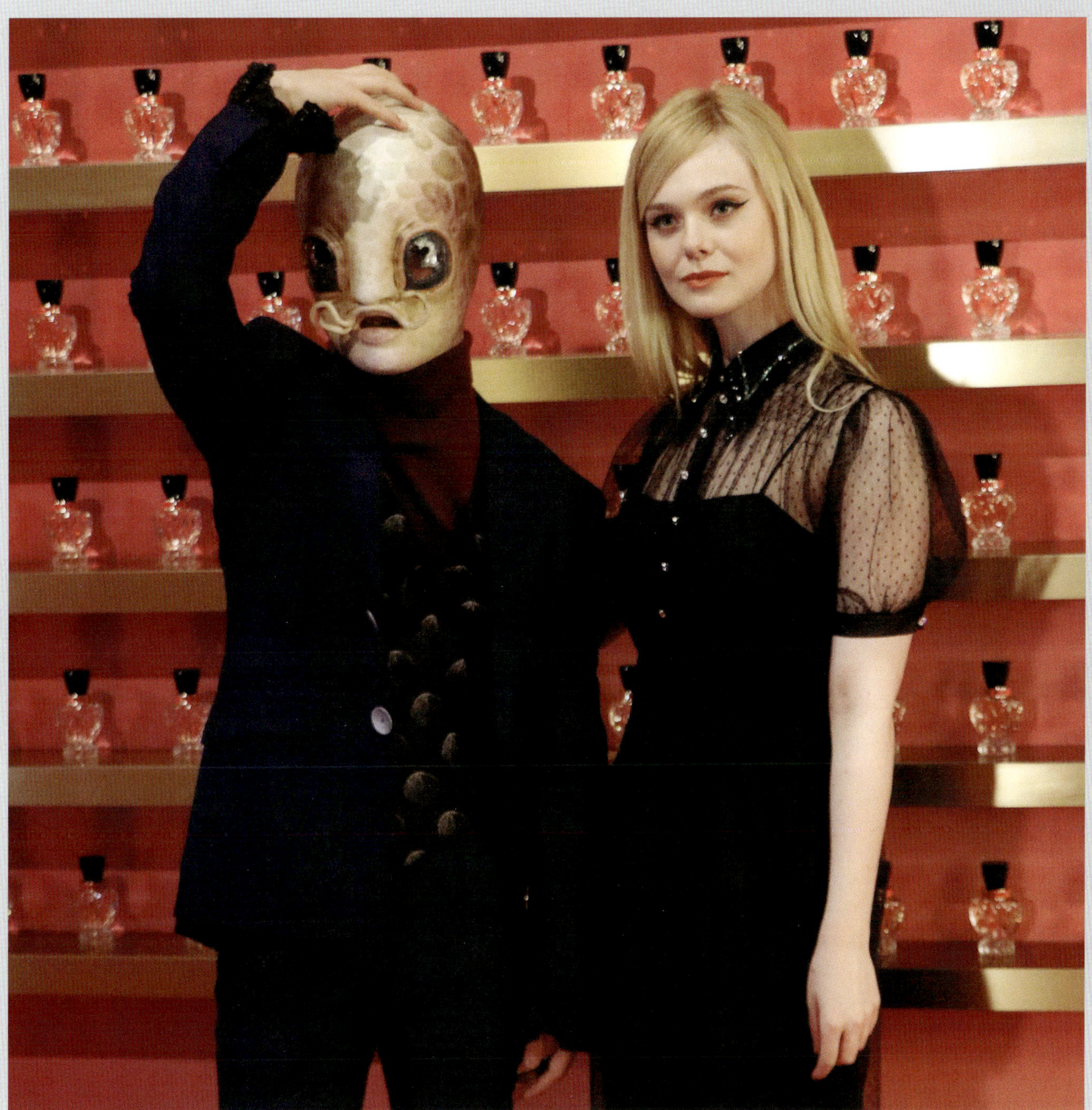

ELLE FANNING

Actress Elle is one of the brand's most visible ambassadors and frequently wears Miu Miu for major events, including film festivals and award shows. She's also appeared in several ad campaigns.

ABOVE: Elle Fanning attends a promotional event for Miu Miu in Shanghai, China, 26 March, 2019

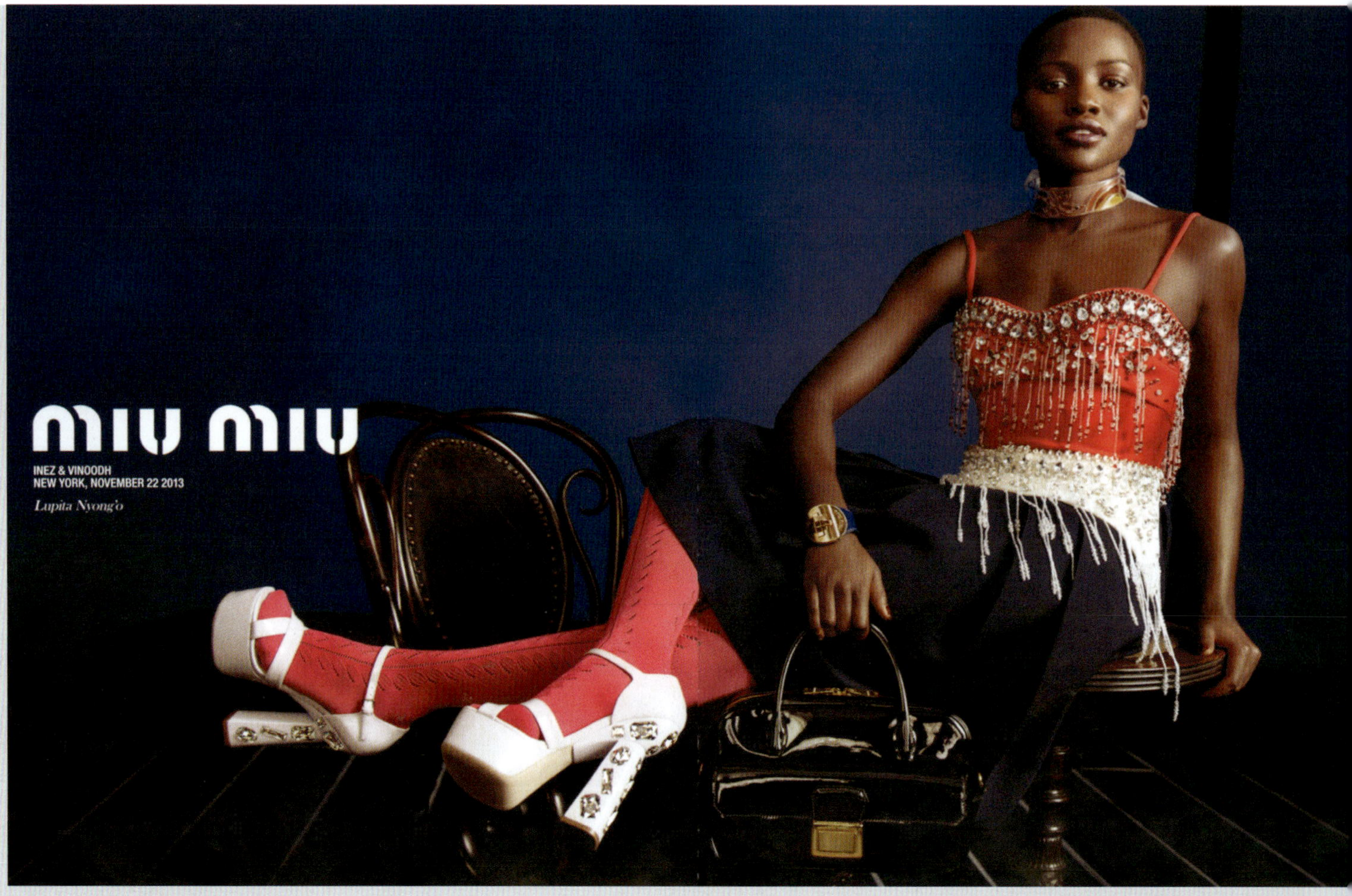

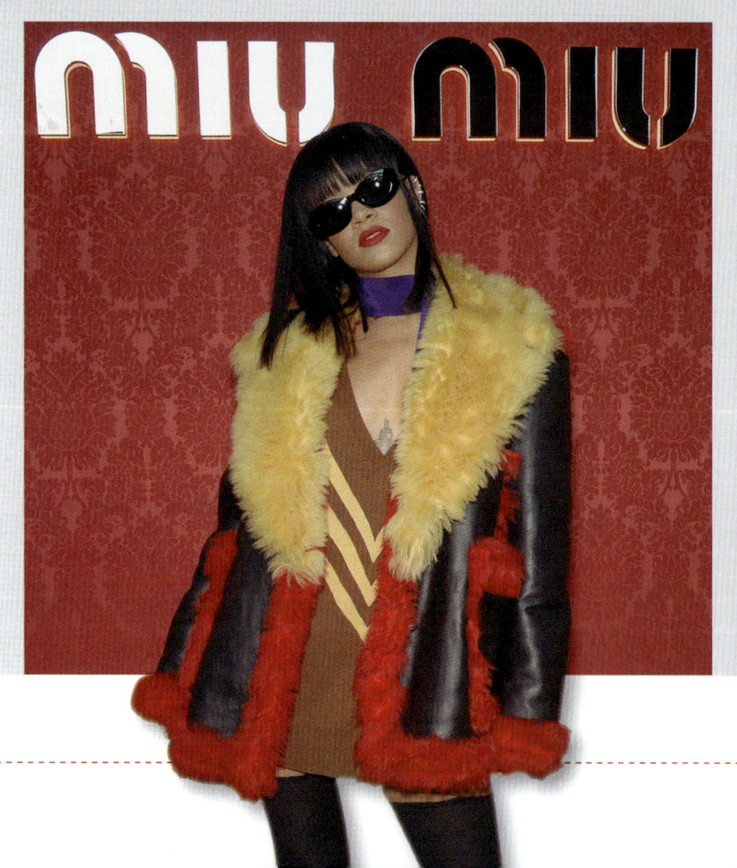

LUPITA NYONG'O

The brand is a red carpet go-to for Lupita who is also a Miu Miu ambassador.

RIHANNA

Rihanna is known for her daring fashion sense and she has worn Miu Miu on several occasions – both in formal and informal settings.

ABOVE: UK Miu Miu magazine advert featuring Lupita Nyong'o, 2013

RIGHT: Rihanna attends the Miu Miu show as part of Paris Fashion Week Womenswear Fall/Winter 2014-15

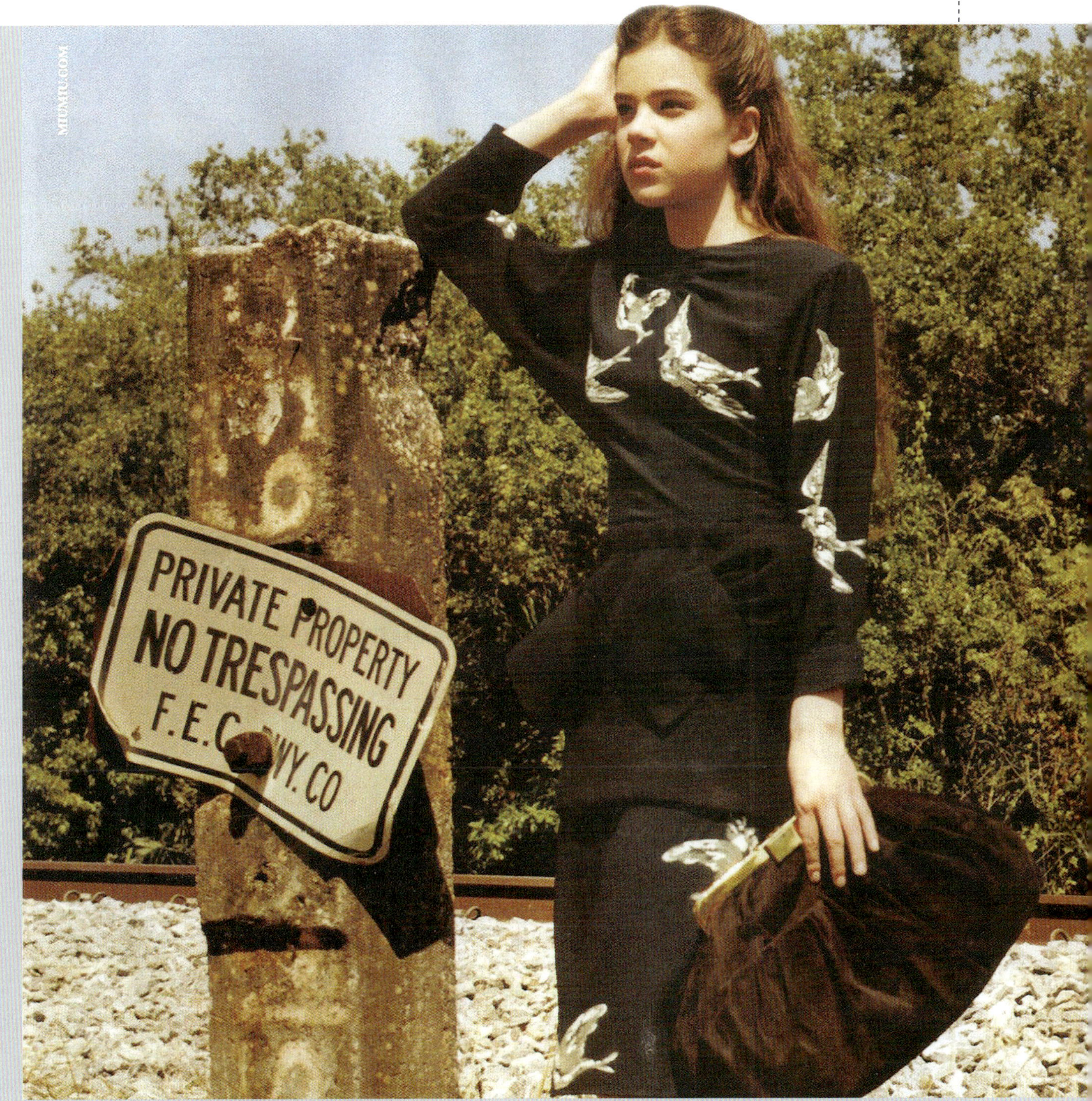

HAILEE STEINFELD

Hailee Steinfeld has been featured in Miu Miu campaigns and is frequently seen wearing the brand at events. Her youthful and edgy style aligns well with the Miu Miu aesthetic.

ABOVE: Miu Miu Fall/Winter 2011 print advertisment featuring Hailee Steinfeld by Bruce Weber

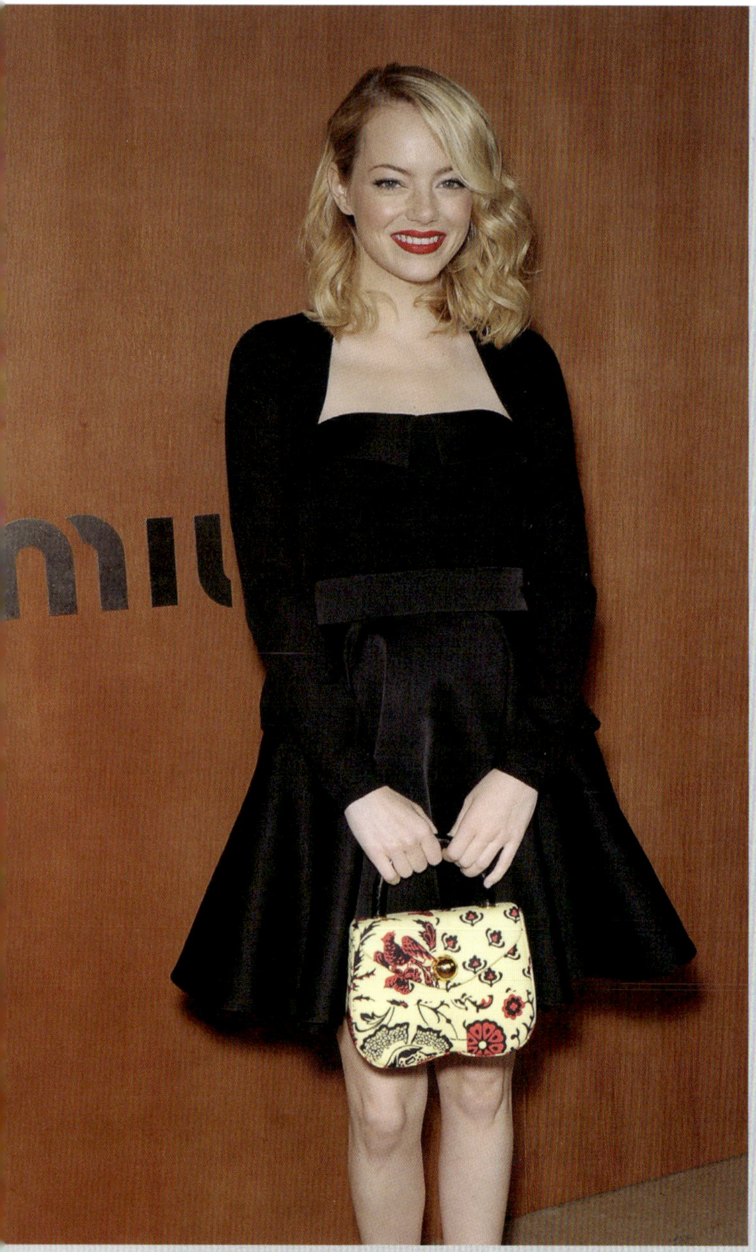

EMMA STONE

Oscar winner Emma Stone has worn Miu Miu on the red carpet multiple times, often choosing their elegant, vintage-inspired pieces for high-profile events.

CHLOË SEVIGNY

Chloë Sevigny is known for her avant-garde style – making her the perfect Miu Miu muse.

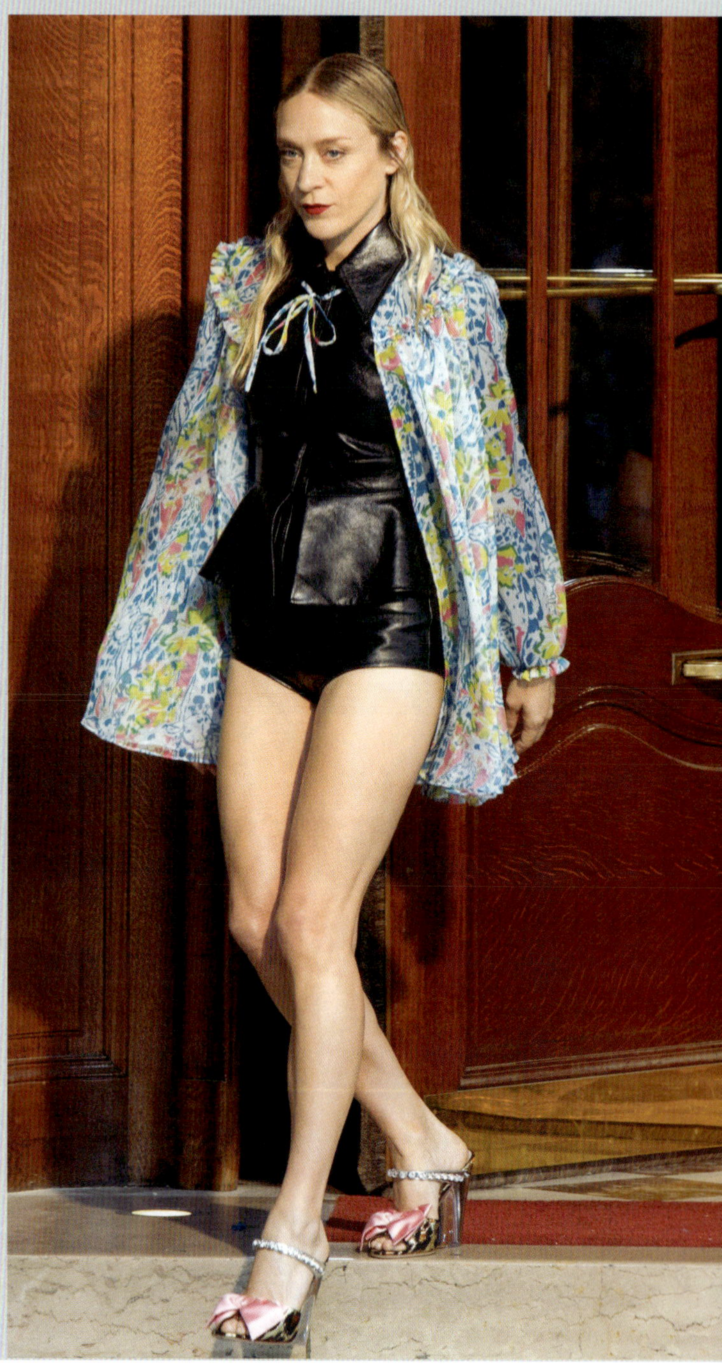

ABOVE: Emma Stone attends the Miu Miu Spring/ Summer 2013 show
RIGHT: Chloë Sevigny during the Miu Miu 2019 Cruise Collection Show held in Paris, France, 30 June, 2018

KENDALL JENNER

Model Kendall has been seen wearing Miu Miu both on the runway and in her personal life. She's been spotted in everything from the brand's statement coats to iconic micro mini skirts.

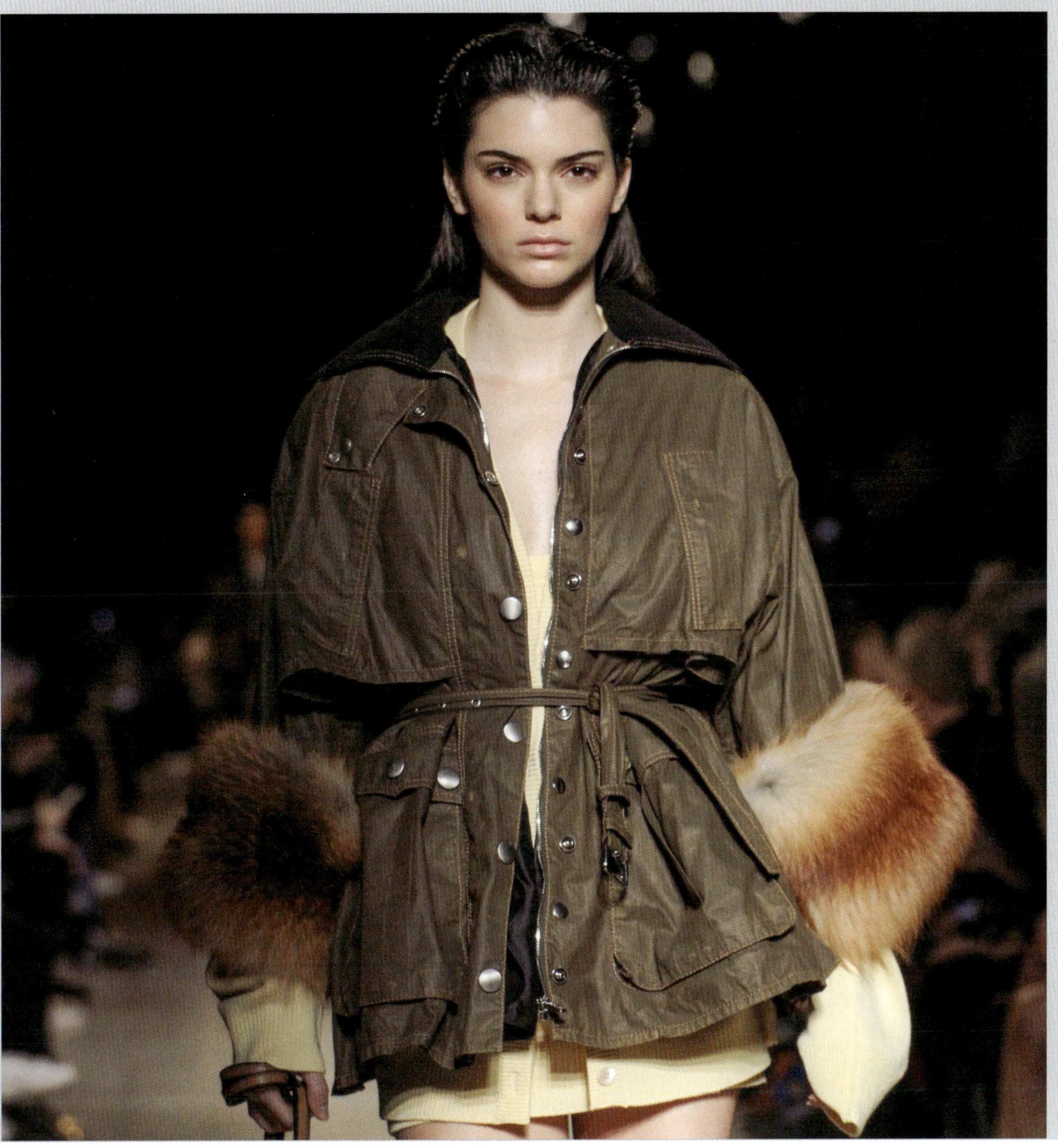

ABOVE: Kendall Jenner walks the runway during the Miu Miu show as part of Paris Fashion Week, Fall/Winter 2016/17, 9 March, 2016 in Paris, France

DAISY EDGAR-JONES

The *Normal People* star is a Miu Miu fan who appeared in Miu Miu's 2022 short film campaign.

ZENDAYA

Zendaya incorporates the brand's playful femininity along with her own bold style, often opting for both glamorous gowns and statement casual looks.

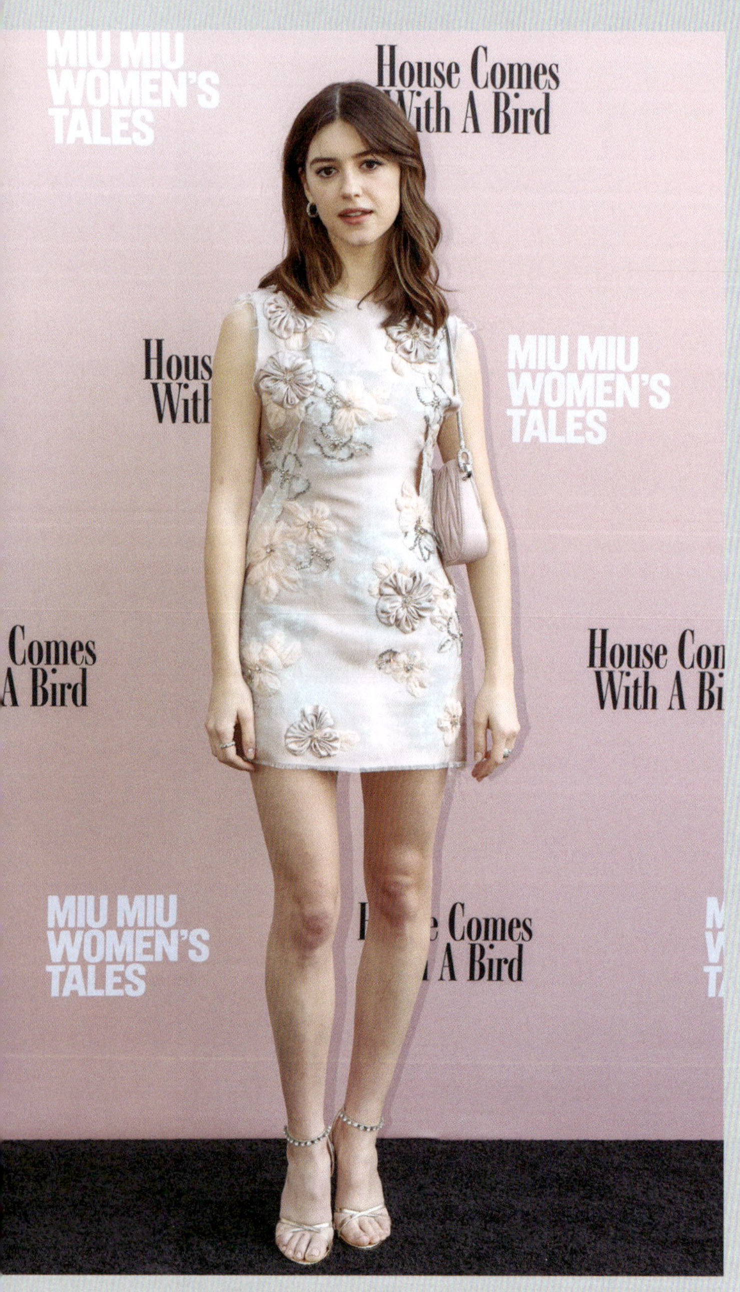

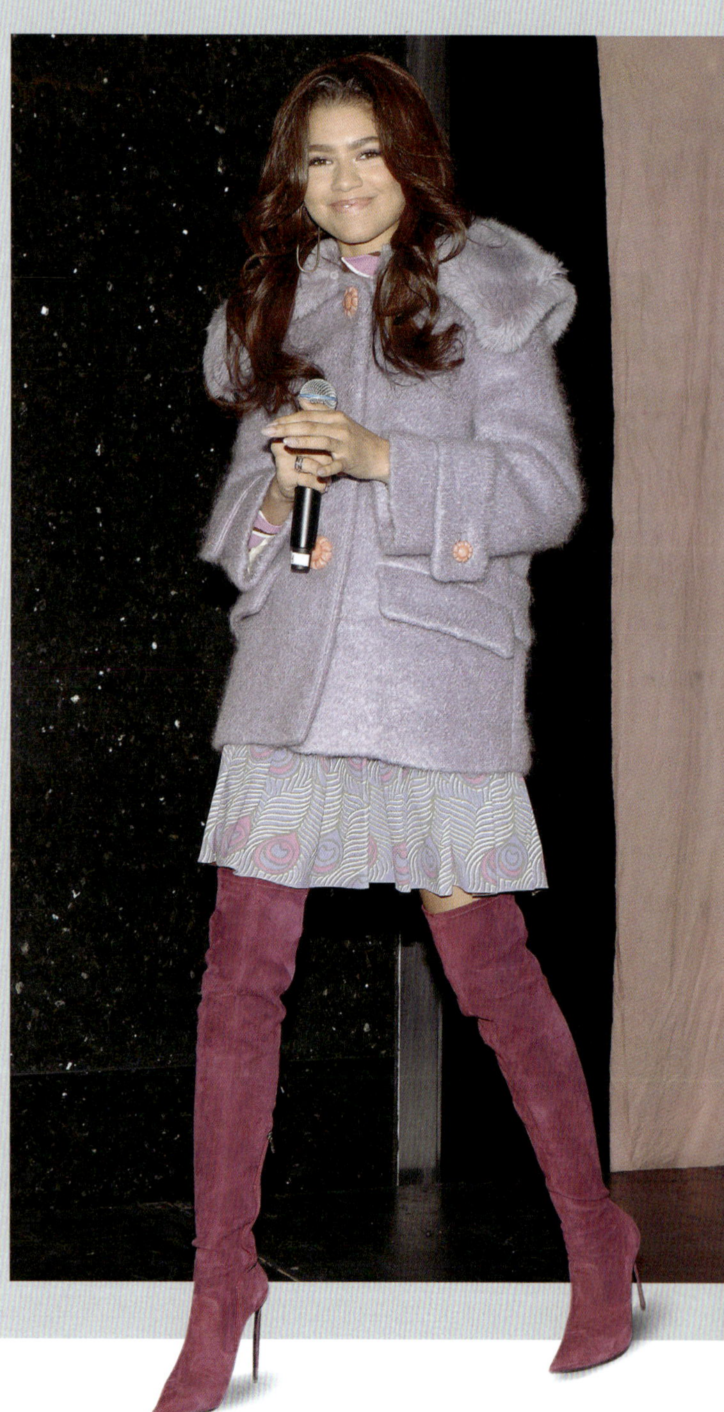

ABOVE: Daisy Edgar-Jones at the Miu Miu 'House Comes With a Bird' Screening and After Party, 23 March 2022
RIGHT: Zendaya attends the Bloomingdale's Holiday Windows Unveiling in New York, 21 November 2017

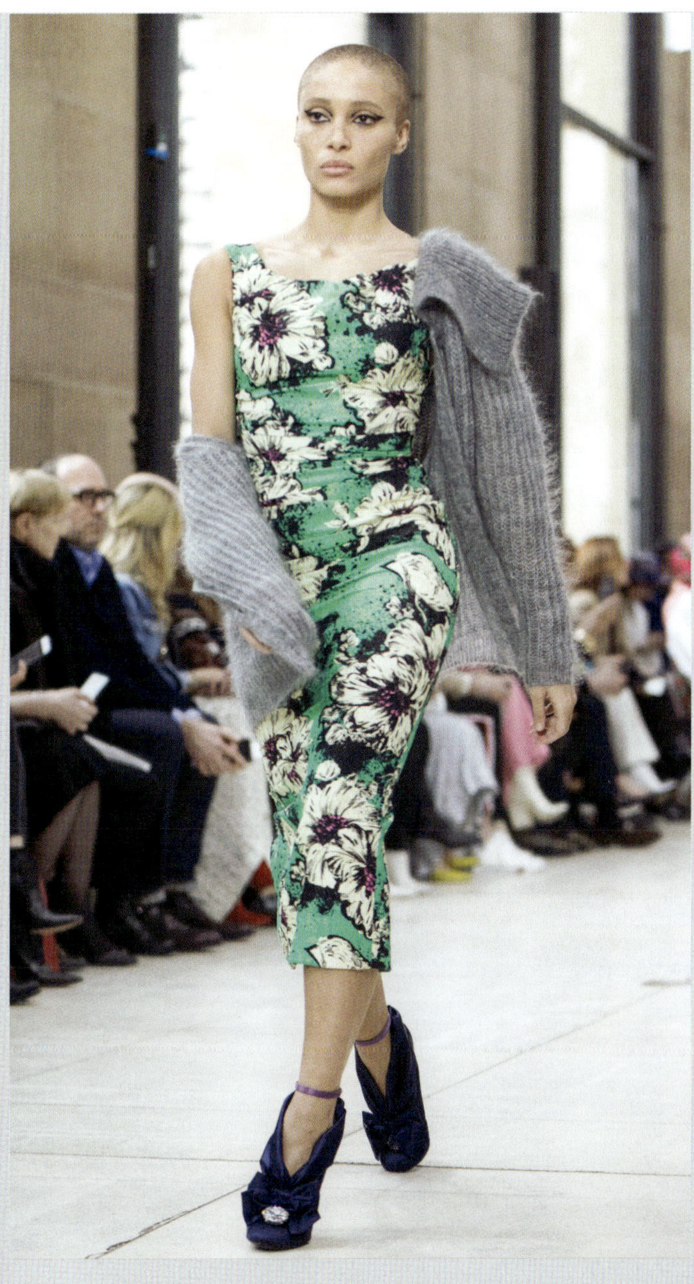

ADWOA ABOAH

The British model and activist has been a Miu Miu muse for years, featuring prominently in their ad campaigns. She's a perfect fit for the brand.

BELLA HADID

Model Bella has walked in Miu Miu's runway shows and has been spotted wearing the brand off-duty.

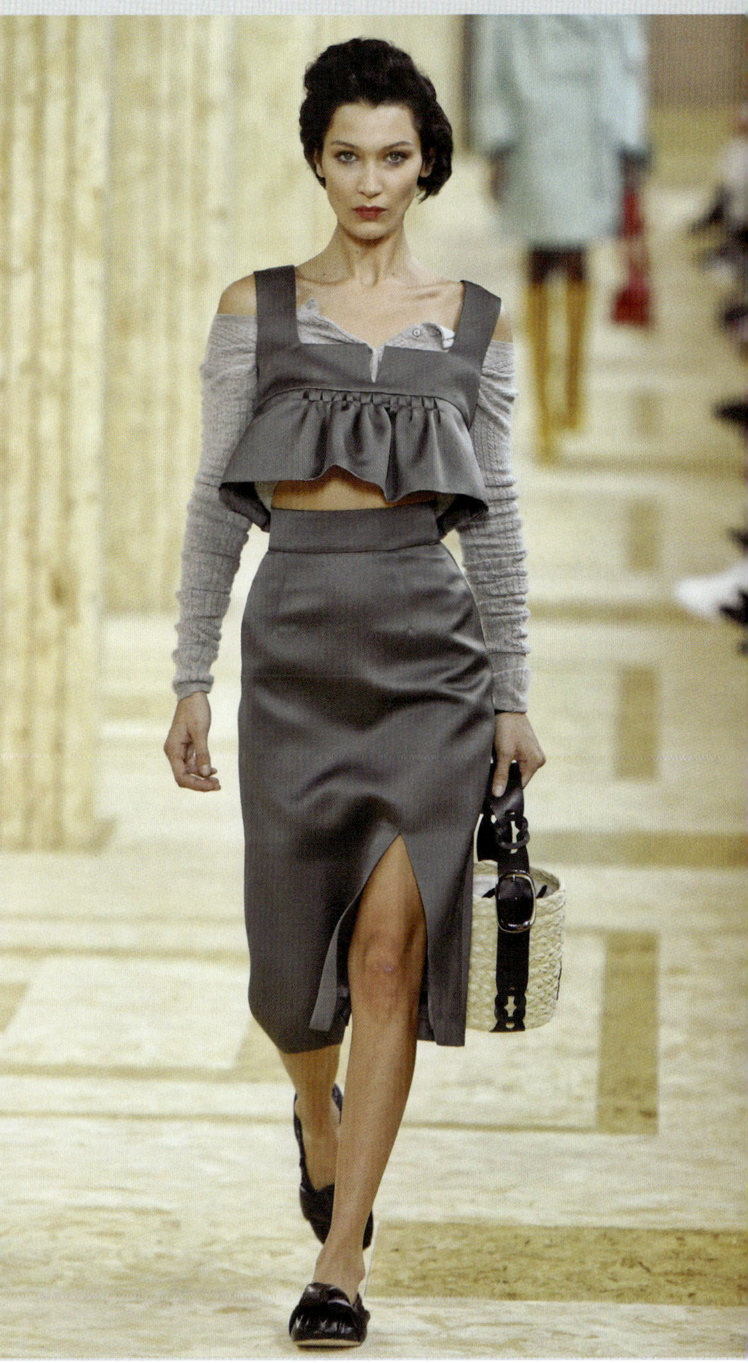

ABOVE LEFT: Model Adwoa Aboah on the Miu Miu Fall/Winter 2018/19 Collection runway, 6 March, 2018
ABOVE: Bella Hadid on the runway during the Miu Miu Ready to Wear Spring/Summer 2020 show

LÉA SEYDOUX

The French actress is a regular in Miu Miu's cinematic campaigns and favours the brand's designs on the red carpet.

ALEXA CHUNG

Fashion icon Alexa has a long-standing relationship with Miu Miu and often wears the brand's pieces, whether it's for fashion shows or everyday looks.

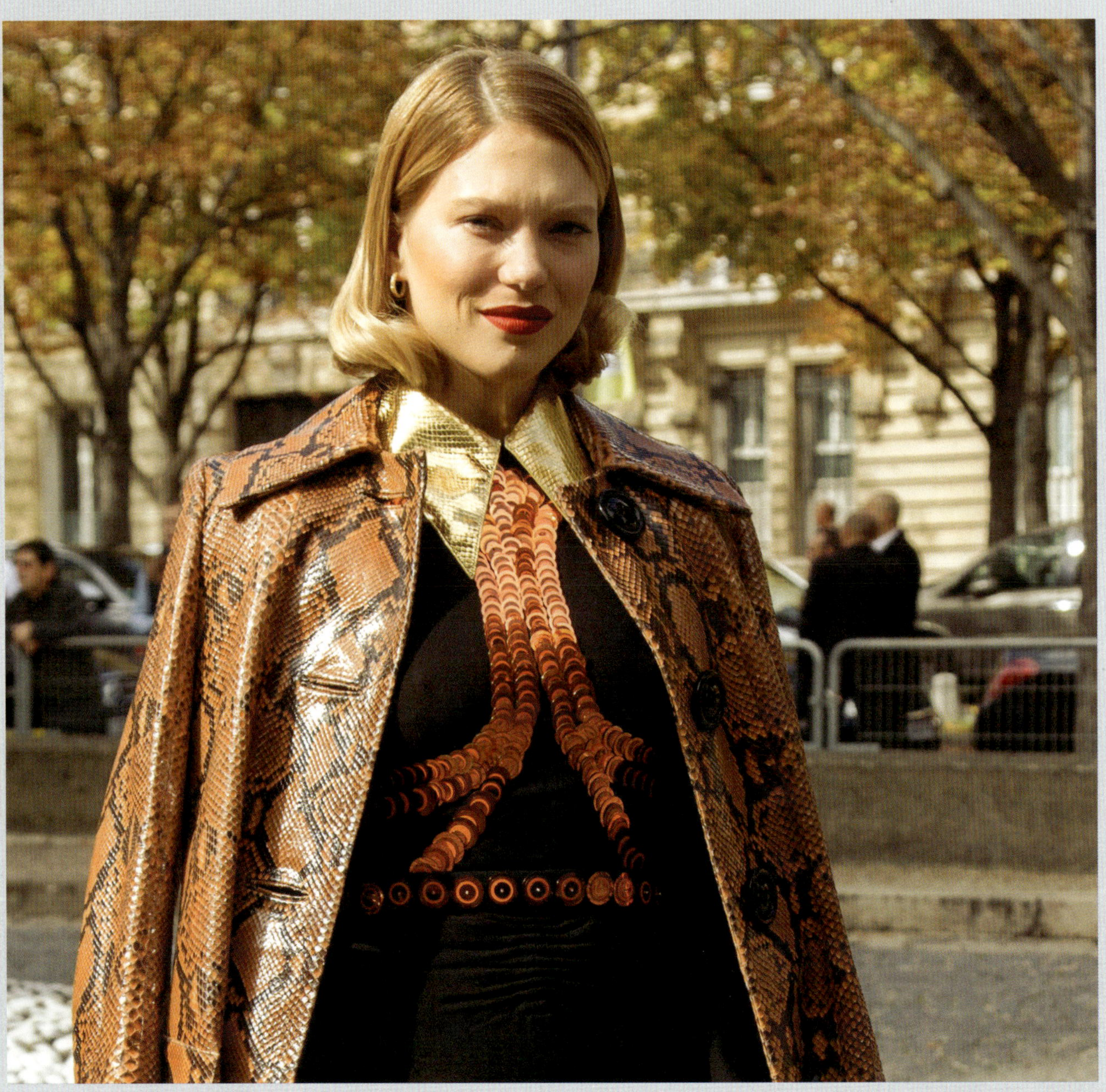

ABOVE: Léa Seydoux attends Miu Miu Show at Paris Fashion Week, 7 October, 2015 Paris, France
OPP PAGE: Alexa Chung wears a creation as part of the Miu Miu Spring/Summer 2025 collection, Paris, France

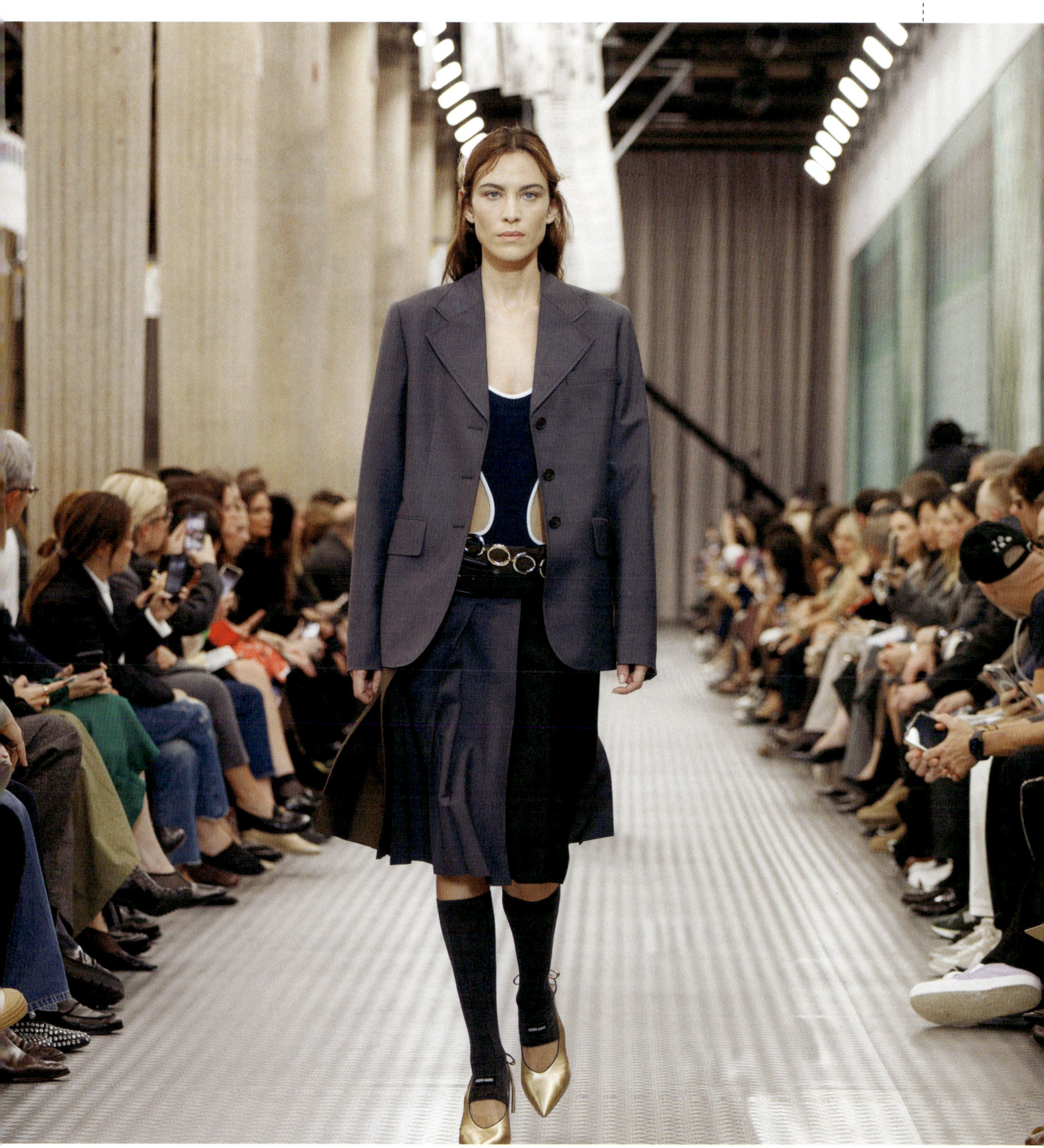

PRADA AND CULTURE

"From the very beginning, through the Fondazione's activities, I wanted to address the investigation of human culture in its variety and complexity"

Miuccia Prada on the Fondazione Prada in Milan

Prada's influence can be felt far beyond the perimeters of high-end fashion. It's influence permeates film, music, art, and even everyday language. Its minimalist yet luxurious designs and avant-garde ethos make it a symbol of sophisticated elegance – bar none. From the film *The Devil Wears Prada* to TV shows and musical references through to the worlds of art and social media, Prada is woven into the very fabric of culture.

FONDAZIONE PRADA

The Foundation is a cultural institution, established in 1993 by Miuccia Prada and Patrizio Bertelli, dedicated to contemporary art and culture. Its main venue is located in Milan at Largo Isarco 2 - a former distillery dating from the 1910s. The architectural

RIGHT: 200,000 gold leaves by Giusto Manetti Battiloro adorn the tower at the headquarters of the Prada Foundation, Milan, Italy

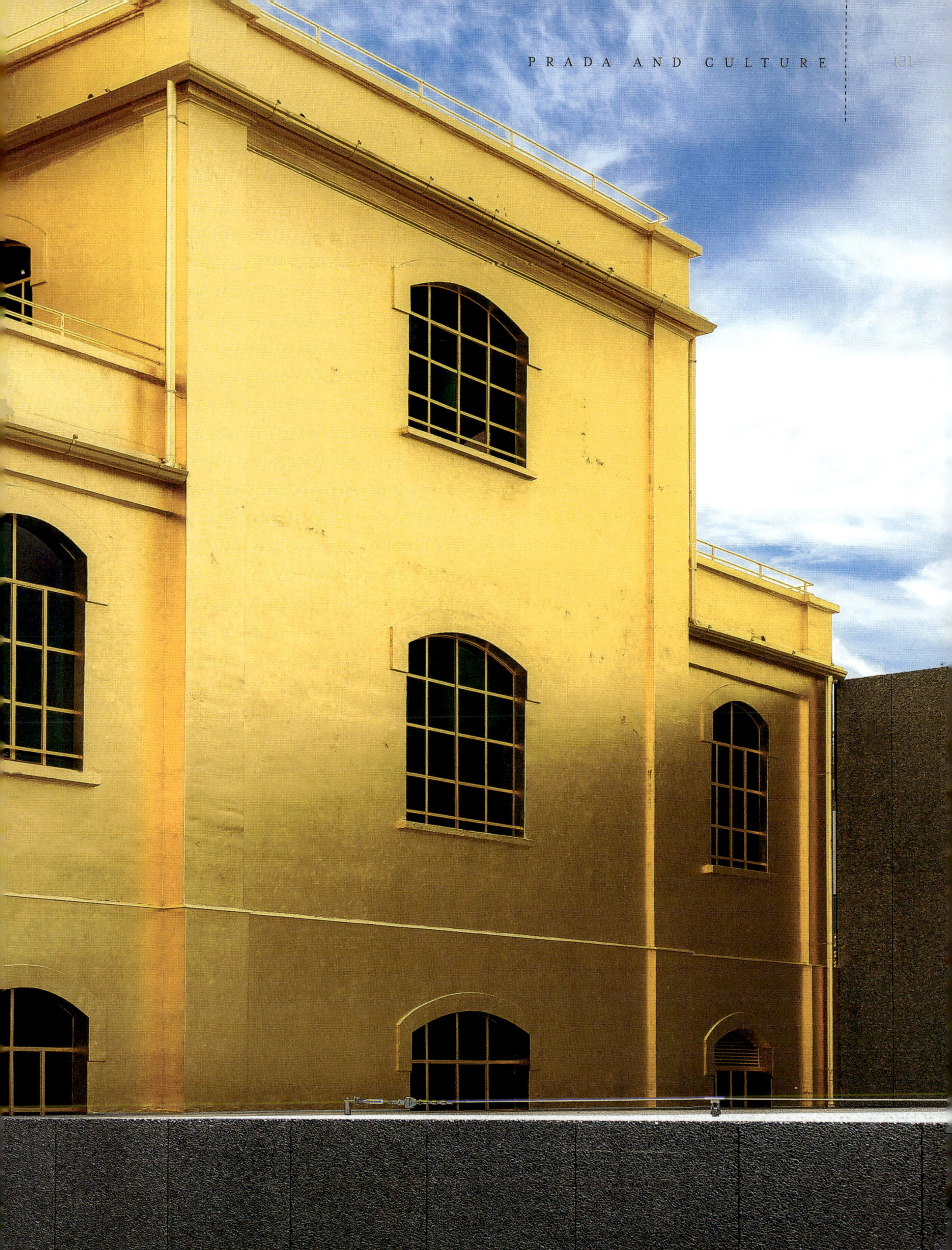

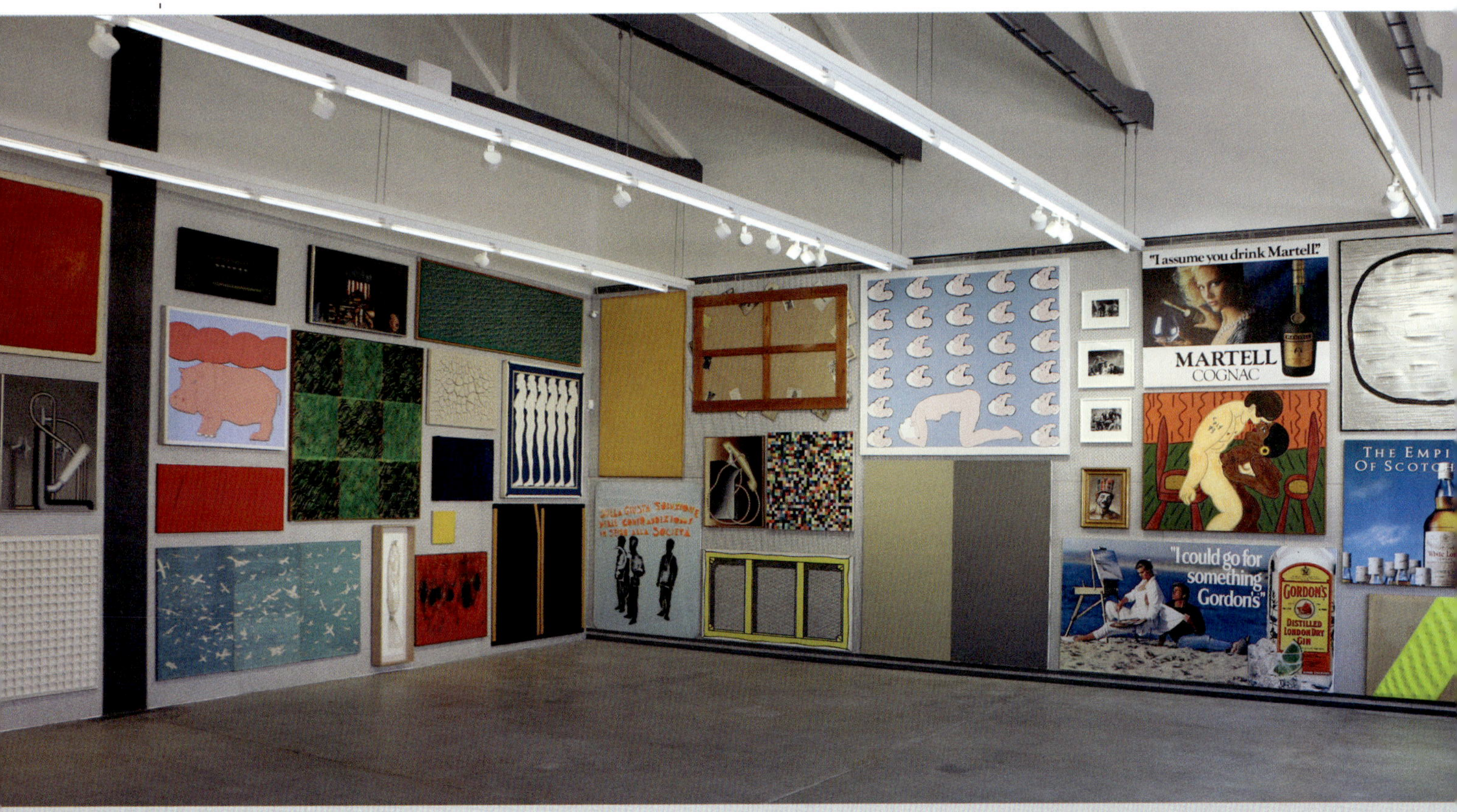

design combines existing industrial structures with new buildings, creating a unique space for artistic exhibitions. The Foundation hosts a variety of temporary exhibitions and permanent projects, exploring different artistic and cultural disciplines. In addition to its Milan headquarters, Fondazione Prada has a presence in Venice at the Ca' Corner della Regina palace and also in Tokyo.

'THE DEVIL WEARS PRADA'

The 2006 movie is arguably the most recognisable popular culture reference to Prada. Starring Meryl Streep as Miranda Priestly, a tough, fashion-forward magazine editor widely thought to be based on real life Vogue legend Dame Anna Wintour, and Anne Hathaway as her assistant, the movie explores the fashion industry's inner workings. The title alone associates Prada with wealth, ambition, and luxury, cementing the brand's place in mainstream consciousness. The film also made fashion a more accessible subject for wider audiences, blending high fashion themes with popular entertainment. Although Prada didn't officially design costumes for the film, the brand is central to its plot and setting. Many of the costumes in the film are inspired by the Prada aesthetic. Some pieces were used although costume designer Patricia Field sourced outfits from many luxury brands. *The Devil Wears Prada* stage musical with the score and music by Elton John and starring

Vanessa Williams premiered in Chicago in July 2022. It opened in London's West End in November 2024.

PRADA IN MUSIC

Prada is frequently name-dropped in music, principally in genres like hip-hop where luxury brands symbolize affluence, style, success and wealth. Several high-profile artists reference the brand in their lyrics. In his song "Fashion Killa", ASAP Rocky raps about Prada, among other luxury brands, to highlight the lavish fashion tastes of his muse. Drake also mentions Prada in tracks like "I Get Paper" – 'I buy Prada I spend dollar after dollar I get money' - highlighting again the brand's high status, exclusivity, and luxury. Then there's Cardi B in "I Like It" where she namechecks Prada and other exclusive brands. Prada's willingness to embrace and celebrate hip-hop culture has not only solidified its relevance but also fostered a deeper connection with a diverse audience.

PRADA IN TV

In *Sex and the City*, Prada is frequently alluded to as part of the main characters' luxurious lifestyles. Carrie, Samantha, Miranda and Charlotte regularly shop 'designer' which includes Prada. Similarly, in *Gossip Girl*, the rich Upper East Side, New York teens often sport Prada as part of their high-fashion wardrobes, further embedding the brand into pop culture's representation of wealth and privilege, luxury and status.

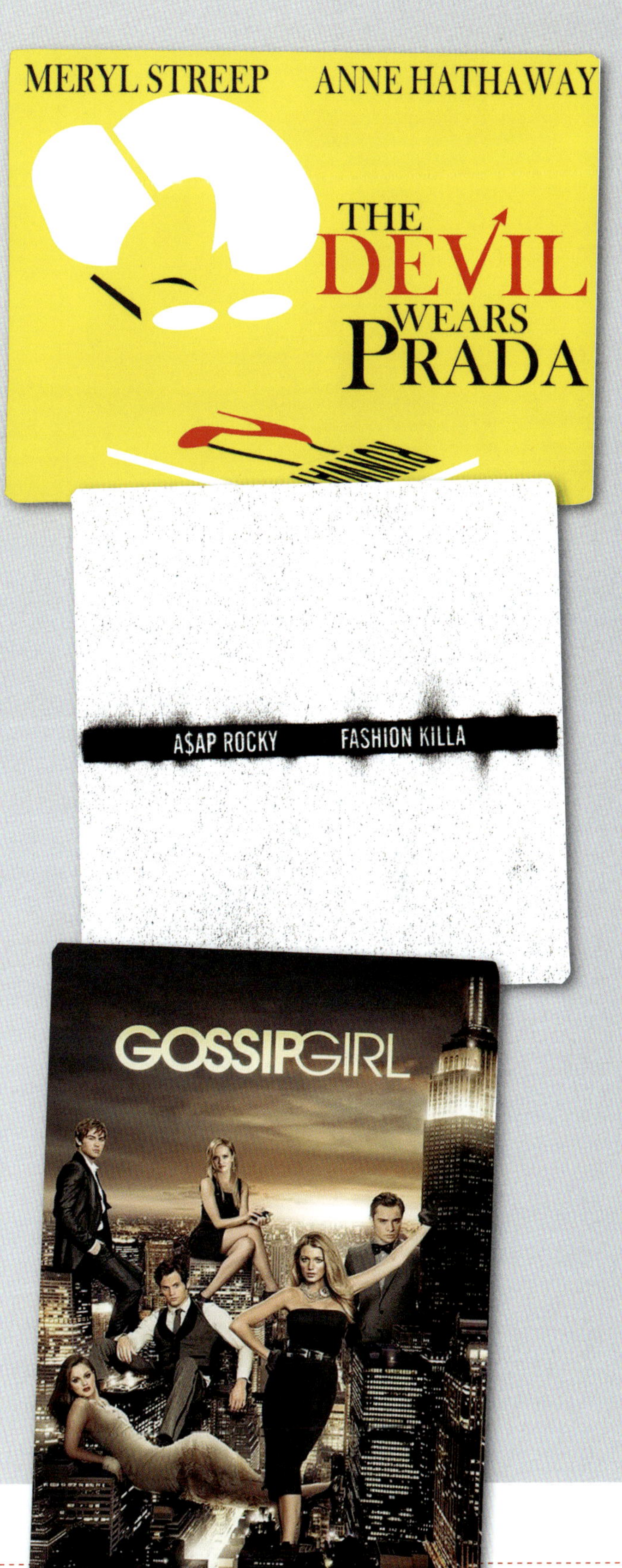

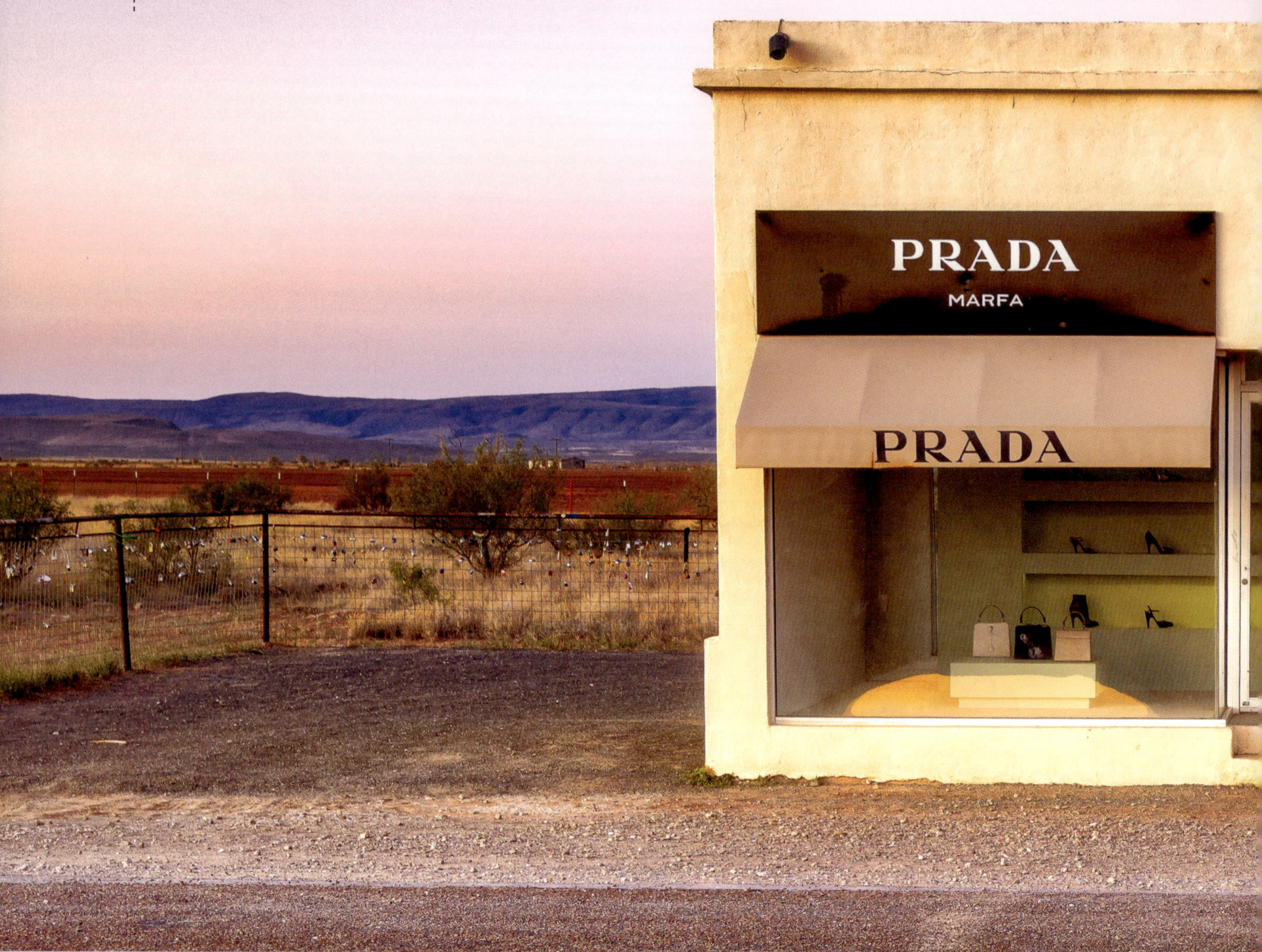

PRADA ART INSTALLATION

Prada Marfa is an art installation by artists Elmgreen & Dragset which is located in the middle of the Texas desert and looks like a real Prada boutique. On the front of the structure, two large windows display actual Prada wares, shoes and handbags which were selected by Miuccia Prada from the Fall/ Winter 2005 collection. While the installation was not commissioned by Prada, Miuccia appreciated the project's concept, which was designed as a commentary on consumerism and luxury in an unexpected desert location.

PRADA AND INFLUENCERS

Prada's influence extends to the world of fashion bloggers and social media influencers, who

ABOVE: Prada Marfa in the Texas desert
OPP PAGE: Prada often features on young influencers social media posts like K-pop artist Chanyeol's Instagram

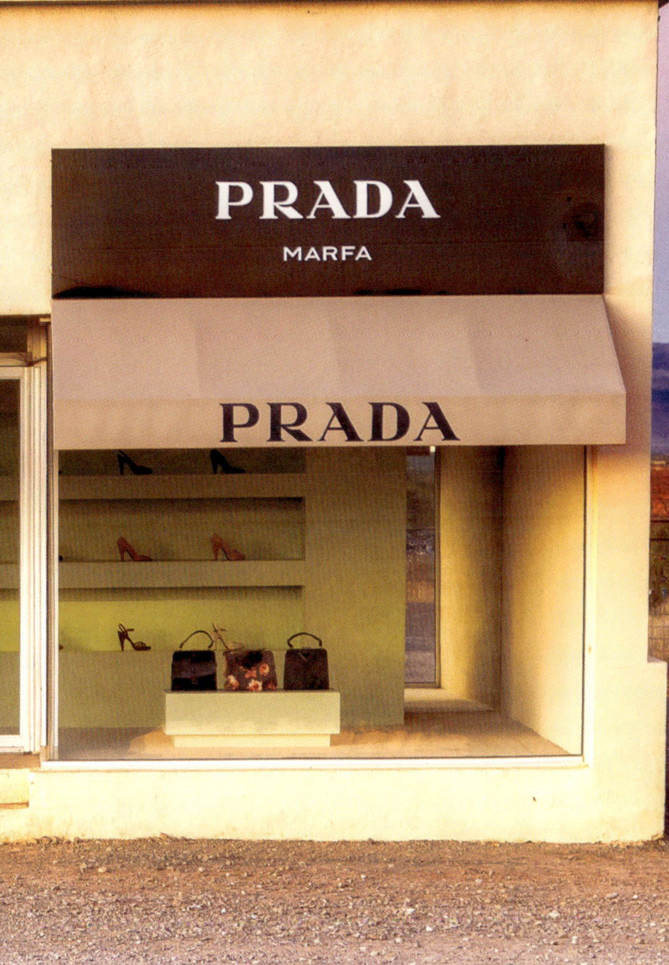

frequently showcase the brand in their posts, videos, and collaborations. Prada's presence on platforms like Instagram, TikTok, and YouTube is substantial, making it a key brand in the influencer-driven fashion space. The brand's accessories, like the Prada Re-Edition nylon bags and its signature triangle logo, are often featured in fashion hauls and styling videos, further solidifying Prada's presence in digital pop culture.

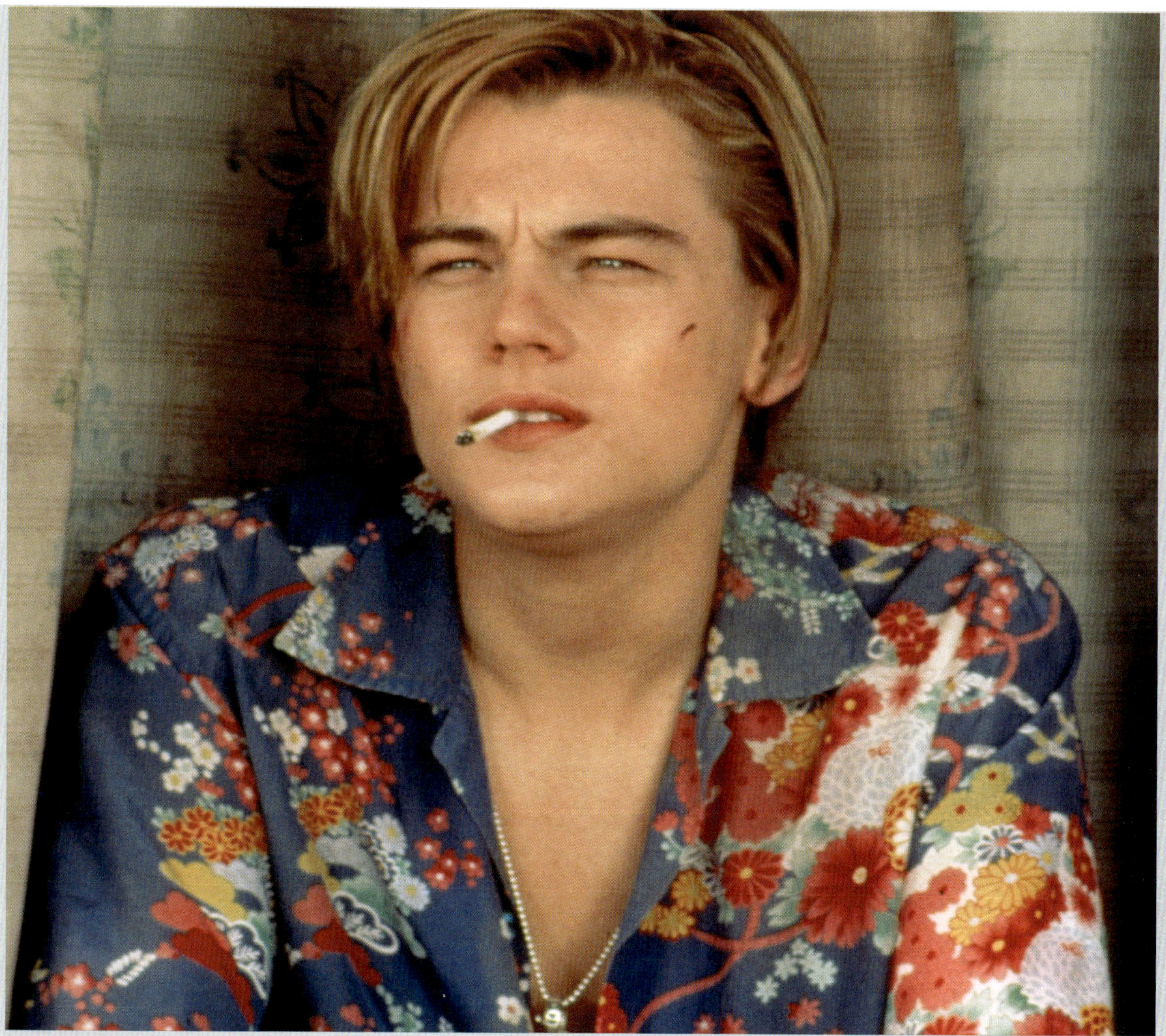

PRADA AND COSTUME DESIGNERS

Prada is frequently chosen by the costume designers of films to dress movie characters who require elegant and sophisticated yet minimalist high-fashion looks. Prada's involvement often elevates the visual storytelling of the films. Here are some notable movies where Prada has contributed to costume design:

ROMEO + JULIET (1996)

Prada worked closely with Catherine Martin for this modern reimagining of Shakespeare's classic tragedy – the costumes blending contemporary fashion with Elizabethan undertones. Prada designed outfits for Leonardo DiCaprio's Romeo, giving him a sleek, modern look that complemented the film's youthful and rebellious energy.

THE GREAT GATSBY (2013)

Miuccia Prada worked with costume designer Catherine Martin to create 40 looks for the film, drawing from Prada's own archives. Prada designed various flapper-inspired outfits that highlighted the opulence and extravagance of the 1920s - crucial for the film's lavish party scenes. Prada's creations were worn primarily by the character Daisy Buchanan, played by Carey Mulligan, and other party guests.

IO SONO L'AMORE (I AM LOVE) (2009)

Miuccia Prada, along with Raf Simons (then at Jil Sander), designed costumes for Tilda Swinton's character who was a member of a wealthy Italian family. Prada's elegant and understated designs for the character reflected the transformation of the character and also the emotional complexity of the film.

LA GRANDE BELLEZZA (THE GREAT BEAUTY) (2013)

Prada designed several key costumes for this Oscar-

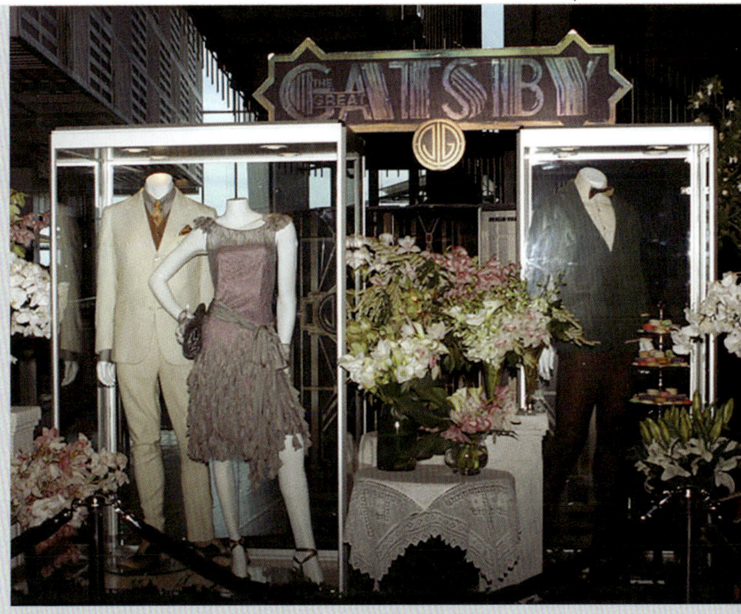

winning Italian film, particularly for the character Jep Gambardella (played by Toni Servillo). The brand's sharp tailoring accentuated the high-society world that the film explores.

TÁR (2022)

For this psychological drama starring Cate Blanchett as Lydia Tár, Prada collaborated to her tailored and androgynous outfits. A minimalist yet powerful wardrobe highlighted the character's authority and artistry as a world-renowned orchestra conductor.

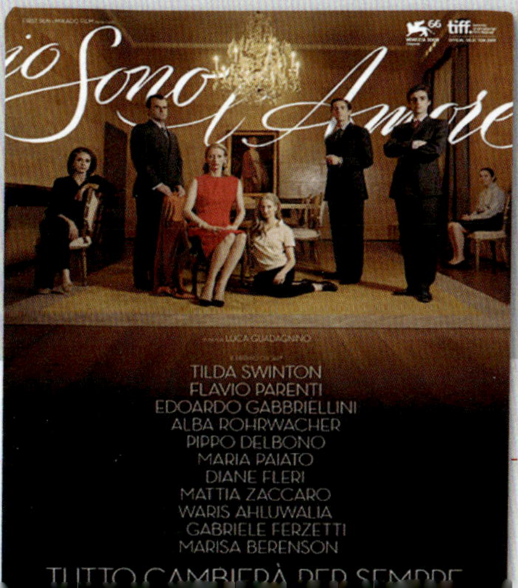

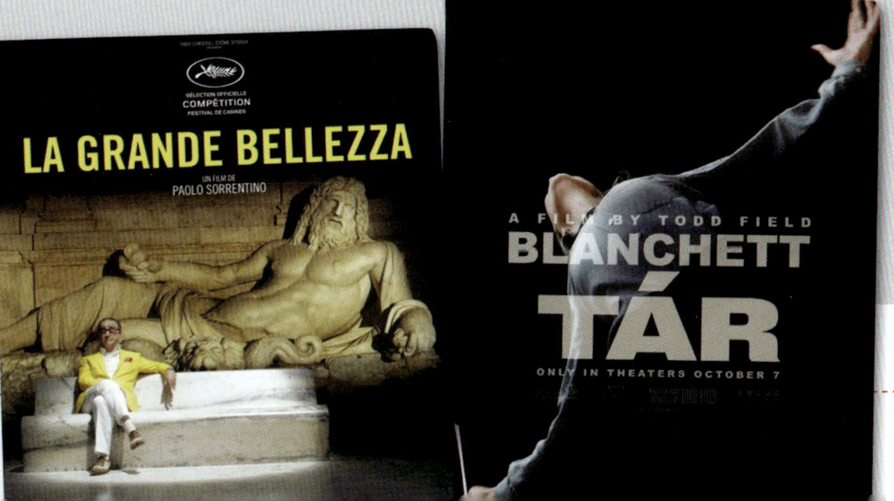

MIUCCIA'S WORDS OF WISDOM

"Fashion is instant language. When you dress, you are somehow embracing or rejecting ideas, which is why fashion has such political significance."

"What you wear is how you present yourself to the world, especially today, when human contacts are so quick. Fashion is instant language."

"I hate the idea that you shouldn't wear something just because you're a certain age. I mean, don't put yourself in a cage."

"I've always been interested in the idea of uniformity and anonymity, and yet clothes are so personal."

"You have to embrace the world if you want to live in it now. That's what I'm trying to do - be honest and embrace everything that happens, not shut yourself off from the world."

"Fashion is about the everyday and the ordinary, but also the extraordinary."

"I always try to introduce some sort of imperfection. That's really what I'm about. The beauty of imperfection."

"I like to be as comfortable as possible, but I am also aware that if you want to be respected, you have to have a certain kind of attitude, and that's not necessarily comfortable."

"I'm interested in that contradiction between people's appearances and what they are feeling and experiencing inside."

"Fashion is a way to express yourself. It's something to be taken seriously because it's a reflection of how we want to present ourselves to the world."

"Fashion is not necessarily about labels. It's not about brands. It's about something else that comes from within you."

"I always wanted to be different. I always wanted to be first."

"I always loved being a woman. But I wanted to be a clever woman. I never wanted to be a housewife."

"I always loved the idea of women's strength, and dressing in a way that expresses that strength."

"I don't want to be exclusive. I think that's old-fashioned. I want to be democratic."

"I'm always attracted to a new challenge. A new idea, something that is a bit strange and dangerous – that's exciting."

"I'm not interested in trends. I'm interested in things that last for a long time."

"I am interested in things happening in the world – politics, art, and culture. Fashion can be a way to talk about all of this."

"I'm never satisfied with what I'm doing. I always want to try new things and take risks. I like the idea of challenging myself and pushing boundaries."

"What you wear reflects your freedom, your style, and how you want to live. Fashion gives you a way to explore that."

"To be intelligent in the fashion industry, you have to question everything all the time."

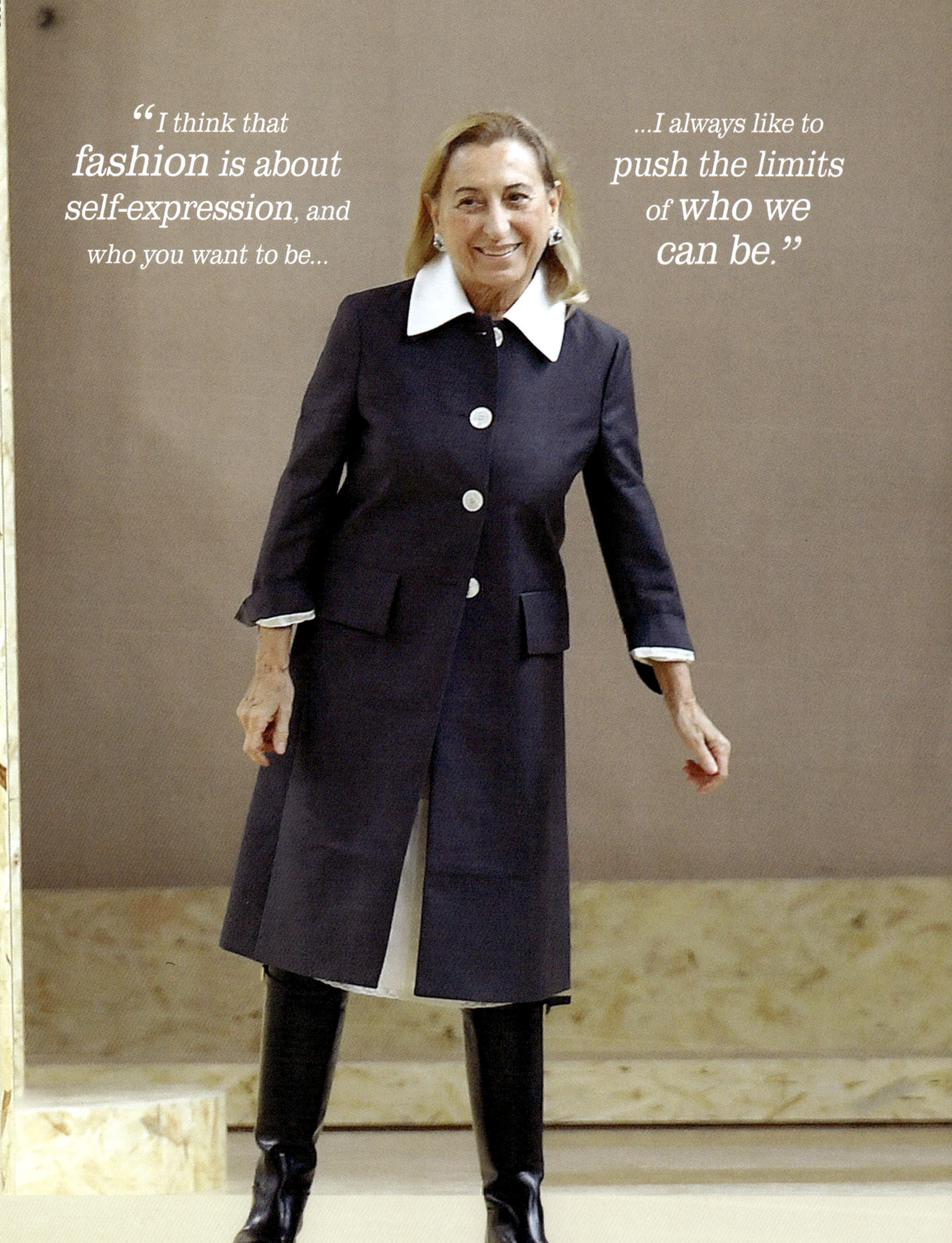
"I think that fashion is about self-expression, and who you want to be...

...I always like to push the limits of who we can be."

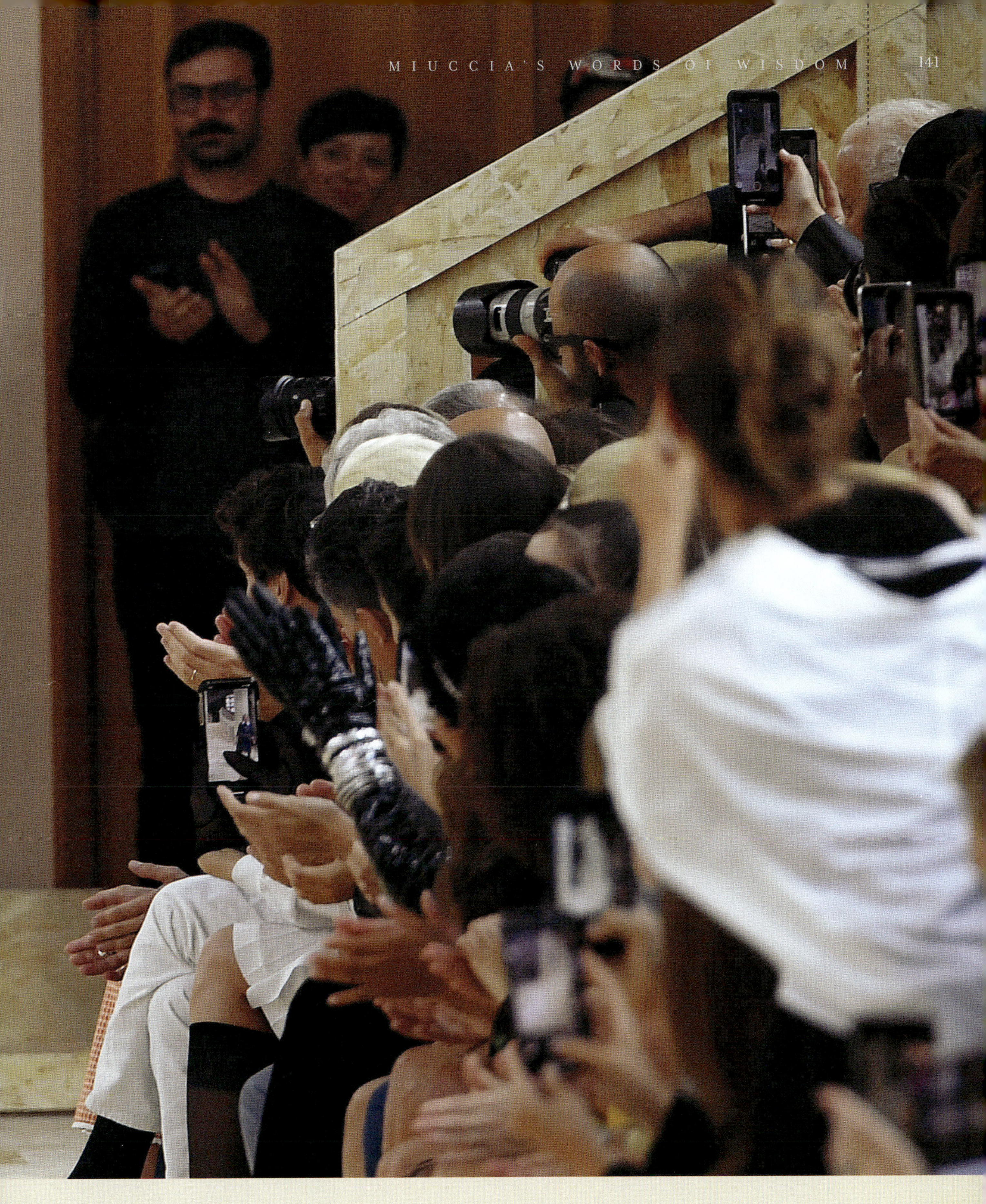

ABOVE: Miuccia Prada walks the runway after the Miu Miu Womenswear Spring/Summer 2020 show as part of Paris Fashion Week on 1 October, 2019 in Paris, France

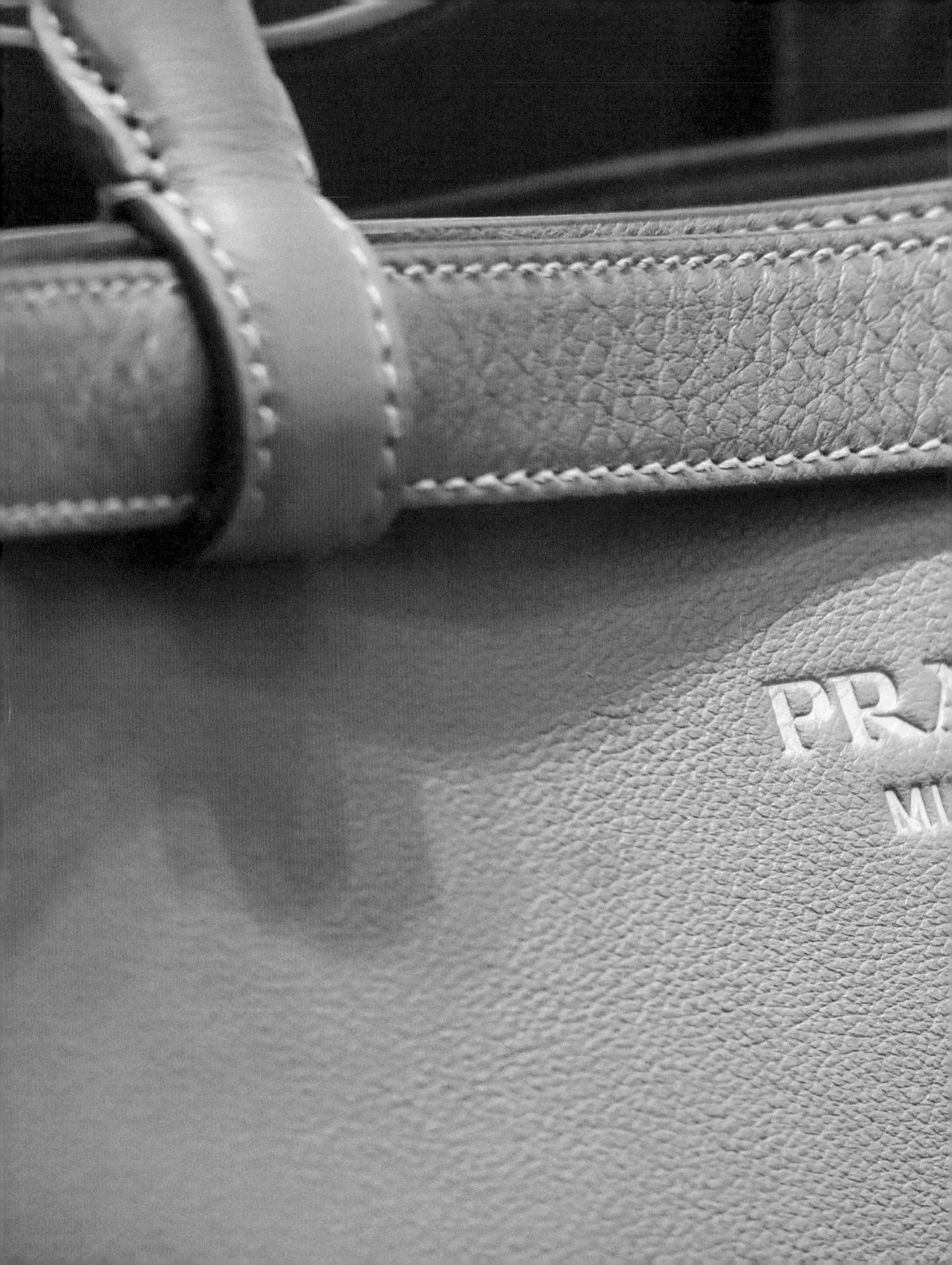